SHARK TANK

SHARK

TANK

*Greed, Politics, and the Collapse of
Finley Kumble,
One of America's Largest Law Firms*

KIM ISAAC EISLER

ST. MARTIN'S PRESS | NEW YORK

Design by Janet Tingey

Library of Congress Cataloging-in-Publication Data
Eisler, Kim Isaac.
    Shark tank: greed, politics, and the collapse of Finley Kumble, one of America's largest law firms.
    p. cm.
"A Thomas Dunne book."
ISBN 0-312-03340-0
1. Finley, Kumble—History. 2. Kumble, Stephen.
3. Lawyers—New York (N.Y.)—Biography. 4. Law partnership—New York (N.Y.)—History. I. Title.
KF355.N4E38 1989 340'.06'073—dc20 89-30509

First Edition

10 9 8 7 6 5 4 3 2 1

To my mother and father

ACKNOWLEDGMENTS

WRITING A BOOK about a failed enterprise is hardly a joyous experience. During the course of my research and writing, the fate of Finley Kumble rested in the hands of a United States Bankruptcy Judge, Prudence Abram, who tenaciously attempted to get two hundred feuding lawyers to come to an agreement on how to parcel out the debt that had been accumulated, so everyone involved could get on with their lives. Despite the strain that the firm's breakup had created, I am indebted to the many former partners and associates who gave away their valuable time to help me put together this story.

The prime mover behind this project was my agent, Jane Dystel, whose interest and enthusiasm never flagged, even when my own was hitting a valley.

I was aided by three very special friends. Chris Calhoun was a constant source of inspiration and a sounding board during my many trips to New York. Judy Sarasohn constantly reminded me not to do anything stupid. Joel Chineson, a friend now of twenty years, was full of both encouragement and good suggestions. I would also like to thank Tom Dunne and David Hirshfeld of St. Martin's Press and Linda Venator, who did a terrific job as copy editor.

In the interests of full disclosure, I would like to talk for a moment about my relationship with Steve Brill, who emerged during interviews as a major character in the book.

Since October 1985, I have been employed at Brill-owned

publications, first at *American Lawyer* in New York and, since August 1986, at *Legal Times* in Washington, D.C. Since undertaking to write this book, I have been on part-time status. During this period I have received $1,500 per month from *Legal Times* in exchange for helping to edit the weekly paper on its two busiest days, Thursday and Friday. There may be those who will feel that my treatment of Brill was influenced by this fiduciary arrangement. So be it. I have tried to present a balanced assessment of both his strengths and shortcomings. Like all of us, Brill has plenty of both. Those who refused to talk to me because of the relationship between myself and the controversial magazine editor, should know that Brill had absolutely nothing to do with the research, reporting, writing, or anything else having to do with this book.

CHRONOLOGY

July 3, 1933: Steven Kumble born in Brooklyn.

June 1959: Kumble graduates from Harvard Law.

September 1959: Kumble joins Goldstein, Judd and Gurfein.

January 1964: Kumble joins Amen Weisman and Butler.

February 1967: Leon Finley recruited to Amen Weisman and Butler.

August 1968: Finley and Kumble lock Weismans out of firm, win court fight, and rename operation Finley Kumble Underberg Persky and Roth.

April 1970: Kumble hires star litigator Norman Roy Grutman.

November 17, 1970: Newberger Loeb brokerage house threatened with expulsion by New York Stock Exchange.

December 1970–February 1971: Corporate partner Robert Persky leads negotiations to recapitalize Newberger Loeb.

March 1, 1973: Persky indicted by grand jury for filing false statements with the Securities and Exchange Commission. Name dropped from firm title.

April 1973: Kumble hires Andrew Heine as new corporate department chief. Firm becomes Finley Kumble Heine Underberg and Grutman.

May 1973: Persky sentenced to four months in prison.

May 1975: Finley Kumble opens first branch office in Miami.

June 16, 1975: Grutman defends Finley Kumble against charges stemming from Newberger Loeb representation.

December 1975: Former New York City Mayor Robert Wagner
becomes partner in firm. Name changes to Finley Kumble
Wagner Heine Underberg & Grutman.

September 1, 1976: Judge in Newberger Loeb case issued $1
million judgment against firm. Grutman quits in dispute
with Kumble over who should pay. Firm name changes to
Finley Kumble Wagner Heine and Underberg.

May 23, 1978: Steven Brill publishes article in *Esquire* about
Manatt Phelps partner Marshall Manley, who has no
qualms about "stealing lawyers, clients" from rivals.

July 1, 1978: Manley leaves Manatt Phelps.

January 1979: Miami partners leave firm.

February 1979: Steven Brill starts *American Lawyer* magazine.
Marshall Manley opens Los Angeles office of Finley Kumble.

February 1979: Robert Casey, former name partner at Shea and
Gould joins the now seventy-lawyer firm. Name changed to
Finley Kumble Wagner Heine Underberg Manley and
Casey.

July 1979: Finley Kumble reopens Miami office.

November 10, 1979: Kumble meets former Maryland Senator
Joseph Tydings, managing partner of Washington's Danzansky Dickey Tydings Quint and Gordon at Laurel Race-
course.

October 16, 1980: Danzansky Dickey agrees to merge with Finley Kumble, making it one of the twenty-five largest law
firms in the United States.

November 1980: Firm featured in *American Lawyer* as "fastest
growing firm in the nation."

August 6, 1982: Unhappy Miami partners leave and set up own
practice.

September 9, 1982: Kumble meets Miami lawyer Tom Tew.

December 25, 1982: Tew's twenty-lawyer firm becomes anchor
of Finley Kumble's new Miami outpost.

February 1, 1983: New York Governor Hugh Carey becomes
Finley Kumble partner.

October 3, 1983: Marshall Manley is divorced. Kumble orders Manley to pay $400,000 for firm legal expenses. Manley threatens to take one hundred lawyer L.A. office to rival firm if he is not made co–managing partner of firm. Feud develops between Kumble and Heine after Heine throws support to Manley's demands.

January 1984: Finley Kumble loses representation of Samuel Heyman, who was attempting to take over GAF Corporation. Heyman criticizes Finley Kumble's litigation team.

July 3, 1984: Manley, who has built practice of 150 lawyers in L.A., opens office in Newport Beach, firm's fourth in California alone. Firm now totals over five hundred lawyers.

September 1984: Harvey Myerson, fancy litigator from Webster and Sheffield, hired to beef up Finley Kumble litigation practice.

March 1985: Manley named president of Home Group Inc., Finley Kumble's largest single client. Remains Finley Kumble partner earning $1 million per year.

April 1985: Heine and Kumble exchange vicious memos over handling of client American Bakeries.

July 1985: Finley Kumble takes in Washington, D.C.'s Perito Duerk and Pinco to become second largest firm in nation with 650 lawyers.

February 1986: Finley Kumble opens London office. Becomes one of the premier firms in nation doing international film deals.

May 16, 1986: D.C. Mayor Marion Barry declares "Finley Kumble Day" in Washington.

June 1986: Manley resigns as co–managing partner. Replaced by Myerson and D.C. partner Robert Washington.

July 29, 1986: Myerson, representing Donald Trump and the United States Football League, beats NFL in massive antitrust case. Wins $1 in damages.

September 1986: Bob Washington engineers coup in which firm signs two retiring United States senators, Russell Long and Paul Laxalt, as partners for $1 million each.

January 1987: Strapped by costs of expansion, Kumble borrows $27 million to pay partners.

February 1987: Myerson and Washington depose Kumble as head of New York office. Myerson takes over.

April 1987: *American Lawyer* publishes portions of American Bakeries memos between Kumble and Heine.

Spring 1987: Kumble threatens to torpedo firm's financing arrangements with banks if Heine isn't fired.

June 1987: Heine is removed as head of firm corporate section. He announces plans to leave.

September 1987: *American Lawyer* magazine reveals firm is paying huge partner salaries with $27 million in loans.

October 1987: Finley Kumble partners begin deserting law firm. Unable to collect its bills, firm's debt climbs to $83 million.

February 1, 1988: Firm dissolves and goes into bankruptcy.

INTRODUCTION

I COULDN'T HAVE BEEN more than twelve or thirteen when
my father put a copy of Louis Nizer's *My Life in Court* on top
of my nightstand. Even then I realized that the arrival of Nizer
in my room was a none too subtle hint. There was never any
doubt in my parents' minds that my brother was going to be a
doctor and I would be a lawyer. Neither of us eventually pursued these careers, but the memory of *My Life in Court*, especially the tale of Quentin Reynolds and Westbrook Pegler, was
permanently ingrained in my memory. I was the only kid in my
seventh-grade class who could discuss Nizer's defense of Ethel
and Julius Rosenberg intelligently. Unfortunately, such information has little impact on your grade. Later I discovered, on my
own this time, Clarence Darrow's *The Story of My Life.* A
whole new set of wondrous cases and trials enthralled me. After
some time, I'd sometimes confuse the two books, picturing the
McNamara brothers union bombing case with Nizer instead of
Darrow. But it didn't matter. Both men stood for the same
things: total integrity, courage, persistence, and a willingness to
stand up for an underdog, no matter how unpopular.

In 1965, when I was fourteen, a landmark civil rights case had
set my hometown of Lynchburg, Virginia, afire. A seventeen-
year-old black kid had been sentenced to die after an extremely
dubious rape conviction. It was a big brouhaha, with national
civil rights figures such as Stokely Carmichael and Martin Luther King getting involved. In from the evil north came William

Kunstler, in his pre–Chicago Seven days, to defend this itinerant dishwasher. My father and I dressed up to go downtown, and we attended the trial. Dad turned to me at one point and, aptly for the times, observed about Kunstler, "He looks like Lincoln." For the blacks of my town, he *was* Lincoln. Bill Kunstler was also a great lawyer; he saved the youngster's life.

I wasn't personally involved with lawyers until 1974, when I started covering the courts for the Greenville, Mississippi, *Delta Democrat Times.* Some great lawyers practiced in that sandy flatland: a one-armed federal judge named Bill Keady who could dictate the most beautiful and profound rulings from the bench, a brilliant three-hundred-pound black lawyer from New Jersey named Charles Victor McTeer who could have been a six-figure partner anywhere, but devoted his career to the poor people of Mississippi.

I didn't realize it at the time, but in observing the bar in a backward place like the Mississippi delta, I was seeing lawyers as they had been 100 years ago. They didn't try their cases in the newspaper; they honored their agreements, and they spent time representing clients rather than trying to enrich themselves. Some lawyers in Greenville would even take their fees in barter, because people there didn't have much money. They were men of their community. That a law firm from a big city like Jackson might move into Greenville was improbable. And the idea that lawyers from another state might come in and set up a practice was ludicrous. They wouldn't get a client, and if they did, the hometown juries would toss them out of court with dispatch.

In the early 1970s, that provincialism was the reality in not only small towns like Greenville, but in most cities in this country. Even the giant New York City law firms had little inclination to branch out. When a satellite office was established, more often than not it was because a certain loyal client had an interest in that other place. But usually a big national company would use different lawyers for each of its various offices—New York law firms in New York, Los Angeles law firms in Los Angeles, and so on. But that was just one way that the law business was split. Within each city a firm might use several different groups of lawyers, one for tax work, another for labor problems, another for merger-and-acquisition work, another for collections, and yet another for antitrust problems. When a case actually went to court, special litigation firms took over and presented it at trial.

By 1978 two "visionary" attorneys, one in Los Angeles and one in New York, had come to believe that this multifurcated system should be a thing of the past. Each man, Marshall Manley at L.A.'s Manatt Phelps Rothenberg Manley and Tunney, and Steven Kumble at New York's Finley Kumble Wagner Heine and Underberg, set out to make his firm the biggest in the country. Under the roof of a megafirm, Manley and Kumble surmised, all the different types of legal work could be accommodated. Furthermore, they believed that by establishing branch offices in other cities, a corporate client would only need one law firm. Neither had any remorse about stealing lawyers or clients from rivals.

Had each pursued his goal independently, perhaps little would have come of it. But through a totally unexpected series of circumstances, the two men were brought together as partners. Their concepts and practices transformed law from a gentleman's profession into a coldhearted business. But Finley Kumble's big-and-tough public image masked the Keystone Cops manner in which the firm's managers lurched from crisis to crisis.

As the firm that eventually became Finley Kumble Wagner Heine Underberg Manley Myerson and Casey gobbled up small law firms, other firms felt compelled to follow. Almost overnight it seemed that law had entered the era of the megafirm. Chicago's Sidley and Austin, Cleveland's Jones Day Reavis and Pogue, and Philadelphia's Morgan Lewis and Bockius all jumped on the bandwagon. None were as successful. In just eighteen years, not long in a profession whose traditions can go back one hundred years, Finley Kumble became one of the largest law firms in the country. Only Baker and McKenzie, which had hundreds of lawyers overseas and had developed for nearly a century, was bigger.

By 1984, just six years after Manley and Kumble had joined forces, dozens of law firms in the country had over one hundred lawyers; thirteen had more than three hundred. The small and medium-size law firms were faced with an impossible choice. They could either accept the merger offers of the expansion-minded larger firms, or they could stand on the outside and watch the big groups steal their clients and their livelihood. The profession of law seemed to be duplicating what had happened throughout American industry. Steve Kumble believed that eventually there might be just a handful of big national law firms, just as the accounting industry was controlled by a "Big Eight." Had Kumble succeeded, even lawyers in towns like Greenville, Mississippi, might one day be working for the local office of Finley Kumble or Jones Day, just as the local accountants in such towns worked for Price Waterhouse or Arthur Andersen. The lawyers would all be making a lot more money, of course. But they wouldn't be able to accept a pound of bacon in payment for a bill or take a case for no fee. In the Finley Kumble world, the law profession was run like a business. Deadbeat clients were not tolerated, and partners were actually employees. The carefully devised lawyer's code of ethics was simply not important.

In 1984 I was called to a hotel room in Los Angeles to meet Louis Nizer. Naturally I was excited. The person who made the arrangements had not said what the occasion was, and I didn't feel the need to ask—I would take any opportunity to meet my old hero. I met the great man in his suite, and we settled down opposite each other in easy chairs. The floor was littered with depositions and court briefs. Nizer's big news was that his New York firm, Phillips Nizer Benjamin Krim and Ballon, was starting a Los Angeles law firm—hardly the thing I wanted to talk to him about. I asked the great defender of the underdog about the case on which he was working. His client was an oil company.

CHAPTER

1

IT WAS THE MORNING of January 5, 1987, and for the first time in a golden career, David Ellsworth's professional life was in turmoil.

Striding into the bright daylight of southern California, Ellsworth stared at the sun's reflection against the surreal landscape of Century City, where tall, angular monoliths of steel and glass housed the great lawyers and accountants of the west. For seven years he had reigned as one of those great lawyers although he didn't try big cases and in fact rarely went anywhere near a courtroom. Trials weren't important, not here in this futuristic office complex on the old movie lot where once Twentieth Century-Fox had filmed fanciful Tom Mix westerns. There were no monuments in Century City to Clarence Darrow, or even Perry Mason. The one-time movie adventureland was now all business.

In Century City, this Brasília-like enclave just southwest of Beverly Hills, Ellsworth had achieved greatness where it counted. An expert in international resort development and condominium time-sharing deals, the forty-six-year-old had amassed a fortune that most people his age could only dream about. Money—that was what mattered here.

Ellsworth owned at least two homes near L.A., neither exactly modest. One was in Malibu, the other in Beverly Hills. He had memberships in the Wilshire Country Club as well as the prestigious Vintage Club. On the East Coast, in Sarasota, Florida,

Ellsworth owned more property where he kept his stable of handsome palomino horses. His net worth, according to court documents, was conservatively estimated at $2.5 million.

But on this brisk winter day in 1987, David Ellsworth was shaken. His career, for the first time ever, was in chaos.

Once he had toiled in downtown Los Angeles with one of the oldest, most conservative law firms in the city. Meserve, Mumper and Hughes was the kind of firm where, once a young lawyer made partner, he had a job for life. It offered good, stable work and the opportunity to make more and more money as you got older and older. But like a lot of lawyers in the 1970s, Ellsworth had been led to believe that there was no reason to wait to get rich.

In 1980 David had decided to quit the downtown L.A. partnership and join forces with Sherwin Memel, an egotistical lawyer-businessman who subscribed to the newfangled philosophy that law firms should reward the aggressive go-getters who bring in the business and produce the income, without regard to how long they have been with a firm. After all, the craftsmen of legal documents, the scholars and the draftsmen, all owed their livelihood to the business getters. Therefore, the theory went, they were not as valuable and certainly should not receive equal compensation. Furthermore, the prevailing notion in most conservative downtown firms that all partners should be considered equal and pay scales should be set strictly on a seniority basis was discarded by Memel. Law, he believed, had entered a new generation.

A native of Buffalo, New York, Memel was the son of a soft-drink distributor, and working on his dad's truck was one of the most horrid memories of Sherwin's early years. Before he was fourteen, Memel had cut grass, shoveled snow, sold costume jewelry, hawked wares at cheap carnivals in Canada, and played the drums in a jazz band. When his parents decided to abandon Buffalo and move to California when he was fourteen, he told his mother that he thought he had been reborn in heaven. He spent his evenings hanging out near the Hollywood Bowl hoping to meet his hero, Gene Krupa. Eventually Memel went to law school at UCLA and was graduated second in his class. He then made one of the key career decisions of his life: he married the daughter of a doctor. Needless to say, Memel became an expert in health care and hospital law. His father-in-law, who owned a small hospital, became his first client. Memel's practice grew to include a large number of small hospitals, which he then organized into an interest group with political clout. As general counsel for the small hospitals, Memel developed into one of the country's leading experts on health law. In the late 1960s, he left the practice of law and became an executive in a small hospital chain, figuring that he could make more money acquiring hospitals on his own than he could by doing the same thing for clients.

But his career in business didn't turn out very well. Memel was hit with a suit, filed by shareholders in the company he had joined. The management of the firm settled the complaint for $1.8 million, of which Memel had to pay $270,000. It was a large enough sum to persuade him to return to his law practice. But the sour experience didn't quench his ambition. By 1975 he had founded a law firm of his own, originally called Memel and Jacobs. Six months later Memel convened a meeting of the five lawyers who worked with him. On a blackboard he drew a diagram of the growth he was projecting for the firm. Among the cities in which he predicted Memel Jacobs would become a force were Paris, London, and Tokyo. His own partners chuckled, discreetly.

Originally specialists only in health care, Memel decided in 1980 to expand his firm and branch out. That was when he hired David Ellsworth to build the real estate practice. For five years Memel Jacobs grew more explosively than any firm in Los Angeles. By 1984 Sherwin Memel had built a law practice of 120 lawyers, and while he didn't have offices in Tokyo, Memel Jacobs had become an important legal name in Washington, D.C., San Francisco, Dallas, Paris, and Hong Kong.

Memel Jacobs was certainly on the map. Major legal trade publications featured Memel prominently in articles on fast-growing new practices, and Memel Jacobs was routinely cited as

4 | Kim Isaac Eisler

one of the three or four fastest-growing law firms in the country. There was now money to be made in law, and Memel made a pledge to each his partners: he would make them all millionaires.

That opportunity had first presented itself in 1975, when Sherwin suggested to his partners that they purchase their Beverly Hills office building for $15 million. It seemed too big a risk to everyone but Memel, and the partnership refused. When the building was sold five years later for $45 million, Memel's prescience was well established.

So in 1984, his partners listened when Memel outlined his plans to build a twenty-two story, $90 million office complex on L.A.'s Wilshire Boulevard. The firm would occupy only a quarter of the building and rent out the rest. The optimistic Memel had options to take over eleven of the floors over the next thirty-five years. "I have never decided to do something that I haven't done," he told doubters. "So it has never occurred to me that it won't work."

By August 1986 the money and time being sunk into the new construction began consuming the law firm. Short of cash, Memel began asking associates to defer a portion of their salaries to help the firm make it through lean times. Some did. But most began looking elsewhere for jobs, and by December the firm that had started the year with 144 lawyers had only 80. The income that Memel was expecting to receive from the work of those lawyers moved with them to their new firms. Partners who decided to leave found that Memel was unable to return to them their full share of partnership equity in the firm.

Among those who were summarily fired during one belt-tightening bout was Lester Seidel, a former Washington, D.C., prosecutor who had been lured to Memel Jacobs just a year earlier. Seidel gave up a lifetime job with a smaller firm to handle labor litigation for Memel. Seidel alleged in a lawsuit he subsequently filed against Memel Jacobs that shortly after arriving, he began to complain that the firm's Washington office was cheating clients. Settlements were deliberately prolonged to make it seem as if the lawyers were working harder on cases than they were. If the legal fees for a case were covered by insurance, that case could drag on forever.

Seidel claimed that his constant complaints about this alleged unethical behavior were not ignored, however. Just a year after being hired, Seidel was confronted by Memel during a trip to Washington. "We're letting you go without cause," Memel said matter of factly. "It would be best if you left immediately."

A stunned Seidel vigorously protested. He hadn't sought out Memel Jacobs. They had needed a labor litigator. They had come to him. He had given up a wonderful job for this new life—and a guarantee that he would never again make less than $150,000 per year.

Memel was unmoved. "It's just one of those things," Memel said. "Just like when you make a bad investment." That was how it was in Century City.

Seidel filed suit against his former partners alleging fraud, defamation, and retaliatory expulsion—a suit that was well publicized in the legal press. As the acrimony became public, clients began moving their business elsewhere, lest the turmoil interfere with their cases. When legal recruiters recognized that the firm was unsettled, they began actively trying to lure Memel Jacobs partners to rival firms. As more lawyers left, those who remained felt more unsettled. As the firm became more disrupted, more headhunters began making unsolicited calls. Those partners who weren't being pursued flooded the city's legal newspaper, the *Los Angeles Daily Journal,* with classified employment ads. Word filtered down from the classified department to the editorial department. Such letters were considered confidential, but anyone could see that most came in on stationery with the Memel Jacobs letterhead. Anybody could see what was happening. The paper's reporters began making inquiries. Among the reporters' best sources were the headhunters. While the lawyers lied to the newspaper, the headhunters, off the record of course, confirmed to reporters that Memel Jacobs was failing. So the insistent calls, now from both headhunters and reporters, continued. The lawyers who thought things would work out grew more nervous and ultimately receptive to new offers.

On Sunday morning, February 1, 1987, the remaining partners of the firm, including David Ellsworth, gathered at Memel's Century City office and voted to dissolve the firm. The following morning office staff and associates got the word—all were out of work. At the Dallas office, an associate named Mark Mesec had one last request: could he possibly be reimbursed $283.41 in out-of-pocket expenses, incurred for the Dallas office Christmas party? "To be stiffed on the Dallas office Christmas party is a bit much," complained Mesec. "What am I supposed to do, just lock the door and let the plants die?" He never got an answer to any of his questions. Mesec was stiffed.

For the associates and the office help, the demise of Memel Jacobs was a calamity—they had to begin searching immediately for new jobs. Men like Memel and Jacobs weren't exactly going to miss meals or start riding the bus to work, but at their station in life, the firm's dissolution was a huge professional humiliation. If clients dislike one thing, it's confusion and instability among their lawyers. Attorneys can't be operating out of their homes. Indeed, a fancy office is considered so important that one entrepreneur built office suites for lawyers that he would occasionally rent out by the hour.

So Memel and Jacobs wasted no time in attempting to rebuild their shattered professional lives. But firms weren't beating down the doors to hire former Memel Jacobs partners. It had a reputation for being overly aggressive, and the dozen or so malpractice suits it was fighting at the end were testimony to the controversial nature of its legal work. Stanley Jacobs, by far the most sociable of the name partners, decided to start his own firm. And even before the official vote to dissolve the firm was taken, Memel and Ellsworth had quietly hired headhunters of their own to find them other positions.

Ellsworth had long ago outgrown all but the largest law firms in the country. The work that he performed for his developer clients required his own efforts as well as those of three other senior attorneys, all of whom had been partners at Memel Jacobs. In addition, Ellsworth was generating enough work to occupy twelve associates, the more junior attorneys who did the grunt work for his clients. Wherever Ellsworth went, his team would also have to go. So for any firm, Ellsworth and crew would be a major hire. The new firm also had to have national and, ideally, international offices. Ellsworth was the nation's leading expert in the legal complexities of resort development. Any time a major U.S. developer was interested in opening up a foreign resort, there was a pretty good chance that Ellsworth would be retained to make sure the deal was completed.

In the days before the demise of Memel Jacobs, Ellsworth had already begun a methodical search for a new law firm. He had made a list of some fifteen national firms, most of which had already contacted him as soon as word began circulating that he might be available. Among them were such respected fast-growing national practices as Philadelphia's Morgan Lewis and Bockius.

In late December 1986, Ellsworth received a call from Keyth Hart, a well-known Los Angeles headhunter. For several years Hart had been placing lawyers for a New York–based legal behemoth with the eel-like name of Finley Kumble Wagner Heine Underberg Manley Myerson and Casey.

"Finley is looking for a partner to head up a new international real estate development practice," Hart excitedly told Ellsworth. "Will you talk to them?"

If there were a successful prototype for what Memel and Ellsworth had tried to accomplish in terms of building a giant national law firm quickly, Finley Kumble was it. Not yet twenty years old, the New York firm had grown to become the second-largest in the country, and there were few who wouldn't bet that within several years it would pass Chicago's venerable Baker and McKenzie to become the largest law firm in the world.

Finley Kumble was impressive. Its client roster included foreign governments, *Fortune* 500 companies, and yes, even President and Mrs. Reagan themselves. Their list of partners was unsurpassed, at least in terms of fame. The firm was home to a former mayor of New York City, a former governor of New York State, the former chief of protocol for the United States, three former U.S. senators, and an equal number of ex-congressmen. But Finley Kumble was most impressive in the way it compensated partners like David Ellsworth. Ellsworth was, in the parlance of the legal profession, a rainmaker. He didn't so much do legal work himself as he attracted clients to the firm. Any law school graduate could draft documents, and what did the client know from documents anyway? At Finley Kumble, which in many ways had served as a model for Memel, rainmakers were kings. Ellsworth was a rainmaker, and he and Finley Kumble seemed a perfect match.

Originally Finley Kumble hadn't been on Ellsworth's list of fifteen potential employers, despite its reputation as the fastest-growing firm in the country. Law in Century City wasn't exactly practiced by the book. The previous year, for example, one of the city's best-known entertainment firms had paid a $1 million malpractice settlement for representing both a thieving Hollywood business manager and the crook's clients. When a lawyer in the firm found out the manager was stealing, he counseled the business manager but never told the victims (who included comedian Mort Sahl and Bruce Weitz, who played the savvy undercover cop Mick Belker on "Hill Street Blues"). The firm claimed the victims weren't "clients." But even in the rough-and-tumble legal environment of Century City, the word on the street was that Finley Kumble had never come across a deal it wouldn't try or an unscrupulous corporate client it couldn't find a way to represent, regardless of potential conflicts of interest. It was also known to put tremendous pressure on clients to pay their bills, lest clients be sued by their own lawyers. Such practices made even the most suspect Century City firms seem staid by comparison.

Largely for those reasons, Ellsworth's initial reaction was to give Hart an unequivocal no. He would talk to almost anybody, but that didn't include Marshall Manley, the charismatic but infamously aggressive chief of the firm's huge L.A. office.

Hart, however, was used to such negative initial reactions.

Hadn't Ellsworth heard of the firm's coup, just a couple of months earlier? Ellsworth drew a blank. Hart reminded him that in September Finley Kumble had been on the front pages of all the legal and business papers after they had snared the two most eligible retiring U.S. senators in Washington, Paul Laxalt and Russell Long.

Laxalt at the time was still a serious possibility for the Republican presidential nomination and was the closest friend of the Reagans. Long, the shrewd son of Huey P. Long, had chaired the Senate Finance Committee and knew more about taxes, retirement plans, and federal regulation than practically anybody. Just a couple of months earlier, Hart reminded Ellsworth, Long and Laxalt had joined Finley Kumble. "Are you sure you don't want to talk to them?" she asked.

The Laxalt/Long argument was persuasive—neither man was known to be prone to rash decisions. Paul Laxalt was thinking about running for the White House. Maybe Hart was right, Ellsworth thought. Maybe the rumors and street talk that had prompted him to keep Finley off the original list stemmed from jealousy. In many ways Finley Kumble was recognized as one of the great success stories of American law. It was just natural that people would bad-mouth them. Ellsworth agreed to talk.

According to Ellsworth, in a phone conversation with Marshall Manley on that golden January day in 1987, Ellsworth bluntly outlined some of his concerns. "I've just come from a firm that overborrowed itself to death," Ellsworth said. "I have no interest in repeating the same situation."

"You're listening to rumors," Manley chided him. "Our firm is solid. We have the same $8 million to $9 million worth of debt that Memel did, but we're anticipating $160 million in revenue. That's nothing."

Nevertheless, Ellsworth made it clear that he was interested in a financially strong, stable firm. He had been embarrassed in front of his clients once. A second such disaster, and Ellsworth's carefully crafted career could be crushed.

Manley again assured Ellsworth that he had nothing to worry about. Any concern about instability was laughable. If there was one thing Finley Kumble, and especially its founder and New York managing partner Steven Kumble, was known for, it was business acumen. Articles in the legal press routinely printed stories with such headlines as "Kumble Shows Business Side of Law." No less a prestigious publication than *Fortune* had just done a major feature on the firm, describing it as a "taut financial ship."

"But," Ellsworth insisted, "I hear the management of the firm is testy. Isn't there a struggle for power?"

This too was nonsense, said Manley. The firm had had its share of problems in the past, but they were all resolved. Things had never been smoother.

On January 8 Ellsworth met some of the leaders of the L.A. firm at a Beverly Hills restaurant. Maybe he was being overly cautious, Ellsworth said, but he'd like to see copies of the Finley Kumble financial statements. "You guys don't know what I've been through," he told the Finley partners.

L.A. partner Alan Schwartz, one of the country's most successful entertainment lawyers (he represented Mel Brooks and Dustin Hoffman, among others), laughed at Ellsworth's worried expression. The firm was growing so fast, Schwartz told him, that last year's financials were already outdated. Forget about it. David was persuaded.

Besides, the Finley Kumble partners said, "Our financials wouldn't tell you anything. We've just gone from eight offices to fourteen. We're close to hitting seven hundred lawyers."

"Well, I just want to know one thing," Ellsworth asked Manley, "because this turned out to be a disaster at Memel. Do you ever pay partners out of borrowed funds?"

"We don't do that, and we have no intention of doing anything like that," Manley assured him.

Practicing in Century City as he did, Ellsworth was street wise. He played tough. He had asked all the right questions, and Manley, to his credit, had looked him in the eye and parried every negative possibility. Maybe all the talk about Finley Kumble was just rumor. Ellsworth remembered how all the namby-pamby lawyers at his old downtown firm had warned him about the evils of Century City when he went to Memel Jacobs. As far as Ellsworth was concerned, that was hokum. He could practice law in the jungle. He had done it.

As Ellsworth recalled it, on January 24, more than a week before the partners voted to dissolve Memel, Ellsworth went to Manley's palatial Beverly Hills home. In return for the delivery of some $6 million worth of client billings, Ellsworth would be paid $600,000 a year and receive an expense account for an additional $75,000. His three partners, Richard Davis, Douglas Dodds, and Michael Simondi, would receive salaries ranging from $195,000 to $275,000 per year.

With the deal complete, Ellsworth would walk into the firm as one of its ten top earners. Few corporate executives were as well compensated as the top tier of partners at Finley Kumble. Several, including Manley, were already making over $1 million per year. Starting at $600,000, it didn't seem like it would take Ellsworth very long to achieve that level.

There was one small requirement of course: the matter of Ellsworth's equity participation in the firm. Partnership in Finley Kumble did not come cheaply. He would be asked to sign a note to Manufacturers Hanover bank in New York, pledging a loan of $322,000, which Manny-Hanny would turn over in cash to the firm's coffers.

But to Ellsworth, the old Century City pro, this didn't seem to be a big deal. The money from the loan would go to the firm, the payments would be made automatically by the firm out of Ellsworth's partnership draws, and the loan would be guaranteed by the firm. It all seemed relatively smooth and neat. If he should happen to leave, the capital contribution would be returned to him.

In addition to the $322,000 pledged by Ellsworth, the three real estate lawyers who would come with him as partners would contribute an additional $220,000 in anticipation of annual earnings of $275,000, $190,000 and $175,000 each. That made Finley's haul for the day a tidy $542,000. But, of course, nobody thought of it in those terms. Surely the firm wasn't hiring partners just to bring in needed cash; such a thing was unthinkable.

Hart had been right, Ellsworth finally concluded. Finley Kumble was young, vibrant, and muscular. A hot young lawyer would have to be crazy not to want to work there. Crazy.

On February 1, the same day they voted to dissolve Memel Jacobs, Ellsworth and the three more junior partners from that firm took the plunge to financial security and professional stability. They joined the law firm of Finley Kumble Wagner Heine Underberg Manley Myerson and Casey. After the nightmare that had become Memel Jacobs, their futures were again secure.

CHAPTER

2

LAWYERS LIKE DAVID ELLSWORTH, looking for a firm where law was treated more as a business than as a gentleman's calling, could thank one man that such an institution existed: Steven Jay Kumble, who had almost single-handedly moved the practice of law away from the weak-kneed worshippers of Darrow and tilted the profession more in the direction of Howe and Hummell, the two rascal lawyers who in the 1880s were disbarred and jailed after hiding a witness in a brothel. By the time Ellsworth arrived on the scene, Kumble and Manley had amassed a crowd of almost seven hundred lawyers with one common credo: to make as much money as they could as fast as they could. Such sentiments were of course nothing new to lawyers. But for decades, using its often ignored canons of ethics promulgated by the stuffy American Bar Association, the profession had worked overtime to mask what had become the primary motivation for many of its members. Kumble, however, had taken greed and made it respectable. He firmly believed that, just as there were eight large national accounting firms, the so-called Big Eight, one day a similarly small number of law firms would dominate the country's corporate legal business. He was determined that his firm, Finley Kumble, would be one of them. It was a goal he had pursued relentlessly, ruthlessly, since his earliest twenty-hour days at Harvard Law School.

A calculating charmer, Steve was often accused, even by those in awe of his talents, of having been born "on the dark side of the moon." Those critics weren't far wrong. He had been born in 1933 on the coldest July 3 that anyone in Brooklyn could remember. Along the south shore, lifeguards under heavy wraps patrolled deserted beaches, and visitors to the maternity ward donned topcoats for the day. It was a bad day in other respects as well. Mary Pickford and Douglas Fairbanks' "House of Happiness" dissolved with the breakup of their marriage. At Broadway and Wall Street, evangelist E. S. M. Nutter verbally attacked speculators, warning a packed crowd that "no society that is based on acquisitiveness alone can survive."

By the time Steven reached high school his family had escaped Brooklyn for New Jersey. There, in a quiet meadowed corner of Westfield, his father, Oscar, operated a nonexclusive swimming, tennis, and golf club called Shackamaxon, named after the village (now the Kensington section of Philadelphia) where, on June 23, 1683, a tribe of Delaware Indians, led by their supposedly wily chief Tammany, handed over most of what became southeastern Pennsylvania to William Penn.

Shackamaxon, now the site of an attractive suburban club, in those days was frequented by what one contemporary visitor described as a rather low-class clientele, most of whom came in from New York City on weekends. The men were hairy-chested creatures who, to the visitor, physically resembled stereotypical mobsters. The women were heavily made up, said to be part of the first set to adore bright plastic pocketbooks.

Steve Kumble, as handsome as a matinee idol, tended the golf greens and lifeguarded at the pool his summer before law school. One close friend who visited the Kumbles at the club described the elder Kumble as "witty, but unpolished." Although Steve Kumble would later insist he had an excellent relationship with his father, former close friends say his relationship with his father was at best complicated. According to someone who was close to Steve Kumble, Steve frequently expressed a desire for a better life than his father's. Steve would work impossible hours if need be, but he would get into Harvard Law School.

Although he grieved deeply over the death of his father, Kumble was, according to friends, embarrassed at the financial condition in which the family had been left. The family's financial life had always resembled a roller-coaster ride. But in Oscar's final days the roller coaster had been on the downswing. There had been no savings.

Kumble rarely revealed to his Yale classmates that his family owned the Shackamaxon. Some people were told that his father had managed the tonier Copacabana. Others, including some who were extremely close to him, believed that Oscar had owned a resort in the Catskills or that he was a wealthy businessman who bought and sold golf courses. Still others, some who had known Kumble for years, had no idea where he came from. "It was as if he had sprung from the earth," longtime friends complained. A favorite topic of speculation was whether Kumble was even his real name. But how could anybody have made it up?

His father's experiences made an indelible mark on Kumble. He vowed from high school days to make a fortune, telling one friend, "I may not be the smartest guy in the world, but I'll work harder than anybody."

At Yale, from which he was graduated Phi Beta Kappa in 1954, and at Harvard Law, from which he was graduated in 1959, fellow students remembered him as someone who would associate only with people who might do him some good down the road. The standard answer around campus when somebody asked for Kumble was, "Why should I have seen him, I'm not a contact."

"If there wasn't some way that you could help his career," classmates would say, "Steve Kumble didn't care about you." Shortly after returning to Harvard Law, he married his girlfriend, Barbara, a student at Wellesley who hailed from the prestigious Shaker Heights suburb of Cleveland.

He also had an early reputation as a bullshit artist. Some of his most outlandish, even ghoulish, stories stemmed from his time in the army, during which he was assigned to Fort Sills, Oklahoma. In one of Kumble's favorite tales, he was flying in a military airplane that ran out of gas. A commanding officer told Kumble and his companion to bail out. The companion did, but, as Kumble told the story, was "turned to hamburger" when his parachute failed to open. Kumble refused to jump and survived. Kumble told different versions of this story to different people, which cannot be confirmed in any of its permutations because military records of the period were subsequently destroyed in a warehouse fire in St. Louis. But there must have been some truth to it: he was white-knuckled with anxiety every time he boarded an airplane.

If Kumble was imaginative, he was also brilliant. He was graduated with honors from Harvard and won a job at one of New York's most distinguished Madison Avenue law firms, Goldstein, Judd and Gurfein. He instantly made an extremely favorable impression on Burton M. Abrams, the Goldstein partner with whom he was assigned to work, mostly on banking and corporate matters and especially on new stock issues. Abrams was the newest partner at the firm and Kumble the youngest associate. But Kumble didn't make a name for himself with good solid legal work alone. One day Abrams came into the office complaining that his golf bag had mistakenly been thrown out of the garage. The next morning Kumble arrived and presented his mentor with a glistening new set of clubs, housed in a bright new bag. After that, Abrams was always careful about saying that he wanted something, lest Steve produce it.

To the others at Goldstein, Kumble was immediately identified as a lawyer to watch. He had no rough edges, in his dress or his speech. But he was also considered one to be wary of. While many young Harvard lawyers were considered aggressive—they wouldn't have made it to Harvard in the first place if they weren't—Steven's reputation quickly went beyond that. He was known as "predatory." It was an image he relished and often embellished with his stories. Partners didn't know what to think when Kumble told them how he once had been caught in a boat on a Catskills lake during a thunderstorm. Afraid the vessel was too heavy to maneuver to shore with both couples, Kumble claimed, he forced the other couple into the water while he and a companion rowed to shore. The other couple eventually made it back as well, the story went.

His career at the prestigious firm did not last long. With name partners Orrin Judd and Murray Gurfein both about to be appointed to federal judgeships and Goldstein not the easiest man to work with, Abrams and Kumble decided that they made such a good team that they would go off on their own.

It just so happened that another partner, Robert Haft, also had the same idea. His idea turned from talk into action when he was offered an opportunity to join the firm Cohen and Stamer by partners Howard Stamer and Barry Cohen.

When Kumble got wind of Haft's intentions, he talked to Abrams and then approached Haft.

"If you're leaving, we'd like to join you," he said.

Haft had reservations about including Abrams in the deal. Abrams had a fiery temper, but he was also smart as hell, generated a lot of business, and had a terrific background working with financial statements and annual reports. That he was something of a bully, which didn't always make him very popular around the office, sometimes spawned unbelievably good results at a negotiating table.

So Cohen and Stamer agreed to bring in Haft and Abrams as partners in the firm, with the young Kumble as a junior associate. A hint that this would be the kind of firm that would appeal to Kumble was given in the name selected for the new firm; Cohen, Abrams, Stamer and Haft. The telex number made no secret of the glue that presumably would bind the four: CASH.

It was, after all, the era of Camelot. The Eisenhower years were over, and John F. Kennedy talked about going to the moon. "Our horizons are unlimited," Haft told his new partners. "Let's go out and make all the money in the world."

Such talk was seductive for the ambitious twenty-seven-year-old Kumble. When he told senior partner Nathaniel Goldstein that he was already leaving, the mentor turned red with anger. Screaming at Kumble and waving his finger excitedly, Goldstein cried, "You're going to get yours some day, Kumble." Fifteen years later Goldstein, his own firm no longer viable, would be working for Steven.

The year 1960 was a good time for new law firms, and Kumble

and Cohen felt sure that this was the way to make their impact on the legal profession. But twenty-four hours after the firm was created, problems developed between Abrams and Stamer. During the negotiations on who would get what, Abrams was in one of his uncontrollable moods, and friction developed between him and Stamer. The principals couldn't agree on how the shares of the new partnership would be divided. They all wanted CASH, but that was about all they could agree on. Finally, after an all-night negotiating session, during which Abrams at one point threatened to throw Stamer from a twenty-three-story window, the still-born firm broke in half. Kumble decided to stay with Cohen and Abrams. Haft and Stamer went off on their own.

It was as a Cohen and Abrams associate that Kumble made what he would always consider his first big business deal. It involved the owner of Frontier Airlines, Miamian L. B. Maytag, who wanted to sell his share of the Denver-based carrier so he could buy his hometown-based National Airlines. Kumble had handled some proxy work for a San Francisco company called Goldfield Consolidated Mines, a client of Cohen's. At Cohen's direction Kumble called a friend at the company and asked if it might be interested in acquiring Frontier, which at the time served most of small cities in the ten Rocky Mountain states where Goldfield had most of its mines.

The twenty-four DC-3s and seven Convairs in the Frontier fleet were just what Goldfield was looking for, and the purchase was made on March 13, 1962. Kumble's finder's fee came to $50,000. But exactly who should get the fee quickly became a matter of controversy among the partners.

Had Kumble still been an associate at the firm, he would have been entitled to one-third of the fee. But a few weeks earlier, he had begged Abrams to make him a partner, and Abrams had agreed. As a partner, Kumble had no special claim to the fee at all; the money went into the firm's coffers, to be divvied up at year's end.

Steven was frantic, insisting that he had been an associate when the deal was made. He was entitled to the $50,000. Finally

Abrams and Cohen relented. It was the first big lump of money Steve Kumble had ever seen, and he promptly quit his job and moved to Florida. But in just six months, he blew the entire sum in bad investments.

On his return to New York, Kumble joined another law office, Amen Weisman and Butler. By the time Kumble arrived, both Amen, who had been one of the chief interrogators at the Nuremberg trials, and Butler were long dead. Herman Weisman was very much alive, as was his son, Robert, and numerous other relatives who worked in and with the firm. Weisman himself was nearing sixty. His career had been distinguished, particularly in Jewish affairs. He had been vice-chairman and then chairman of the United Jewish Appeal during the critical years of 1944 to 1948. He had served as president of the American Jewish Congress from 1942 to 1955, and finally in 1965 he became president of the Jewish National Fund.

Herman Weisman had no dreams of grandeur when it came to practicing law. He hoped to make a good living and to pass the firm along to Robert. But that was before he was hit by the whirlwind named Steven Kumble.

At twenty-nine, the Harvard-Law-educated attorney had two years on poor Robert, a graduate of the less prestigious Florida Southern College. And he quickly began to show Weisman's son a style that had never been seen at Amen Weisman and Butler.

Aggressively seeking clients, Kumble latched onto the representation of a young real estate developer named Richard Cohen. The brother of the millionaire owner of the E. J. Korvette's discount chain, Richard was said to have been challenged by his real estate attorney father Louis D. Cohen to outdo his older sibling, Arthur. The result was an intense rivalry between the two. As Arthur eventually became one of the most powerful men in New York City real estate and the owner of the Gotham Hotel, Richard became one of the country's largest developers of shopping centers. Among his biggest were centers in Bakersfield, California; Columbus, Ohio; and Huntington, New York.

When Richard Cohen's attorney gave up his practice to become the developer's business partner, an acquaintance from

Harvard Law School suggested Kumble might be a good replacement. The two hooked up, and Kumble switched from being an expert in new corporate issues to a specialist in real estate and lease law. Cohen's business boomed, and Kumble's work seemed never done. Kumble finally had to hire an assistant to help him, a thirty-seven-year-old real estate lawyer named Neil Underberg whom he had found working for a real estate company. Weisman also hired two other young lawyers, a corporate specialist named Robert Persky and a litigator, Herbert Roth.

By the end of 1966, Kumble had forced Herman Weisman to give him equal status with Bobby Weisman, who was producing very little new business of his own and thus generating practically no fees or growth for the firm. Kumble frequently complained about this state of affairs; rather than risk losing him and the more than $100,000 per year in income he was generating for the firm, Herman agreed to give Kumble a one-third share in the equity of the firm. But while that sounded good, it didn't really amount to much because the two Weismans still had 66 ⅔ percent equity, and no father and son had ever been closer. The chance for Kumble to have any real say in the firm was still minimal.

But Kumble's success nevertheless bothered Herman Weisman. Steven was twice the lawyer that Bobby was, twice the business getter. To his colleagues, up-and-comers such as Persky, Roth, and Underberg, Kumble was a tornado. On one rare day when he elected to eat with his fellow lawyers rather than with a potential client, he recognized his addiction to money and success. "I can take about five minutes of my wife," he said. "I can stand to read only one chapter of a book. I can't get through the first act of a play. All I think about is getting business."

Steven Kumble had already bullied his way into the partnership, the only non-Weisman family member to do so since firm founder John Harlan Amen himself had died in 1960. But where would he stop? Would it become Kumble's firm, or Bobby's? That's what worried Herman Weisman. It became clear to him that Steven had to be brought under control, and the old man thought he had found a way to do it.

In February 1967 Weisman teed up for a round of golf at the Palm Beach Country Club. His playing partner that day was a fellow New York lawyer, an equally enthusiastic duffer by the name of Leon Finley. Also involved in Jewish affairs and organizations, opera buff Finley had been born Leon Finkelstein and had officially listed that as his name until 1965, when he took a partner and opened a law office called Finley and Gore. One of Finley's more endearing habits was to ask other Finleys he met what their names were before being changed. Finley was four years younger than Herman Weisman but, like Weisman, was starting to think about winding down his law practice. Like Weisman, he was a name partner in his own small firm. His clients were largely banks and savings institutions.

The eccentric Finley had practically a city-wide reputation for unbridled chutzpah. He would ask perfect strangers for huge favors, and clients were requested to give him almost anything he wanted. He frequently imposed upon friends to get him memberships to various clubs, often to the friend or colleague's considerable embarrassment.

Although a good gabber and politically well connected, Finley was considered by many of his colleagues to be a blowhard, not best known for his legal scholarship. When Finley landed clients, which he did with shocking frequency, he referred many of their problems to a more scholarly attorney.

What Finley lacked in legal education, he made up for with common sense. No one in the city of New York was more adept at finding hidden traps in written agreements. If someone wanted to know if he was being snookered, Leon Finley could usually tell him almost instantly. If Finley had been struck with one moment of genius, perhaps inspired by self-awareness of his own shortcomings, it was in deciding to associate himself with a brilliant lawyer, Donald Zimmerman, destined to become a New York Supreme Court judge and widely considered to have one of the sharpest legal minds in New York. Zimmerman had been hired to work on a case for Finley back in 1963. The results were so favorable that Leon asked Zimmerman to take an office in his firm's suite, with the promise of plenty of referral work from Finley's clients. Zimmerman agreed, and the two made a perfect match. Finley brought in the clients; Zimmerman solved their legal problems. From Weisman's perspective, Finley alone might be considered something of a mixed bag. But with Zimmerman in the picture, Finley's little law firm almost had luster.

So it was that, on a breezy Florida day in February 1967, Herman Weisman decided to become better acquainted with Leon Finley. Weisman was preoccupied that day, not with golf but with attempting to solve the Kumble problem. By the fifth hole, Finley, a pretty good talker himself, found he was meeting his match in the loquacious Weisman. Herman described his firm in minute detail, extolling the virtues of his young lawyers. He had an exciting litigator by the name of Herbert Roth and a brilliant young corporate law specialist named Robert Persky. And none was more brilliant nor more capable, Weisman declared, than his own extraordinary son, Robert.

Finley listened with uncharacteristic thoughtfulness. The last thing he wanted to do was look eager. But eager he was.

Not only was Finley tired, ready to be freed up for golf, but his major client, First Federal Savings and Loan, was growing restless. They wanted, as much for prestige as for anything else, to be represented by a larger firm, and Finley was under considerable pressure from the bank officials to join a large firm. But at his age, and with his somewhat eccentric reputation, Leon wasn't about to be invited into any of the established large white-shoe firms. He listened to Weisman with interest but made no commitments.

A few months later, back in New York, Finley stopped by Weisman's brownstone near Sixty-third and Madison. He wanted to talk more about the merger.

Weisman was thrilled and set up a meeting at the Hotel Pierre, where Finley could meet his son for the first time. Weisman presented to Finley an impressive list of his firm's clients. Among them were the Carvel Ice Cream chain, Arlan's Department Store, and Swingline's Jack Linsky. Weisman himself was involved in a $35 million arbitration proceeding that involved his major client, Schine Enterprises, the $150 million real estate, hotel, and theater chain founded by brothers J. Meyer and Louis Schine in 1920. A dispute had arisen over the sale of twelve hotels, sixty movie theaters and seven thousand acres of land in Florida. A court had ordered the problems among different factions of the Schine family settled by arbitration, and Weisman stood to be awarded a big fee once the case was settled.

Weisman was willing to go to any length to attract Finley. Among Finley's demands was that the name of the firm be changed to Amen, Weisman, Finley and Butler. Weisman agreed. Weisman then suggested that, as the two senior partners, he and Finley share a 30 percent interest in the firm's profits. Both Bobby's and Steven's shares would be reduced from their present one-third interest to 20 percent. The other partners—Roth, Persky, and Underberg—would be paid what really amounted to salaries based on performance and production of business.

When Kumble was presented with the new arrangement as a fait accompli, he was initially furious. But Kumble was calculating, not prone to making rash decisions. He agreed to accept his reduced percentage after being assured that, with Finley's business, his gross would be greater. Kumble agreed to the merger, and on August 21, 1967, the partners, anticipating that the new firm was too big for the brownstone, signed a ten-year lease at $6.25 per square foot at 477 Madison Avenue. The new arrangement worked harmoniously for about two months, if that long.

It didn't take Finley long to see that Robert Weisman wasn't exactly setting records for billable hours. That's why he was so irritated when the Weismans continued to badger him about some $360,000 in estate fees that he had listed as accounts receivable before the merger had taken effect. The Weismans wanted the money thrown into the firm's partnership pot. Finley, quite simply, wasn't about to share it. The costs related to the merger were fairly substantial, causing a temporary cash shortage as the end of the firm's fiscal year neared. In December Bobby approached Leon and begged him to collect all his bills as soon as possible. Finley didn't like the idea of pressing his clients. He didn't work that way. Instead, Finley suggested that the partners loan cash to the firm to tide them over until the new firm's receivables began to come in. But the Weismans refused.

It was already clear that the arrangement was flawed, but the partnership managed to survive. Herman Weisman spent a lot of time traveling. Bobby was frequently out of the office looking after the family's real estate holdings. When Weisman did come to town, Finley badgered him about the way the books were kept and complained that the firm's accountants were Herman's brother and nephew.

Finally, in late May 1968, Finley, whose good nature did not extend to giving away money, undertook a study to see exactly how much each partner was bringing into the firm. He calculated that from February 1, 1968, until May 24, 1968, the firm had earned $459,000. Of that total Finley was responsible for $167,000 in billings. Kumble accounted for $112,000. Herman's total billings, largely because he was spending so much time on the Schine matter, for which no fees had yet been awarded, barely totaled $82,000. All but $7,500 of that had not been collected and was just paper money, carried on the books as an account receivable. Finley figured Bobby's share to be $12,500.

Livid at these revelations, Finley roared into Robert Weisman's office.

"Everything you and your father said to me was a lie," said Finley.

"Nobody has ever called my father nor myself liars," Bobby responded tersely.

Finley waved his documentation high in the air. "Here are the facts," he cried. "They speak for themselves."

"If you're calling us liars, then you're a cock sucker," Bobby replied.

The color drained from Finley's face as Weisman rose angrily from his chair, opened his door, and physically hurled the older man into the corridor.

Finley staggered back to his office and had his secretary phone Kumble. It was an awkward moment for Kumble—he was in the middle of a real estate closing that he couldn't leave. But he had never heard Leon in such a state. "If you're not here in twenty minutes," said Finley, "I'm leaving the firm."

"What did he say to you?" Kumble asked.

Replied the shaken Finley, "He used language so vile the exigencies of good taste preclude setting forth the exact words."

The obvious solution was for Finley to withdraw from the partnership. He was a wealthy man, and he could afford the disruption. But once again Kumble urged caution.

The ten-year lease had been negotiated on extremely favorable terms. Furthermore, the firm's name had value. Amen Weisman and Butler was long established and signified quality. Starting over with a new identity would be more difficult. The solution, Kumble said, was not for him and Finley to leave, but for the Weismans to be forced out. They were interrupted by a phone call from Herman Weisman in Palm Beach.

"Don't do anything rash," the diplomatic Weisman said. "I'll cut my vacation short and be back tomorrow."

But a reconciliation meeting in the ninety-three-degree heat of July 23 only made matters worse. Finley demanded that Bobby Weisman apologize for calling him a cock sucker.

"You call me a liar again, and I'll call you a cock sucker again," Weisman said.

Kumble did most of the talking at the meeting because Finley had recently had a throat operation and was so emotionally roiled that he could hardly speak. Kumble itemized the complaints that both he and Finley, the two largest business producers, had with the firm. Why should they produce three-quarters of the income and receive only half the profits? It wasn't enough. Furthermore, Kumble said, the office was run like a "goddamn plantation." The accountants were relatives, being paid between $100,000 and $150,000 a year by Herman. Weisman's personal secretary was his sister-in-law, and she received as large a salary, $22,000 a year, as some of the associates. It's got to change, Kumble insisted. And the change needed is for the partnership to be terminated and for the Weismans to leave.

Herman Weisman, who never wanted to regard the troublesome Kumble as anything more than a law clerk with a charming and attractive speaking manner and an admittedly good ability to bring in business, became angry. Bringing in business is not practicing law, he said. Practicing law was practicing law. He couldn't understand the emphasis that Kumble kept placing on business production. That wasn't important. But it was to Kumble. So the fight went on.

"Look, if you don't like the system here," Weisman told Kumble one day, "you should leave the firm." Bobby kept his fingers crossed. Herman's face turned redder and his language angrier. "You can take your clients and get the hell out," he repeated.

"I'm not leaving,' said Kumble, mindful of the good deal that had just been made on the office space. Another meeting had stalemated.

The usually gregarious Finley then showed an instinct for the jugular that few realized he had. He began a personal investigation of Herman Weisman that culminated in the discovery of a 1957 case in which Weisman had been accused of representing two competing sides in a negotiation. Weisman's actions had brought a reprimand from a New York State judge. Excitedly Finley revealed his discovery to Kumble. This might be grounds for severing the partnership, Finley said. The two conspirators agreed that the obscure case (never even officially published— Finley had found it reported in an old copy of the *New York Law Journal*) might prove the key to throwing the Weismans out of their own firm. Observed Kumble: "I guess this explains how Herman has been reduced to one measly client with an outstanding balance of $450,000."

To make sure the scheme went smoothly, Finley and Kumble first hired Sullivan and Cromwell, one of New York's most prestigious white-shoe firms, to advise them on a breakup. But the lawyers there declined to get involved, suggesting that before they fly off the handle completely on this malpractice case, which after all was ten years old, they should once again try to talk to the Weismans, try to end the partnership with some degree of civility.

So in yet another reconciliation meeting, Kumble outlined the indignities he and Finley had endured. The Weismans were not bringing in business; they refused to allow outside accountants to audit the books; Weisman's sister-in-law was overpaid. "It's a family plantation," Kumble repeated. The partnership must dissolve, and the Weismans would have to go.

Kumble announced that he and Finley would be keeping the lease and that the other attorneys—Persky, Underberg, and Roth, as well as thirty-year-old Alan Gelb, who had worked closely with Weisman on the Schine arbitration—would be remaining. It was good-bye.

"You can't unilaterally terminate a partnership," sputtered Weisman. "We must draw up a plan of termination."

"If you don't leave," Kumble announced coldly, "we're going to starve you out. From now on Finley and I will be retaining all fees and disbursements from clients, and we will be turning over no money to the firm."

Kumble knew that, without the fees generated by Finley and Kumble, the Weismans couldn't last long. The only thing that could save Herman would be the Schine fees, but no one knew when that case would be settled and the fee awards allocated by the judge.

Following the meeting, Kumble and Finley began screening the office mail and removing all payment checks from clients before the Weismans could see them. Clients were informed that the Weismans were leaving. New bank accounts were set up, and when Herman Weisman insisted on seeing the books, Kumble refused. The Weismans were indeed being starved out. But on August 14, 1968, they struck back, hiring William Meagher and Stephen Axinn of the then seven-partner New York law firm of Skadden Arps Slate Meagher and Flom to have Finley and Kumble evicted, restoring the firm to its rightful owners: them.

The breakup became uglier. Finley's accusations of Herman Weisman's ethical shortcomings in the 1957 case and Bobby's failure to contribute were matched by countercharges involving deals that Finley had made. The name calling became worse.

Kumble actually compared the Weismans, who had had the audacity to mount a surprise counterattack, to the Vietcong. "They're a bunch of parasites," Kumble announced.

Finley was scornful. "If Kumble and I extended ourselves to our limits, it was possible for us to make enough money to keep the Weismans in luxury while they produced nothing but additional expenses for the firm."

In court documents the Weismans accused Finley and Kumble of launching a "vicious, unsupportable, and futile attack . . . brashly impugning a reputation for honesty and competence that had been painfully structured over a period of forty years."

But Herman Weisman, whose only true blind spot had been his unstinting loyalty to his son, would not win his court plea for common decency. On almost all points, Justice Samuel Gold ruled in favor of the insurgents and against the Weismans. Gold was moved in part by Kumble's testimony, news to his partners, that Weisman had secretly yielded an additional 3.5 percent of Bobby's partnership interest to Kumble. Weisman's denials of the testimony were not believed by the judge. That interest pushed the Finley-Kumble share over the 50 percent mark and made them the holders of the lease, as well as the valuable February-ending fiscal year. The judge drew the line at the firm's distinguished and valuable name, which the Weismans managed to retain. When a surprised lawyer in the firm asked Steven where the other 3 percent had come from, Kumble was coy. According to this colleague, he stated mysteriously, "We were born in sin."

The victors, Finley and Kumble, now needed a name. What better idea, Kumble thought, than to have the Weismans name our firm. Kumble picked up the complaint that he had been served in August. "Here's the name of our new firm," he said, reading from the paper. "Finley, Kumble, Underberg, Persky and Roth." It had a certain ring to it, but the resonance would not last long.

CHAPTER

3

INDEPENDENCE FROM THE WEISMANS had not come without cost. In the early days after the revolution, massive legal bills remained from the court fight. Clients were confused about where to send fees, and many simply stopped paying. Others decided to stick with Herman Weisman, who had returned with his son to the old brownstone. Sometimes the new firm didn't even have enough cash on hand to pay the staff. But Finley would reach into his personal fortune and bail out the firm, so nobody left. That Finley was willing to go to such lengths was testimony to his decency. In the early days of the new firm, Finley was toying with the idea of going back out on his own and leaving the firm to the younger guys. He had always expected to be senior partner of the new group; as he liked to phrase it, "I'll be the papa of the candy store." But the candy store wasn't to be managed by a papa, although his name would lead on the letterhead. It would be run by a czar, a czar named Kumble.

Seemingly always armed with a long yellow legal pad, Kumble made it his business to make sure fees were collected. The partners were organized into four working groups: the litigation, corporate, and real estate departments, and a catchall estate and banking section. Every month Persky, Underberg, Roth, and Alan Gelb would be called in and questioned about the fee status of every client. No client could be taken on without cash up front. Deadbeats were to be threatened with lawsuits until they paid. Kumble obnoxiously harangued them about the necessity of bringing in new business. The firm couldn't count on Richard Cohen's shopping center work forever. Every partner had to bring in new business. Kumble's motto was Close the deal, get the fee—in reverse order if necessary. He often bragged, "I don't get heart attacks, I give them." He also attracted more clients to the new firm, including some of the most aggressive young real estate developers in New York City. His hardheaded style was paying off, and the firm began making money. Two years after its founding, more than forty lawyers busily crowded what had once been the Weismans' Madison Avenue offices.

From the earliest days, Kumble had demonstrated more interest in making deals for himself than in representing clients. He set up his own venture capital concern, Shelter Capital Inc., to finance friends and partners who wanted to invest in real estate investment trusts. When Cohen and several of his associates purchased controlling interest in Chelsea National Bank, Kumble ended up on the board of directors. His wheeling and dealing left his partners standing still.

Most tried to avoid involvement in Kumble's convoluted personal transactions. On one occasion Kumble arranged a complex system of financing for New York City real estate developer Richard Maidman. The deal involved Kumble's own firm, Shelter Capital; Cohen's company, GIT Realty; and Chelsea National Bank, which issued letters of credit. Kumble acted as the attorney for each of the three entities. When the deal went sour, as did many real estate transactions during the 1972 to 1973 recession, Kumble called Maidman into his office and nastily threatened to take over his properties.

Kumble's emphasis on bringing in fees began producing revenue that partners with less confidence than he couldn't imagine. And it also often resulted in legal shortcuts by Finley Kumble attorneys.

Rival firms quickly realized that you had to be extremely careful in dealing with crafty Steven. Frequently lawyers for other parties in complicated public offerings or tax shelter transactions, deals that included banks or underwriters, insisted on coming into the office and examining every sheet of paper. In one deal involving Cohen's GIT Real Estate Investment Trust, a meeting was scheduled with attorneys from Dewey Ballantine Bushby Palmer and Wood. Because of certain requirements that the trust had to fulfill to be qualified, a proposed Cohen purchase of a shopping center was being held up. When the time for the meeting arrived, no lawyer from Dewey Ballantine had arrived.

"Where the hell's Dewey Ballantine?" asked one of the parties.

The answer: "They won't come in if Kumble's in the room."

William Rosenblum, Jr., a newly hired thirty-five-year-old associate of Kumble's, was forced to conduct the meeting on Cohen's behalf. Kumble waited outside.

Later, in a report of the meeting with Cohen, Rosenblum blurted out that Cohen's trust had tax problems. Kumble's face turned red with anger, and he accosted Rosenblum in a cab afterward. "That was a stupid thing to say," he told him. "Telling Cohen that he has a tax problem." Rosenblum eventually paid for his candor. When the time came to be offered a partnership in the firm, he was told by Finley, "Kumble doesn't want you." That was that.

Eventually Cohen himself tired of Kumble's antics, moving most of his business to another firm, Simpson Thacher and Bartlett. But by the time he had, Finley Kumble was well endowed with other clients, and the loss was viewed as only a disruption.

It hadn't taken long for Finley Kumble to develop a reputation from Wall Street to Park Avenue: at least some attorneys at the firm cannot be taken at their word. Make sure everything is written down.

Just as Kumble had little patience for lawyers who told clients unpleasant things, he also had little patience for lawyers on his staff who found reasons not to approve proposed deals. Tax lawyers, Kumble felt, did that a lot, and for that reason Kumble often ignored the one tax lawyer he had brought into the firm, Stanley L. Golden. Golden's concerns about some of the tax shelter deals just slowed up the works. Kumble didn't want that.

He wanted to close the deal and get the fee. After Golden died of cancer in August 1971, Kumble rode back from the funeral with a group of partners, and they began discussing business. One of them began expressing doubt about a particular deal on which the firm was working.

Kumble cast a seering glance into the back seat. "You say anything like that again, and I'll throw you in that coffin with Golden," he barked.

Likewise, he had little regard for his accountants and other support staff. It was not unusual for Kumble to stop his accountant on the way from work on a Friday evening to say, "Oh, did I tell you I need the firm's financials for a partners' meeting on Monday." The hapless accountant would kiss his weekend good-bye and disappear back into the office to produce the needed numbers. On Monday morning he was invariably greeted by a smiling Kumble. "Gee, I guess I didn't make it clear," Steven chuckled. "I don't need them until next Monday."

Kumble's unique attitude toward the practice of law can be summed up by another of his favorite sayings: "Praise the adversary. He is the catalyst by which you bill your client. Damn the client. He is your true enemy."

Nor was such sentiment purely rhetorical. One of Kumble's biggest and most profitable clients had long been the the fast-expanding Arlan's Department Stores, which had recently come under the control of Richard Cohen's father, businessman Louis D. Cohen. Founded in 1948 in New Bedford, Massachusetts, Arlan's had developed 119 stores stretching all the way to Michigan, Colorado, and Wisconsin by 1970. But the rapid expansion had a price. In 1971, with a recession looming, sales began falling behind the revenue needed to pay for the rapid expansion. From 1970 to 1973, Arlan's lost $65 million, closed 40 percent of its stores, and laid off four thousand employees. Banks were demanding some $21 million in loans, and Arlan's was bouncing its payroll checks. The store owed an additional $35 million to trade creditors and was on the hook for another $15 million owed to landlords.

On April 12, 1971, Kumble already recognized that the future of Arlan's was dubious at best. Barring something extraordinary, bankruptcy was on the horizon. So Kumble did what seemed most natural. He concocted a plainly unethical deal with another law firm designed to squeeze as much in legal fees out of the corpse of Arlan's as possible. On that day Kumble wrote a letter to bankruptcy specialist Ronald Itzler of Ballon Stoll and Itzler, retaining that firm as special bankruptcy attorneys. In exchange for this referral, Kumble demanded and received a promise that one-third of all Ballon Stoll and Itzler fees from Arlan's would be turned over to Finley Kumble. In less genteel professions, such an arrangement might be called a kickback; it was totally contrary to the most rudimentary code of legal ethics. In addition, Ballon Stoll promised that if, during the bankruptcy proceedings, a nonbankruptcy special counsel was needed, Finley Kumble would be appointed. Needless to say Kumble wouldn't be splitting the fees from such an appointment. Not only was the bankruptcy court not informed of the agreement, but it later found it "highly unlikely that Arlan's was privy to the agreement." The deal put Finley Kumble in the potentially conflicted situation of profiting from their client's misfortune.

If anyone needed proof that this was a sleazy deal, on May 14, 1973, Ballon Stoll decided the time had come to file for bankruptcy. But before they would do so, the firm insisted on a $125,000 retainer. The money was obtained by Arlan's executives, who went around to the cash registers of the company's Michigan stores after they had closed for the weekend and removed $124,993.98 for the retainer from the various cash registers in dimes, quarters, and small bills. The satchel of money was then shipped by air to Ballon Stoll's New York office, where partner Ronald Itzler sat up all night counting it. An SEC report later found no justification for a law firm receiving such a large retainer from a cash-starved company that may have still had some hope of recovery.

Trouble arose when Kumble called, demanding that the 1971 agreement be adhered to and that one-third of the cash be turned over to Finley Kumble. Ballon Stoll refused, virtuously pointing out to Kumble that the agreement they had signed went against every legal canon of ethics. They had the money, and they were keeping it.

But playing hardball was Kumble's forte. Totally unconcerned about the propriety of what he had done, Kumble shocked Itzler by suing Ballon Stoll in an open New York State court for the $41,666.66 he felt Finley Kumble was owed. A year later, after threatening to depose Itzler, Ballon Stoll agreed to settle the dispute for $22,500, mainly to get Kumble off their backs. Five years later, after Ballon Stoll had expended what was estimated by their attorneys to be some $250,000 in lawyers' time on the Arlan's bankruptcy, a federal judge, calling the arrangement "patently improper," denied the bankruptcy attorneys all fees for their work on behalf of Arlan's. Moreover, Ballon Stoll was ordered to return the $125,000 retainer. The primary reason for the decision was Ballon Stoll's failure to inform the court of the fee-splitting agreement with Finley Kumble. Had Kumble not called Itzler's bluff and filed the suit in open court, neither the bankruptcy court nor the Securities and Exchange Commission would likely have ever known about the secret fee-splitting arrangement.

Ballon Stoll's attempt to stick Finley Kumble had turned out to be a costly mistake. In the entire deal, only Kumble had managed to turn a profit. After the court ordered all fees returned to the estate, Itzler called Kumble and asked that the $22,500 in settlement money be returned. Kumble was unequivocal. "Go screw yourself," he roared.

Getting screwed was a fate that seemed to frequently befall lawyers in Kumble's path, as his own partner Bob Persky was about to discover.

CHAPTER

4

ROBERT SAMUEL PERSKY, the new firm's corporate lawyer, was artistic, brilliant, and politically connected. A native New Yorker, Persky had a range of interests and abilities that friends found staggering. In high school he had been in both the band and orchestra, as well as serving as business manager of the yearbook and chairman of his school's scholastic fraternity. There seemed to be nothing that the one-time Eagle Scout didn't have the time or inclination to do.

He had been graduated from New York University at the age of nineteen and from Harvard Law by twenty-two. From there Persky had enlisted in the U.S. Army, serving time in both the Philippines and Okinawa. Returning to New York in 1953, he chose to take the New York bar examination, ignoring his eligibility for a military waiver.

As befitted a law graduate of Persky's ability, he won a job as clerk to a federal judge. His stellar career remained on track when he was hired as assistant counsel to New York's Waterfront Commission, the organization that regulated the rough-and-tumble world of the docks.

In 1957 Persky helped to organize his own firm, Harold Luca Persky and Moser. He became extremely active in Democratic politics, especially through his close friendship with New York City congressman William Ryan. Persky's reputation for honesty inspired Ryan to trust the twenty-seven-year-old lawyer with the always sensitive job of campaign treasurer. In his spare time, Persky served as volunteer counsel for the Catholic Trade Unionists, an organization devoted to protecting the rights of black and Hispanic union members. More free time was spent giving lectures on the problems of the brokerage industry at Princeton University.

By 1965, however, Harold Luca Persky and Moser wasn't succeeding financially. All four were good lawyers, but they were more interested in practicing law than scouring the city for business. Each of the four partners decided to go his own way. Persky landed the dream job. With his liberal leanings, his interest in Jewish affairs, and his academic bent, it almost seemed that Persky had been born to work at Amen Weisman and Butler, a firm that put little emphasis on business production and a high premium on quality law practice. Ideologically, Persky was comfortable with Herman Weisman, who also gave time generously to liberal and Jewish causes.

Persky never had ownership interest in the firm, and in his best year he was never paid more than $40,000. But in 1968 that wasn't such a bad living, and Persky was as interested in his outside activities as in his profession.

Like his six-foot, six-inch colleague Herbert Roth, nicknamed the "wild beast" by several partners, Persky had been caught in the middle of the vicious fight between the Weismans and Finley and Kumble. Herman Weisman pleaded with both Roth and Persky to stay with him and promised at least $50,000 a year if they did. But as much as Persky and Roth respected Herman personally, they shared his adversaries' feelings for what nearly everyone outside the family regarded as Weisman's "one blind spot," his loyalty to his son, Robert. In addition, Weisman was nearing the end of his career. Amen Weisman and Butler's glory days were in the past with John Harlan Amen, not the future with Bobby Weisman. In the final analysis, it didn't really seem a hard decision to make. Finley Kumble was a firm with a future. With more sadness than uncertainty, Persky and Roth refused Herman's final plea and cast their lot with Kumble.

Persky and Roth thought Kumble's brand of lawyering a bit frightening but possibly worth trying. Indeed Kumble's ethic was already firmly in place when they transferred to the new firm the client Microthermal, a small Miami company that was the creation of a Miami inventor named Morton S. Kaplan.

Kaplan had developed something that he called the "lost wax theory" of jewelry making. His product involved the packaging of jewelry, and he had sold his invention to one big customer, the Hamilton Watch Company. Then a dispute had developed between Kaplan and Hamilton Watch. Kaplan filed suit, seeking some $500,000 that he claimed he was owed by Hamilton. Roth had worked on the litigation.

Persky, whose specialty was securities work, had also done Microthermal corporate work, making sure the company had the proper registrations with the state of Florida and with the SEC. Persky was officially listed as both the company's general counsel and its secretary. As part of his fee, he had been promised some 15,000 shares of Microthermal stock, which stood to be worth something if the company ever won its lawsuit. When Amen Weisman and Butler became Finley Kumble, Steven Kumble insisted that he turn over three-quarters of the shares to the firm, because he had received them as a fee. As the originator of the business, Persky was allowed to keep 3,750 shares for himself.

In early 1969 Kaplan decided to take Microthermal public, selling 200,000 shares of stock at a public offering price of $4 per share. Persky handled the drafting of the prospectus, which included, among other things, a section promising stockholders that the proceeds would be invested in interest-bearing certificates of deposit. Unfortunately for Persky, the money never found its way to the bank. Instead, it was sent to and squandered by a pair of high-powered investors-turned-swindlers.

John Peter Galanis and Akiyoshi Yamada were the financial wunderkinder of the late 1960s. By the age of twenty-eight, Galanis, who had started as a broker at Merrill Lynch, had become director of his own highly successful mutual fund. Yamada had become a vice-president of Kuhn, Loeb and Company by the age of twenty-five. He too had decided to go off on his own, organizing what was known as a hedge fund, an investment vehicle for wealthy investors. Called Takara Partners, it had among its investors the chairman of the board of RCA, the president of the New York Stock Exchange, and the Rockefeller brothers. In later swindles, for which Galanis would eventually receive a twenty-seven-year prison sentence, the victims included bankers, entertainers, and star athletes.

When Yamada's hedge fund began developing problems, he joined forces with Galanis in an effort to return the investment fund to profitability. Galanis and Yamada's specialty was the buying and selling of new issues. In an optimistic era when stocks could triple a week after being issued, Galanis and Yamada had learned to move quickly to capitalize on the action—or they thought they had.

By the time Microthermal stock went public in July 1969, Yamada and Galanis, known in financial circles as the "Gold Dust Twins," had gotten in trouble with some of their great ideas and were desperately seeking new cash sources for investments that might reverse their fortunes. Yamada, who knew Kaplan, suggested that Microthermal invest its new proceeds with Takara Partners, promising a much higher rate of return than would ever be possible with conventional CDs. Kaplan agreed, sending Yamada a check for $240,000.

When Kaplan told Persky what he had done, the careful lawyer was appalled. It was totally unlawful, he warned. He insisted that the deal be undone, or at least be revamped to comply with the promises concerning application of proceeds that he had made to the SEC. Persky's reaction led to a meeting on September 28, 1969, in which Persky told Yamada that the deal would not comply with the use-of-proceeds section of his prospectus, and negotiations were begun to work out another deal between Kaplan and Yamada that might provide more security to the stockholders.

In October the deal was revised, with Yamada promising to return the $240,000 check to Persky. The check was mailed, but unbeknownst to Persky, Yamada stopped payment on it. Then, on January 5, 1970, as part of the revised deal, Persky allowed Kaplan to send a second check for $240,000 to Yamada. Persky always claimed that he was led to believe that, under the agreement he had made with Yamada, the money would be put in a safe certificate of deposit. Kaplan had convinced Persky that because of Yamada and Galanis's expertise in such matters, they could get a higher yield than if Kaplan himself deposited the money at a local bank.

The upshot of the deal was that $375,000 of the $800,000 raised in the offering had been squandered. Finley Kumble's 11,250 shares of stock, expected to be worth at least $45,000, were about to become worthless.

In May 1970 Persky discovered that the certificate of deposit that was supposed to have been purchased with the second check apparently had not been bought. He began suspecting that something had gone very, very wrong. In just a couple of years with Kumble, his annual income had nearly tripled, to more than $100,000, more money than the modest Persky had ever thought he could make. Now it was all on the verge of ruin. Trembling at the prospect of facing Kumble's wrath at the suddenly worthless stock, Persky began a series of convoluted machinations designed to cover up the loss and enable him to get the hell out of Dodge. He told Kaplan that they simply had to "unburden themselves" of Microthermal, and Persky felt he was clever enough to do it.

Personally tormented by what had happened, Persky could hardly bring himself to focus on the disaster. In the fall of 1970, he told Yamada, "You're telling me no CDs exist. I don't want to know that." Around the same time, according to later testimony in the case by a Finley Kumble associate, Persky was heard to say, "I don't want to know, I don't want to know whether they [the certificates of deposit] are there or not."

Under increasing pressure, Persky began acting in very un-Persky-like ways. He filed false statements with the Securities and Exchange Commission, and he ordered associates to conduct a stockholders' meeting in which the company's true financial situation was misrepresented. Eventually, on November 20, 1970, a sham transaction took place in a Finley Kumble conference room in which Microthermal purportedly purchased

$400,000 worth of stock in a worthless company in exchange for an empty envelope. Then, to cover their tracks further, in March 1971 Persky and Kaplan sold Microthermal to a company in Washington State. It appeared, for the moment, that at long last Persky had washed his hands of Microthermal. But he wasn't that lucky. Kumble's anger would become the least of his problems.

Meanwhile, Persky had another legal problem, one that seemed far less hazardous personally, but that ultimately became the biggest crisis the young firm had ever faced.

At the same time he was working on the Microthermal deal, Persky was embroiled in another complicated case, this one involving the potential dissolution of an old-line New York stock brokerage house, Newberger Loeb and Company. In 1969, Charles Gross, the proprietor of a smaller trading house, put nearly $1 million into Newberger Loeb and became the company's managing partner. But the brokerage didn't fare well under the new management, and in the summer of 1970, several of Gross's partners offered to buy out his interest if he would go quietly. Gross did so on August 31. A new managing partner was named, and a new law firm appeared to handle legal matters: Finley Kumble.

On November 17, 1970, the financially troubled Newberger Loeb partnership (one of its worst investments had been in the short-lived Buffalo Braves NBA franchise) received a very serious letter from the New York Stock Exchange. In part, it said, "In view of your impaired capital position and loss trend we are left with no alternative but to approach the board of governors and ask for your suspension."

Because a new group of investors, including a close friend of Persky's, Paul Risher, was attempting to save the brokerage house, it was only natural that Risher would call on his clever and creative friend to save the firm from extinction. In just days Persky developed what everyone at the firm, and certainly his clients, conceded was a brilliant plan to restructure the Newberger Loeb partnership into a corporation. Persky persuaded

Havana-born client Alex Aixala, who was married to the heiress of the Bacardi rum fortune, to buy 20 percent of the stock in the new company for $1 million. Aixala, who spent most of his time building boats, had been an industrial neighbor of Mort Kaplan's jewelry company. Through that connection Aixala had played a relatively minor role in the Microthermal situation, though exercising extreme caution whenever his fortune was at risk. Persky assured Aixala that, while the business of securities was risky, "this was a relatively safe investment." To ensure it was safe, Aixala insisted on a stop-loss provision, stipulating that if red ink reached a certain dollar figure, the company would dissolve.

All might have gone well except for the staunch opposition to the proposed changes by Charles Gross. As one who still had a considerable investment in the company, Gross's consent was necessary to the reorganization plan, under which each of the former partners were to receive shares of the new corporation. But Gross wanted cash, and he further complained that the amount of stock he had been assigned was too low. He calculated that he would actually do better if the firm simply dissolved itself and divided up any remaining assets. From December 1970 until February 1971, Persky headed the negotiations between the new group of partners favoring the changes and the seemingly intransigent Gross. Negotiations were tough. Not only was Persky determined to show Kumble that he could play hardball, but he had agreed to an arrangement by which no fee for services would be required if the deal didn't go through. Persky and other lawyers at the firm had invested hundreds of hours and tremendous effort in the reorganization, but they stood to make nothing if Gross's hardheaded attorney, Philip Mandel, continued to insist on liquidation rather than reorganization. Persky reflected the attitude of Finley Kumble when he responded that a liquidation might not produce enough money to pay the attorneys.

Persky simply could not let Gross thwart the deal. Kumble's harangues rang in his ears, day in and day out. Close the deal. Get the fee. Failure was not part of the Finley Kumble ethic, and in this case, with its highly unusual fee agreement, it was unthinkable.

So as part of his legal strategy to force Gross into accepting the new corporate arrangement, Persky discovered the existence of a written claim, one that had never been filed as a lawsuit, against Gross by a disgruntled Newberger Loeb client. The claim had been made by David and Mary Buckley. David Buckley was a millionaire son of one of the owners of the lumber giant Georgia-Pacific Corporation. He lived in a twenty-two-room house in Rumsen, New Jersey, and was an avid subscriber to various financial publications. Although he had worked as a $19,000-per-year executive at Lever Brothers, most of Buckley's income came from his father's large annual gifts.

In 1965 Buckley, a longtime client of Charles Gross, began accumulating stock in a new corporation called Westec. Shortly after the purchase, Buckley's profit amounted to over $500,000. Convinced that the company's value would continue to skyrocket, Buckley poured all the profit and more back into his Westec holdings. But in August 1966, trading in the stock was halted by a New York Stock Exchange investigation. Overnight, Buckley's account went $322,000 in the hole, where it remained as a paper loss until Gross resigned.

When the new managers took over the brokerage, they insisted that Buckley pay up. David refused, claiming that while Gross was manager of the brokerage house, he had "churned" Buckley's account, generating commissions through needless trading. In addition, Buckley said he should be compensated for a stock sale that he had ordered but Gross had failed to execute.

When management filed suit against Buckley, demanding payment of the account deficit, Buckley threatened to countersue for $75,000, alleging that Gross had acted wrongly in churning the account.

Buckley's claim was so dubious and would have been so expensive to prove that it seemed unlikely ever to escalate into a court fight. So Persky made an offer to Buckley's attorneys at the New York City firm of Webster and Sheffield, among them a young litigator named Harvey D. Myerson. The Newberger Loeb partners group that Persky represented would agree to pay Buckley $50,000 if Buckley would agree to let the new managers of Newberger Loeb sue Gross for churning in his place. That ensured that the churning claim would escalate into a court suit, but more important, it gave the Finley Kumble lawyers a powerful club in their restructuring negotiations with Charlie Gross.

Buckley quickly agreed. Armed with the assignment of the suit, Persky went to work. He told Gross and Mandel that if they failed to drop their opposition to the corporate reorganization, he would prosecute the Buckley claim against Gross. "If you stand in the way of this deal," said Persky. "You will be tied up in litigation for a long, long time." In addition, Finley Kumble had prepared a long list of other so-called Gross misdeeds as a Newberger Loeb manager for use against him. When Gross, on February 5, 1971, attempted to get a job at another brokerage firm, Newberger Loeb told his potential employers that Gross was under a restrictive covenant and that, if he was hired, the firm could expect a court fight. Gross wasn't hired.

But despite the threats and all of Persky's efforts, the negotiations were a total failure. The threats only made Gross and Mandel more intractable. Not easily intimidated, Mandel was absolutely certain that Buckley's claims were worthless. The February 12 deadline for Newberger Loeb to fulfill its capital requirements was fast approaching.

On February 11, in the Finley Kumble conference room, the partners favoring the reorganization and their various attorneys came together for the final meeting. Neither Gross nor Mandel appeared. Present at Finley Kumble's Madison Avenue quarters were some twenty other lawyers representing different interests in the dispute. Paul Burak of Rosenman Colin demonstrated what Kumble considered an unacceptable approach to practicing law.

"This deal cannot go forward," Burak announced regretfully. "It requires the participation of all of the partners and, without Gross, would be unlawful."

Burak was wrong, said Persky. His own associate, fellow Harvard Law graduate Michael Bamberger, had researched the law.

The deal could go forward, he insisted. Lest there be any doubt among the other lawyers, said Persky, Finley Kumble was perfectly content to issue the opinion letter on its own stationery and put its own neck on the line in case of any litigation against the action by Gross.

With that guarantee, Burak and the other attorneys in the room consented to the reorganization on behalf of their clients. Notified of the new arrangement, the New York Stock Exchange canceled its threat to expel the firm. Persky was undeniably proud of what he had done. In Kumble's view it had been great lawyering. On their own scale for such things, Persky had scored a ten. He had approached a difficult problem and come up with a solution. When faced with persistent obstacles, he had overcome them. He closed the deal. Most important, Finley Kumble received an undisclosed fee that was later termed by a judge to be "embarrassingly large." In addition, Persky personally received a large block of stock in the company.

But Gross's intransigence was not to be forgotten; nor were Finley Kumble's threats to litigate him into poverty with the lawsuit purchased from David Buckley. In a move Mandel would never forget nor forgive, Persky called Mandel to let him know that the reorganization had gone forward without Gross and that negotiations should continue on what Gross was owed. Five days later, on February 16, 1971, while Mandel waited to hear from Persky again, Finley Kumble filed its suit against Gross, attempting to reclaim not just the $50,000 it had paid to Buckley in the settlement, but $250,000. It would eventually be one of the most expensive lawsuits Finley Kumble ever filed.

Mandel was embarrassed by his own gullibility. What was well known among corporate securities firms had apparently escaped him: Finley Kumble's word was not worth much. Persky's offer of further negotiations, Mandel was now convinced, had been nothing more than a tactic designed to ensure Finley Kumble initiated a suit before Gross could do so.

Furious at having been bested, Mandel instructed Gross that no matter how long the case took or how much it cost, he would see it through until the end. On this there would be no settlement. If Finley Kumble's decision to file the suit had constituted a rifle ambush, Mandel responded with a tactical nuclear strike. In addition to filing a lengthy countersuit against Gross's former partners at Newberger Loeb, Mandel took the unusual step of naming as defendants both Finley Kumble as a law firm and Persky as the central conspirator. And all Mandel asked was $5 million in alleged damages.

"I don't know what we'll eventually get," Mandel told his client. "But winning a dollar from those bastards will feel like a dollar and half from anybody else." Gross couldn't have agreed more.

Initially Finley Kumble was confident it had the upper hand. After all, no one had ever heard of a law firm being sued in this manner for its representation of a client. Mandel's action was seen as vindictive. Kumble was so unconcerned that he didn't even hire outside counsel to represent the firm. Instead he handed the file to Herbert Roth.

But by late 1972, the stink over the Microthermal case was beginning to leak, and some of it was permeating Newberger Loeb.

Several large holders of Microthermal stock had begun making inquiries to the SEC. When investigators learned of the involvement of Galanis and Yamada, who by now were the subjects of voluminous stock manipulation investigations, the Microthermal case was moved to the SEC's front burner and the heat was on Persky. Lest anyone doubt it, in this case Finley Kumble had hired outside counsel, turning to John O'Donnell of Olwine Connelly Chase O'Donnell and Weyher, the same firm that had successfully handled the firm's countersuit against Herman Weisman.

Rumors circulated that Kaplan was negotiating a guilty plea with federal prosecutors. Galanis and Yamada, overwhelmed with legal problems, had agreed to talk to the SEC in exchange for the federal government's help in dropping an investigation into their activities by the Canadian government. Galanis ultimately received a six-month sentence for conspiracy for his role in the Microthermal swindle.

Everyone basically was telling authorities the same story: blame the lawyer.

Confident that he hadn't done anything actually criminal but unsure of Kumble's unwavering support, Persky nonetheless remained in good spirits. Each day, however, the first thing Bob did was check that his name was still on the door.

"Glad to see my name is still in the firm," he would joke every morning. But his colleagues responded only with nervous laughter. Persky was required on three separate occasions to testify before the grand jury. Finally, on February 14, 1973, he was called to a meeting at the U.S. attorney's office. It quickly became clear that Persky was not only part of the probe but, with the chief culprits pleading guilty, also a prime target.

On the morning of March 1, 1973, Robert Samuel Persky was indicted by a federal grand jury for fraud and for filing false statements with the SEC. Kaplan had also agreed to plead guilty. Although Persky shared his dubious honor with a pair of accountants who were also involved in the scheme, Persky had been left twisting in the wind by his alleged coconspirators.

On the morning of the indictment, Persky rode the elevator up to the Finley Kumble suite and faced the glass doors. The letters read Finley Kumble Underberg and Roth. All eyes were downcast as Persky made his way to his office. Each cubicle had new stationery with the firm's new name. Kumble had ordered it all changed overnight. Said one associate, "It was sort of like the scene from *The Ten Commandments* when Pharaoh says, 'Let his name be stricken from every monument.' . . . Thus it was written—Persky was gone."

His trial began in federal court in May 1973. On the heels of the Watergate investigation, it was hardly a good time to be a lawyer. On the testimony of two of the most dynamic and enduring swindlers of the age (in September 1988, Galanis was found guilty of another eighty counts of fraud and handed a twenty-seven-year prison sentence, which U.S. attorney Rudolph Giuliani at the time called "the heaviest yet imposed for white-collar crime."), Persky was convicted. The specter of lawyers using the law so wrongly prompted federal judge Inzer

Wyatt, Jr., to declare: "In my almost eleven years on the bench, this is the most unpleasant trial I have ever presided over."

The former Boy Scout was thrown out of the firm, disbarred, and sent to the federal penitentiary in Allenwood, Pennsylvania, to serve four months of a two-year sentence for filing false statements.

Persky's downfall cast the Newberger Loeb case in an entirely new light. In the midst of the massive pretrial discovery procedures that accompany such complex litigation, Mandel could now lick his chops at the prospect of putting a lawyer who had spent four months in prison on the witness stand.

Kumble decided to take the case away from Herbert Roth and hand it to a newly acquired litigator, Norman Roy Grutman.

Kumble's first major outside hire, Grutman had been two years ahead of Kumble at Yale. Absolutely brilliant, and more than willing to show it at the slightest urging, Grutman had developed a tremendously successful medical malpractice specialty. In 1965, while Kumble was chasing real estate developers, Grutman was already involved in two landmark cases involving damaged infants. In one remarkable case, Grutman won a $10,000 jury judgment against Long Island College Hospital after doctors refused to perform an abortion, even though they knew the mother had rubella and that the child might be born deformed. Even though the verdict was overturned by a higher court, his case won such notoriety that it ultimately prompted a liberalizing change in New York State's abortion laws.

In addition, he had represented several writers and actresses in high-profile contract disputes and other types of personal injury matters. In one of these cases, Grutman had represented cabaret dancer Faith Dane against noted producer David Merrick, claiming that Merrick had stolen Dane's character in his Broadway production of *Gypsy*. But Grutman's most profitable client was the highly litigious publisher of *Penthouse* magazine, Bob Guccione.

Kumble had already decided that a great firm needed a great litigation department and that Roth was not the man. Kumble first offered the job of litigation chief to a former Yale classmate, Robert Goldman. But Goldman, who had witnessed Kumble's humorless, relentless drive to succeed, just laughed. "I enjoy my vacations too much," he told Kumble.

Kumble's next call was to Grutman, who had been introduced to him by a mutual friend from Yale. Grutman did not know Kumble as well, having not been in the same class, but he was impressed by his pitch. Grutman was just turning forty, and the idea of heading up the litigation section of what Kumble promised would, within ten years, be the world's biggest and most important law firm appealed mightily to his huge trial lawyer's ego. Kumble promised that, for every dollar Grutman brought into the firm, he could keep 37 cents; the rest would go to overhead. Since Grutman's practice was so trial intensive, he needed to be in a large firm. So charming, so persuasive, so convincing, Kumble so totally won over Grutman that the Shakespeare-quoting classical scholar agreed to turn over 67 percent of all his work in progress as well, even though Finley Kumble had obviously not provided any services that might warrant such a request. Grutman wanted in and would do anything to get there.

With Persky on his way to prison, Kumble realized the danger that the Newberger Loeb counterclaim now posed. It was too big for Herbert Roth. Grutman, however, assured Kumble that in his hands total victory wasn't just possible, but certain.

Comfortable with the confident Grutman in charge of the Newberger Loeb problem, Kumble once again returned to the business of building a law firm. He reached into a rival firm, Marshall Bratter Greene Allison and Tucker, and plucked a top corporate lawyer, forty-five-year-old Andrew N. Heine, to succeed Persky.

A graduate of Yale Law School and a former clerk to federal judge Samuel H. Kaufman, who had presided over the trial of Alger Hiss, the temperamental Heine had bounced around some of New York's best law firms. The son of a wealthy but overbearing real estate tycoon, Heine had entrée into the white-shoe world that Kumble perpetually felt was snubbing him. Heine had actually worked for Sullivan and Cromwell, the whitest of the white-shoe firms. Not the most popular of people, Heine later went to Rosenman Colin, where he became head of the real estate department. He then moved to yet another firm, Marshall Bratter, where he ground out a reputation as one of the top young corporate lawyers in the city. But he was no more liked at Marshall Bratter than at any of his previous firms.

What made Heine interesting to Kumble was that he already controlled from $2 million to $3 million in business. Even though Persky had been considered a careful and good lawyer before his troubles, the accomplished Heine was in a totally different league. He brought numerous corporate clients to Finley Kumble, including Kane-Miller Corporation, Nexus Industries, and D. H. Blair and Company. Heine quickly proved his toughness by driving a much harder bargain with Kumble than Grutman had.

"This is a firm that's growing," Kumble told Heine.

"I'm leaving Marshall Bratter," Heine acknowledged. "It's just a question of where I'm going."

Showing his keen appreciation of what motivates New York lawyers, Kumble quickly responded, "We'll put your name wherever you want it."

With that, Heine opted for the third spot, bumping Underberg back to fourth place on the letterhead. It was a slight Underberg would never forgive. But neither would he ever do anything about it. Explained one partner: "Underberg was the kind of guy who, if Kumble stopped short, he would disappear up Kumble's ass." But now his relationship with Kumble was being challenged. Heine and Underberg were now partners, but they would never be friends. Keenly aware of the rivalry he might have unleashed, Kumble took both men into his office and asked them to make an agreement. Each of the three would always receive an equal share of the firm's profits. And for the next thirteen years, that's exactly what they would do.

At his old firm, Heine had won a reputation for being almost as difficult and ornery as Kumble. Few partners thought the marriage between them would last.

"You and Andy are going to be like two scorpions in a bottle," Grutman warned Kumble.

"Sometimes it's necessary to live with scorpions," Kumble replied.

Heine seemed particularly nervous in his first days at his new home. Partners informed him that they had a million-dollar "key man" life insurance policy on Kumble, lest anything happen to their primary rainmaker. Heine listened with interest. But he was so accustomed to being disliked that he began to tremble when it was suggested that a similar policy be taken out on his life.

"One of you bastards will push me out the window," said Heine with no hint of a joke.

To the surprise, even shock, of the other partners, Heine and Kumble got along well. At Marshall Bratter, his former firm, Heine had always been pushing for dominance. Now Kumble was letting out the reins. The disdain of others qualified Heine as Kumble's blood brother. The two men developed a business relationship and a personal friendship that became tremendously close. Heine would even brag to skeptical friends, "He never does anything without consulting with me first."

For the first time, Kumble seemed to have found someone as interested as he was in making sure that bills were collected and that the firm was run in a businesslike manner. And although Leon Finley's influence in the firm had been waning since day one, Heine's arrival marked the end of Finley's significance. Finley was from that point on excluded from most of the firm's decision making.

In 1975 Grutman brushed off a $300,000 settlement offer from Mandel and marched confidently into trial, crowing that he had never lost a case. "I'm going to grind Mandel into shit," Grutman declared one day before the trial began on June 16, 1975. He made the comments to some friends from New Haven who he was sure were attending the trial to see him work. Grutman never realized that they actually had come to see Philip Mandel in action.

In his opening statement, Grutman was at his theatrical best. He blamed Charles Gross for the demise of the "proud edifice of Newberger Loeb." He talked about bagatelles and tumbrels. Here was a smart lawyer, all right. Nobody knew more big words than Roy Grutman.

"People became aware of the debacle that this man had made of their company," he cried. "It wasn't Finley Kumble."

"I tell you, mark my words, the proof will be here," said Grutman, labeling Finley Kumble's efforts "the save Newberger Loeb operation."

"Here you are going to see the lawyering. The lawyering that went on and that was presided over by one organization, at the ridgepole to hold up the tent or the linchpin for the chain; it was the Finley Kumble firm. You are going to find out about lawyering in this case. You are going to find out that law is not just the laborious study of a dry and technical system. It is not just the practicing of shopkeepers and the greedy watch for clients and the participation in the mannerless and often violent conflicts over sordid interests."

Grutman continued, "I think that I will tell you on behalf of my firm that you will find from the evidence that Robert Persky drank the cup of heroism in that he wore out his heart after the unattainable, set his course for a star that he had not yet seen, and was worthy of the best traditions of lawyering because he sought to do what was right and fair, he helped people in trouble. . . . We at Finley Kumble believed that there is a solution, an honest solution which ingenuity and adaptation and hard work can help find."

"Finley Kumble had right motives," Grutman said. "Finley Kumble does not belong in this case. Our honor, our integrity, the very heart of what we are as lawyers is at stake in this case. Vindicate us. Reaffirm our right to hold our heads high as reputable honorable members of the bar."

It was classic theater. E. G. Marshall was no more dramatic than Roy Grutman. But Grutman had no words eloquent enough to offset the sight of a former name partner in his firm taking the witness stand as a convicted felon.

Sure enough, Persky was forced to testify, and Mandel was allowed to ask him about the Microthermal indictment and prison sentence. Midway through the trial, Grutman agreed with the judge's suggestion that, because of the length and complexity of the case, the jury be dismissed. Back at the firm, worried looks confronted Grutman, who if nothing else was supposed to have a winning way with juries.

A year after the trial ended, on July 7, 1976, Judge Robert Owen issued his conclusions and findings. Finley Kumble was held to have been totally at fault. "Without question," wrote the judge, "Persky was at the heart of this entire matter, guiding the entire plan, carrying threats and knowingly counseling, advising, and instituting baseless lawsuits to achieve the new team's plans." The churning claim against Gross was said to be worthless. The full amount of the judgment against the firm was approximately $1 million.

"No problem," Kumble announced to members of the firm's management committee. He had already talked to a friend at Manufacturers Hanover. The firm would borrow the million, and the loan payments would be taken out of the partner draws—the firm now had twenty-six partners.

"We'll pay it off like rent," said Kumble. "Nobody will feel it."

"Why didn't you raise this at the partnership meeting?" Grutman protested.

"It's not a matter for those guys," said Kumble.

"It affects their pocketbook," said Grutman.

"What are you trying to say, Roy?" asked Kumble.

"I don't think it should be handled this way. I don't see why lawyers who weren't here at the time should be in any way responsible. They didn't join in the fees."

Neil Underberg blanched. "You want me and Steve to be liable for all of that," he said.

"You got the fees," Grutman repeated.

"Fuck you, Roy," said Kumble. "I'm chairman of the finance committee, and I'm borrowing the money whether you like it or not."

Powerless, Grutman walked back to his office and typed out his resignation, careful to give it to Kumble before he could be committed as a partner to the million-dollar loan.

"Some partner you are," Kumble groused, accepting the resignation.

"I understand what partnership means," replied Grutman. With that, Grutman took his wife, Jewel Bjork, also a Finley Kumble partner, and left to form his own law firm, one that would later come to prominence representing first *Penthouse* and then televangelist Jerry Falwell. The lawyer who began his career by suing doctors who refused to perform an abortion ended up with a Baptist preacher who crusaded against the evils of abortion.

Kumble was not at all sorry to see Roy go. His personal-injury-type practice had never really fit into the type of firm Kumble wanted to build anyway. Grutman's departure would weaken the litigation department. But Kumble couldn't spend his time arguing. There was too much to do, and a loan officer to see.

CHAPTER

5

ROY GRUTMAN'S ABRUPT DEPARTURE may not have brought glee to Kumble, but it did brighten the day of Alan Gelb, who had been persistently pestering Kumble about becoming the head of the litigation section. Gelb had been at Finley Kumble since its founding, working first under Herbert Roth and then under Roy. When Grutman had first arrived on the scene, Gelb seemed determined to mimic the successful style of his illustrious mentor. Other partners in the firm noticed some almost immediate changes in Gelb's speech and dress. Not only did Gelb begin buying his clothes from Grutman's tailor, he began copying Grutman's dinnerware as well. Everything Grutman had, it seemed, Gelb wanted. And it didn't stop with objects.

But problems developed when Gelb and Grutman became attracted to Finley Kumble partner Jewel Bjork, an attractive and sophisticated Mount Holyoke graduate who had been in Grutman's 1955 class at Columbia University Law School. Jewel's attentions became increasingly directed toward Roy. On October 30, 1975, she and Grutman were married. Gelb's sycophancy toward Grutman slowly burned into hatred. Relations between the three were complicated in that they worked closely together on litigation relating to *Penthouse,* far and away Grutman's biggest client.

Penthouse publisher Bob Guccione was involved in several hotly contested suits. One involved a circulation dispute with arch-rival Hugh Hefner. Another concerned a short story about a beauty pageant participant, a fictional Miss Wyoming named Charlene, who engaged in fellatio.

In the article Miss Wyoming was a baton twirler whose act of fellatio with a University of Wyoming football player was so delicious that it enabled him to levitate. In a second incident, Miss Wyoming uses fellatio as her talent at the pageant, and then performs again with her coach.

Written by an English professor at a New Jersey college, the article did little to amuse the real Miss Wyoming, Kimerli Jayen Pring. She hired the most flamboyant plaintiff's lawyer in the country, Wyoming's own Gerry L. Spence, to file a million-dollar action against *Penthouse*. Her complaint alleged that the article made it seem that she, Kimerli Pring, had actually committed these acts. At the trial, Pring and Spence prevailed. Ultimately, however, Grutman was able to persuade a federal appeals court to overturn the verdict.

The third and most important of the suits was a well-publicized $500 million libel suit filed in 1975 against *Penthouse* by legendary attorney Louis Nizer on behalf of La Costa Rancho Resorts.

Grutman had assigned most of the early work in the case to Gelb. As Grutman described it at the time, "I was Pygmalion and Gelb was my Galatea. I taught and protected him into being both more of a person and more of a lawyer."

When Grutman submitted his surprise resignation, Alan Gelb could hardly contain his excitement. And when Grutman asked Gelb for the *Penthouse* case files, Alan told Grutman to buzz off. He claimed to have already communicated with Guccione. The La Costa case is mine, Gelb said. Stunned, Grutman went into his office and began working the phone. Through a friendly intermediary, he was finally able to get Guccione on the phone. The *Penthouse* publisher assured Grutman that he and Jewel could keep the case, no matter where they went.

Grutman picked up a precious Mexican artifact, a piece of pottery, that Gelb had given him as a birthday present. Gripping it tightly, Grutman went back to Gelb's office. The two immediately began bickering about who was keeping the case. Finally, Grutman took the pottery and smashed it against Gelb's wall. Interpreting this act of frustration as a sign that Grutman was conceding the client, Gelb danced into Kumble's office yelling, "I did it, I did it. I got the client." But he was wrong. Grutman eventually got the court files, although it took a court order to force Kumble and Gelb to part with them. Kumble never stopped bemoaning the loss of Guccione. The La Costa case spent five years gathering fees before the trial even commenced in 1982. After leaving Finley Kumble, Grutman made millions of dollars in fees from Guccione, enough to support a forty-attorney law practice. In the mid-1980s he finally gave up Guccione to represent Lynchburg, Virginia's wealthy televangelist Jerry Falwell, a representation that Guccione concluded put Grutman in conflict with his interests because Falwell's organization, Moral Majority, opposed the sale of *Penthouse* in convenience stores. The decision cost Grutman more than his client. In early 1989 Roy's second group of partners decided they wanted nothing to do with Falwell, leaving Roy and Jewel and Jerry as one happy but small family.

Though it pained Kumble and Heine to see a good paying customer walk out the door with Grutman, there was a reason that Kumble felt he could allow Roy and Jewel to go. Six months before Grutman's departure, Kumble had found the path to instant respectability and client acquisition. He had, for a rather reasonable sum, hired the former mayor of New York, Robert Ferdinand Wagner.

Robert Wagner may not have been the greatest mayor in the history of New York, but no one had a better name. And a good Waspy name to set off the Irish-sounding Finley and the Jewish names on the letterhead was just what Kumble thought he needed. The mayor's father, also named Robert Ferdinand Wagner, had been one of the most beloved politicians in the history of New York State. The odyssey of the senior Wagner was one of those uniquely American stories. Born in Nastatten, Germany, on June 8, 1877, he came to New York as a child and worked selling papers in the morning and bagging groceries at night. When he entered New York City's P.S. 88, on East 110th Street, Wagner couldn't even speak English. But when he was graduated from City College of New York in 1898, it was with a Phi Beta Kappa key. Two years later, Wagner was admitted to the bar, and he founded the law firm that would carry his name for the next seventy years—Wagner, Quillinan and Tennant. Among Wagner's original partners was Simon H. Rifkind, later to become the almost legendary leader of one of the nation's greatest law firms, Paul Weiss Rifkind Wharton and Garrison. Rifkind would also become known as the mentor of Arthur Liman, who, as a principal player in major lawsuits and as special counsel to the U.S. Senate's Iran-Contra committee, would become the most famous corporate lawyer of his generation.

In 1904 Wagner ran for a seat in the New York Assembly and won. By 1908 he was a state senator, eventually becoming the Democratic party's majority leader. His state legislative record was still regarded with awe by state politicians more than half a century after his arrival. He was responsible for numerous bills aimed at helping his fellow immigrants, among them a guaranteed five-cent fare to Coney Island. He had fathered bills regulating child and woman's labor, and he was chairman of the state commission that investigated the 1911 Triangle shirtwaist factory fire in which 141 women burned to death.

It seemed that nothing could go wrong for Wagner. In 1919 he was appointed to a judgeship. But that same year something did go wrong. At the family's Woodmere, Long Island, estate, his young wife, Margaret, suddenly and mysteriously died. Among those attending the funeral was Wagner's close friend, New York governor Al Smith. Young Robert, just nine, would be brought up in his mother's Roman Catholic faith, as a tribute to her.

In 1926 Wagner, who never remarried, was nominated by the Democratic party to run for the U.S. Senate. One of his most powerful selling points, especially in the eyes of the ambitious Smith and the soon-to-be-governor Franklin Delano Roosevelt, was that Wagner could never be a rival for the presidency because he was foreign born.

Repeated reelection victories until 1944 gave Wagner rare seniority for a northern Democrat. He became the chairman of the Senate's Banking and Currency Committee. As he had in the New York State Senate, Wagner became a legislative giant. He was the primary author of the National Industrial Recovery Act and the subsequent National Labor Relations Act. He was a staunch supporter of civil rights long before such support was fashionable. He was, in short, a beloved giant of a man.

For young Robert Wagner, life with a famous senator meant summers in his father's suite at the Shoreham Hotel. He hob-nobbed with some of the younger members of the Congress and became a well-known child and then young man around the Capitol. In total awe of his father, Wagner attempted to emulate him by running for the state assembly in 1937. The Wagner name was more than enough to win him a four-year term. When World War II broke out, Wagner joined the army air force, where he served for another four years. On his return he was appointed to the city tax commission. That was followed by a stint as commissioner of housing and buildings. In 1949 Wagner was elected the Manhattan borough president. In 1953, just months after his father's death, he was elected mayor of New York City as a reform candidate.

Very little of this, however, brought young Bob much respect. He was widely perceived as a politician who had ridden his famous father's coattails to high office. No one had more scorn for Wagner than the governor of New York, Thomas E. Dewey. When Wagner came to him with his proposed city budget in 1954, Dewey scanned the documents cursorily and then held them over his wastebasket with one hand on his nose. As Wag-ner watched speechlessly, Dewey dropped the city budget in the wastebasket. Mayor dismissed.

But Wagner was determined to live up to his father's image. Less than a year into his new office, Bob decided to travel to Germany to pay homage to his father's birthplace. Then, two years later, in 1956, Wagner decided that he would regain the Senate seat once occupied by his dad. In three years as mayor, Wagner had silenced many of his critics. He had wrapped him-

self in the mantle of the New Deal and was an outspoken supporter of Democratic presidential candidate Adlai Stevenson.
The *New York Times* observed, "The job of mayor has brought
out in him considerably more than he had previously shown. He
lacks the flamboyance or aggressiveness of a Fiorello H. La
Guardia or the glibness, wit, insouciance and playboy tempera-
ment of a Jimmy Walker. But he has a quiet gregariousness, a
patient affability and a willingness to listen." But even the Wagner name couldn't help in the Eisenhower landslide of 1956.
And New Yorkers, by half a million votes, elected the Republican, Jacob Javits, to the Senate.

In a strange way, Wagner felt almost relieved at the defeat. All
his life he had been overshadowed by his father. Now he could
emerge. He wouldn't be in Washington, forever only the son of
Robert Wagner. He dropped the Junior from his name and returned to the office his father had never held—mayor of New
York City. Wagner continued to grow in office. He became enor-
mously popular, rolling up huge reelection victories. But in
1965 Wagner shocked the city by announcing his retirement.
He had been in public office for a long time. Now he wanted to
make some money. To achieve that end, he rejoined his father's
old law firm, still practicing in the Empire State Building. But he
hardly disappeared from public view. In 1968 President Lyndon
Johnson named him the U.S. ambassador to Spain. After LBJ
decided not to seek reelection, Wagner again returned to practicing law but kept a finger in politics. When his close friend
Congressman Hugh Carey became governor of New York, Wagner's stock ran high. Anyone with business requiring the attention of the governor could do no better than to hire Wagner. His
power grew when he was appointed chairman of the nominating
committee that picked judges in New York City. Wagner was
now making real money and beginning to feel, at last, that he
had carved out an identity of his own.

Among the outside positions that Wagner had accepted was
a place on the board of the troubled Chelsea National Bank.
Kumble and his crew also had an interest in Chelsea because
Richard Cohen had bought a big piece of it and had installed a

close friend, Stanley Kreitman, as president of the bank. Kumble had taken over much of the bank's legal work as well as gained a spot on the board of directors. Wagner had never heard of Kumble, although he was acquainted with and fond of Leon Finley. Once as mayor he had called Finley down to city hall to bestow upon him some meaningless commission post. Finley had nearly floated in Wagner's office, convinced he was about to get a judgeship. It was a typical Finley performance, and Wagner had just chuckled over it.

During Chelsea's board meetings, Kumble was amazed at how business just seemed to fall into Wagner's hands. The former mayor never had to lift a finger. Clients just flocked to him. He was Governor Hugh Carey's friend: that was all that counted. It was all Kumble had ever sought—respectability and a good, recognizable, non-Jewish name. Kumble, son of Oscar the club owner, could only dream about being the wealthy son of a U.S. senator. He could never take the name Wagner, as Leon Finkelstein had co-opted Finley. If he couldn't be Robert Wagner, he could own him. That was the ticket to respectability.

It was a great idea, but Kumble wasn't sure how to broach the subject. Perhaps Finley could do it. Everybody liked Leon. Finley, who had saved the firm many times, was now called upon for his most important assignment. Finley thought nothing of it. Ironically, it would be a suicide mission for him. Once a man of Wagner's political clout entered the firm, Finley would become an anachronism.

Finley called Wagner and took him to lunch. Surprisingly, Wagner was interested. Tennant and Quillinan were getting along in years. The younger lawyers at the firm, Wagner figured, might enjoy being part of a younger, more aggressive law firm. At a subsequent meeting at the Yale Club, Wagner was impressed with Kumble's charm and Heine's smarts. That Kumble had been Phi Beta Kappa, like his father, especially pleased him. For Wagner it seemed a perfect deal. He would get an office and a top salary. All he had to do was bring in business. Wagner wasn't expected to do much legal work himself. Ten times a day,

Wagner could be on the phone dispensing advice to Carey, and all day long the rich and influential would walk down Finley Kumble's corridors to seek counsel with the former mayor. Wagner made little pretense, telling the *New York Times*, "In between I practice a little law. My partners are very understanding."

Each visitor would be a potential client. One afternoon at dinner with Wagner, shortly before the deal was made, Kumble pulled in a $25,000 retainer from a client who only knew that Kumble was Wagner's companion. Turning to a Finley Kumble partner, Kumble smiled, "When he's in the firm we'll be doing that all day and night." Officially, Kumble was more circumspect in describing his newest acquisition's role. "We'll consult him on matters of judgment," Kumble told the *Times*. "People pay big money for judgment."

Almost everybody at the firm was excited about Wagner becoming a partner—everybody except Roy Grutman. He was furious when Wagner insisted that his name be made part of the firm name, immediately following Finley and Kumble. At the partners' meeting where Wagner's status was discussed, Grutman pointed out that when former New York City mayor John Lindsay had joined Webster and Sheffield, the firm's name didn't change. "Name partners," instructed Grutman, "are either founding partners or active lawyers who have earned their way onto the letterhead."

Grutman never understood that it wasn't Mayor Robert Wagner's name that was so important to the new recruit. It was Senator Robert Wagner's name that Bob Wagner was representing. There was really very little to discuss, Wagner said. "If there is no name in the firm, there is no discussion. The merger is off. I'm not coming." Kumble and Heine frowned at the obstreperous Grutman. Kumble assured Wagner that he had always been in charge. Why have Wagner if his name wasn't going to be marketed? From then on, he declared, the firm would be called Finley Kumble Wagner Heine Underberg and Grutman. Grutman, who would soon be gone, could lump it. At last Kumble had a firm name that people would have to respect, even if most lawyers in town, even veteran ambulance chasers, still thought the firm's treatment of its clients, colleagues, and its own partners was disdainful.

CHAPTER

6

IF STEVEN KUMBLE had a secret weapon against sleaze, it might well have been his brilliant twenty-seven-year-old associate and later partner Donald Snider. A top graduate of Harvard Law School in 1968, he had actually turned down an offer from the established white-shoe firm Dewey Ballantine. That firm was too big, too impersonal, too daunting; and money had never been the most important thing in Donald's life. A young scholar destined to become a fine and conscientious lawyer, Snider liked the idea of practicing in the old Amen Weisman brownstone. He was greatly disappointed when, shortly after his arrival, the firm moved to its new horseshoe-shaped offices at 477 Madison Avenue. At Harvard, Snider had studied under Professor Andrew James Casner, then the world's foremost authority on real estate law. When Casner sat down to write his monumental treatise on real property, which would become a standard text in virtually every law school in the country, Snider was selected from all the students at Harvard to help him. His efforts in writing two major sections of Casner's text won the magna cum laude graduate of Harvard a highly complimentary editor's note acknowledging his contribution. "The quality of Mr. Snider's work was so great," wrote Casner, "that the authors were able to adopt this material without substantial change."

After accepting his position at Finley Kumble, Snider delayed his arrival for five months in order to finish work on the book.

It was a sacrifice Kumble was more than willing to make.

Snider was one of the most hotly pursued graduates of his Harvard class. Kumble had outfoxed Dewey Ballantine and God knew who else to persuade the legal prodigy that Finley Kumble was the place to be. Don Snider was a Kumble coup.

He quickly became the in-house academic. When a bar association or an in-house training program required a brain to teach a class, Kumble called on Snider. The only thing he would never become was a top firm earner. In the beginning Snider had been asked to give Persky advice on the triability of the Buckley churning claim. Snider came back to Persky with the discouraging word that Gross hadn't personally handled the account and so couldn't possibly have been guilty of churning.

But since his advice was ignored, he had to appear as no more than a witness.

The most unlikely of all the Finley Kumble partners, Snider came from a relatively poor background. He had had to pass up an offer to serve on the prestigious *Harvard Law Review* so he could make money for law school clerking at Boston's ultradistinguished law firm Ropes and Gray. His modest style of dress— Snider purchased his duds off department store racks—worried Kumble.

One day Kumble called Snider into the office to talk about his dress. "You should always live beyond your means," said Kumble. Kumble applied the same philosophy to clothes. All lawyers were expected to wear only the finest. "Think Yiddish, dress British" was the Kumble refrain. He didn't want partners or associates eating Yiddish, either—Kumble banned the munching of bagels because they seemed too ethnic. When Snider seemed reluctant to adopt this philosophy, Kumble produced a $5,000 gift certificate to Brooks Brothers, which he presented to him as a bonus. "Go buy yourself some clothes," he ordered. Other less-favored associates got the same speech, though not all received the gift certificate. Many were directed to the Manufacturers Hanover loan department, where Kumble had worked out an arrangement that guaranteed almost limitless personal loans for his partners and associates—loans that allowed a Finley

Kumble lawyer to display wealth, but inexorably bound the unhappy lawyer to his employer. If a lawyer threatened to leave the firm, he was quietly informed that his Manny-Hanny loan would be called in. Grutman had a phrase for the practice: "silk and chains."

By 1974 a better-dressed Snider had already become a partner in Finley Kumble. But while fascinated with his brilliantly canny boss and mentor, Donald never felt completely at ease. Kumble's visions of grandeur troubled the modest young man the most.

"One day we're going to be the biggest law firm in the country," Steve would predict.

No one laughed when Kumble said such things. He was indeed, as the steady growth of the firm had proven so far, a man to whom no goal was impossible, no ambition too remote. Nonetheless, for a lawyer who had once relished the thought of working in a brownstone, it was troublesome.

"Why don't we concentrate on being the best?" an irritated Snider asked Kumble. "Then we can think about becoming the biggest."

"When you're the biggest," Steve replied. "Everyone will think we are the best."

As usual, Kumble had the last word. Snider was, after all, an academic, a brain; he didn't have Kumble's business sense or vision. By 1975 Kumble was becoming obsessed with the idea of expansion. The first place he would look to develop was down south, in Miami.

"We need some guys up here, admitted down there," he told the partners. Snider, Theodore Greene, and Herbert Roth volunteered to take the Florida bar and open the office.

For a number of reasons, Florida seemed the perfect place to go. Florida's cracker-dominated legislature would do almost anything to keep out-of-state professionals, especially Jewish lawyers from New York, from doing business in the state. But in a challenge to Florida residency restrictions on out-of-state practices, the Florida Supreme Court had eliminated such requirements as having a Florida partner's name in the firm's letterhead. It wouldn't have done Finley Kumble much good to open a firm in Miami and call it Snider, Greene and Roth.

Rules such as that, though they seemed petty, protected local lawyers by preventing big, well-known firms from practicing in the state. Sullivan and Cromwell, one of the oldest and most famous law firms in the world, wasn't about to open an office in Miami if it couldn't use the Sullivan and Cromwell name. Unlike Washington or Los Angeles, where New York firms were already starting to branch out, Miami was still undrained swampland in the eyes of out-of-state firms. Kumble found it even juicier because most of the big local practices were centered around litigation, not real estate and corporate law. It was not only a potential source of new business but also a likely expansion area for the firm's existing client base. Because Finley Kumble's practice was oriented predominantly toward real estate, some fifty to sixty clients of the firm had ongoing land or development deals in Florida. In later years Kumble would claim that his Florida move was the first step in a grand vision. But it was initially based on more mundane considerations. Kumble had squandered his first fortune, the Frontier Airlines fee, in Florida. He was determined to get it back in the Sunshine State.

Kumble first attempted to establish a permanent colony in Miami using a New York lawyer with Florida connections named Robert Mallow. Mallow was not only a member of the Florida bar, but he was also familiar with the complex world of tax shelters and real estate investment trusts, that legal forest in which Finley Kumble lawyers seemed to spend much of their time.

At the time Mallow was working for a New York firm called Swann and Glass, which had actually been created to handle the legal business for two such investment trusts. In recessionary 1974, that seemed to be a good place to be leaving, and Mallow's search for a new firm dovetailed nicely with Kumble's desire to find somebody that could expand his firm into Florida. It was another match not made in heaven.

In 1975 Mallow, with the help of an associate, opened up the firm's first branch. Supposedly Mallow had been admitted to the firm's management committee. He had no way of knowing it at the time, but Kumble would develop the habit of throwing around management committee assignments with the same ease that he had handed Snider a gift certificate. They didn't necessarily mean much.

Sitting 1,700 miles away, Mallow found himself constantly annoyed by the flood of paper from the firm's management committee announcing decisions when he himself, a member of the elite group, hadn't even been informed of a meeting. And even from that distance, Kumble's harangues to "bill, bill, bill; collect, collect, collect" grew tiresome.

Caught up in the fast-paced events in New York, where the firm was also growing rapidly, Kumble paid little attention to Miami. Snider, Ted Greene, and Herbert Roth had all taken the Florida bar exam, but none of the three ended up spending much time down south. Mallow developed and worked on his own clients, and Finley Kumble made little impact on the Florida legal scene. It might have remained that way, except that in March 1977 Mallow prevailed upon Kumble to bring into the firm his long-time friend and colleague Burton Hartman, the former general counsel of New York Life. Hartman had known and secretly reviled Leon Finley and Steve Kumble from the days when they had practiced with the Weismans. Believing strongly that Kumble was ambitious and too money oriented and that the fatherly Finley was gruff and comical, Hartman nonetheless agreed to accept Mallow's offer to join him in Florida. But not for a minute did Hartman ever seriously consider spending the rest of his professional life at Finley Kumble. As soon as he started working with Mallow, Hartman began trying to find both himself and Mallow a better opportunity. "If we stay here, we're going to get tainted," Hartman warned. Mallow wasn't so sure, but he listened to the warning.

In 1978 a twenty-eight-year-old legal columnist for *Esquire* revealed some of the details of the Arlan's bankruptcy proceedings, which at that time were still slowly filtering through the court system. "If any lawyers are wondering why the public has taken such a dim view of the profession lately," wrote the magazine's Steven Brill, "they ought to read the 91-page memorandum filed last month by the SEC detailing its recommendations for payments to the law firms that handled the bankruptcy of the Arlan's Department Store chain."

The publication of the *Esquire* story erased any doubts Mallow had about Hartman's warnings. Hartman had become so rabidly anti–Finley Kumble that he felt ashamed to tell other lawyers where he worked. Burt began negotiating a deal for himself and Mallow at Philadelphia's Morgan Lewis and Bockius, a distinguished law firm that shared Finley Kumble's grand ambitions.

In the fall of 1979, Hartman and Mallow had already decided to leave but hadn't informed the partnership. On that day in 1979, at Andy Heine's Century Country Club in Harrison, New York, Mallow and Hartman were the only two men present who knew this would be their last firm function.

They were standing together as the firm's newest partner, Marshall Manley, was introduced. He too had been the subject of what they considered an unflattering *Esquire* article. Manley had a reputation for brashness and audacity. In the sea of white tennis shorts and white pullover sweaters and shirts, Hartman spotted Manley walking up the driveway to the austere flagstone clubhouse wearing a brightly colored sweat suit that seemed oddly out of place at the club, founded by wealthy German Jews like the Heines who dressed in white and only white. Partner B. Howard Rappaport was appalled. "He looks like the grounds keeper," Rappaport sneered. Worse was Manley's manner, which seemed to Hartman to be boastful and troublesome. Hartman took one look at his new partner and kicked the ambivalent Mallow.

"We're getting out just in time," Hartman assured his friend one last time. "This guy's trouble." This time, Mallow couldn't have agreed more.

CHAPTER

7

WHEN THE STODGY, self-centered partners of Finley Kumble Wagner Heine and Underberg first saw Marshall Manley, bedecked in bright cottons, in 1978, most predicted disaster.

None was more apoplectic than the Kumble sycophant, Neil Underberg, whose devotion to stuffiness now included occasionally donning a monocle. "Those clothes," partners gasped. It was said that Underberg headed Manley off before he could taint the firm's reputation at the club and drove him into town to purchase more acceptable white garments.

Rappaport told one colleague, "When Heine came Grutman said it was going to be like two scorpions in a bottle. This is going to be like two coral snakes."

Only thirty-eight years old, Marshall Manley had already managed to establish a reputation as one of the most ambitious and aggressive attorneys ever to walk into a courtroom. He had been born in Newark but raised in a tough neighborhood in Brooklyn. His father was a union machinist and labor organizer. His mother worked in an office.

As a kid, Marshall had held jobs as a waiter, a busboy, a flower delivery man, a stockboy, and a button boy in the garment district. It was his stint as a waiter, a job that put him in direct contact with people who had been born with much more than he, that fueled his ambition. Manley longed to be served. At Brooklyn College he was a psychology major, but his future first wife encouraged him to enter law. She would become the psychologist. "You ought to be a lawyer," she told him. That was all the encouragement Manley needed; he changed his major to political science, took the Law School Admission Test, and applied to law school. The first member of his family to be graduated from high school, Manley enrolled at New York University Law School. When he was graduated, his grades and savvy impressed recruiters from the Los Angeles banking firm of McKenna and Fitting. He was offered a job and went west to find fortune and fame.

McKenna and Fitting had been founded by William F. McKenna, the most famous banking lawyer alive. Both he and Paul Fitting believed a law firm was an egalitarian place where all partners were considered equal and where good, solid legal work was the highest priority. Toward that end, McKenna had adopted one of the most traditional—some would say old-fashioned—methods of paying its partners: on the basis of seniority. That McKenna brought in 90 percent of the firm's business and Fitting brought in almost none was irrelevant. McKenna and Fitting had formed the firm together, and they received exactly the same draw. Younger lawyers who had come into the firm together could count on splitting the same percentage of the firm's profits, regardless of who generated the business.

Although extremely democratic, the system meant that once a lawyer had attained partnership, he had it made. The profits were brought into the firm by the hard-working young associates, who would labor feverishly during their seven-year apprenticeship, hoping to achieve the vaunted status of partner and the early retirement that it connoted.

Of all the young associates McKenna and Fitting had ever hired, none worked harder or better than young Marshall Manley. Senior partners didn't know what to make of him. He was simply the most aggressive lawyer they had ever seen. He was driven to succeed and appeared willing to do anything to achieve that success.

Not everyone shared that assessment, however. Some of the anti-Manley feelings were caused by anti–New York feelings. Manley refused to adopt the relaxed ways of the Californian. To some, he seemed fresh from the Brooklyn tenements, and his abrasive, brusque manner was considered offensive by many.

But to some potential clients, Manley's aggressiveness was welcome. Such a client was millionaire George Scharffenberger.

Born in Newark in 1919, Scharffenberger was a true child of the Depression. Absolutely dirt poor—his father died when he was eleven—young Scharffenberger often survived on nothing but string beans. But he was driven by his poverty to novel business enterprises, such as the beekeeping operation he started as a teenager. A good student, George looked so young that, when he applied for his first job after college at Price Waterhouse, he was advised to grow a mustache.

Eventually Scharffenberger landed a job at Arthur Andersen and Company, another of the Big Eight accounting firms. From there he went on to executive positions at ITT and then Litton Industries, where he became a senior vice-president.

Finally he was invited to become the chief executive officer of City Investing, an $8 million company that Scharffenberger turned into a $6 billion conglomerate involved in such diverse activities as the manufacture of water heaters, the maintenance of air force transports, the exploration of oil in Syria, the building of homes in Texas, the management of budget motels, and the printing of such magazines as *Forbes, Oui,* and *Golf Digest.*

In 1972, when a City Investing unit developed a problem with some land they were hoping to develop, Scharffenberger approached McKenna and Fitting and asked Manley what he could do.

What Manley did was considered brilliant by people who care about the intricacies of real property law. After a California Supreme Court ruling just about knocked Manley's lawsuit out of court, Marshall refiled the action on an entirely new set of grounds and eventually prevailed. Most lawyers advised giving up after the initial ruling, but he wouldn't. The only person more thrilled than Scharffenberger was Marshall himself. From then on Scharffenberger had himself a lawyer, and Manley had found an angel.

As Scharffenberger's billion-dollar empire grew, so did the

work he offered his young legal prodigy. Nothing was too much trouble for Manley. Whatever Scharffenberger wanted, Scharffenberger got. Manley's success won him a McKenna partnership despite the hostility of several older partners. No one could deny his accomplishments. In McKenna's lockstep compensation system, Manley was feeding the families of the older, non-producing lawyers, just as some younger colleague would support Manley when he got old and wanted to play golf.

But Marshall Manley wasn't the type to wait that long. He had come to California to find gold. He had struck the mother lode, all right, but as the youngest partner, when all the sifting was done, the nuggets in his junior partner's pan were always the smallest. Manley bellowed and cried. But Bill McKenna and Paul Fitting were set in their ways. There was no reward for hustling business, no special deals for lawyers who brought in more money. It wasn't seemly. To his partners, Manley wanted only to "go, go, go. He was driven." Manley was profoundly unhappy at being just one of many in the firm. He wanted stardom—that's why he had come west in the first place. His constant carping about money was making his older partners miserable, although some of his peers, who quietly agreed with him, admired his chutzpah. So there were no tears when Manley took his big client and quit. His departure was made easier by a friend he had made through Saturday morning touch football games at UCLA. That friend was Alan Rothenberg, who in 1973 coaxed Manley into joining the six-lawyer Los Angeles office of Manatt Phelps Rothenberg and Tunney, a firm that was destined to become, at least for a brief time, one of the nation's most influential practices.

It had sprung from the bowels of one of the biggest and most prominent Los Angeles law firms, O'Melveny and Myers. In 1965 Chicago-born Charles Manatt, a twenty-seven-year-old banking lawyer at O'Melveny, decided to take his eight most loyal clients and join the more Hollywood-oriented practice of famed entertainment practitioner Eugene Wyman. But after little more than a year, Manatt decided to hang out his own shingle in L.A.'s sprawling San Fernando Valley. One of his last acts at O'Melveny was to interview Alan Rothenberg, a 1963 law graduate from the University of Michigan who was eager to start a law practice in California.

After a year at O'Melveny and Myers, Rothenberg was persuaded to enter Manatt's firm. Manatt had already been joined by another O'Melveny renegade, Thomas Phelps. Rothenberg quickly confronted a series of confused choices. He was with Manatt for less than a full year when a friend from O'Melveny recommended him to billionaire Los Angeles Lakers owner Jack Kent Cooke, who was looking to cut his legal expenses by hiring a lawyer of his own.

A self-confessed sports nut, Rothenberg thought the opportunity was simply too good to pass up. So he left Manatt and joined Cooke. But after a year with the bothersome billionaire, Rothenberg decided he didn't want to be owned by anybody. Unlike Marshall Manley at McKenna and Fitting, Rothenberg didn't want an angel. He told Cooke that he had decided to return to Manatt.

But by that time, Cooke had become completely enamored of the likable Rothenberg. Rather than feeling betrayed by Alan's quick exit, he insisted that Rothenberg continue to represent him at his new firm. In making that agreement Cooke moved all of his legal business from O'Melveny and Myers to Manatt Phelps.

Rothenberg was almost sheepish when he went over to O'Melveny and Myers to pick up Cooke's files. He knew it was a great opportunity, but he was embarrassed about taking the client from his friends and former colleagues. But Cooke had insisted, and Rothenberg had no choice.

By 1973 Manatt Phelps had grown to include eight attorneys, and the firm was doing so well that the three senior partners decided to move into L.A.'s prestigious and more expensive Century City area. Their long-range strategic plan called for the firm to have thirty lawyers in five years.

One of the first moves of the newly relocated firm was to bring in two of the city's most aggressive and successful young lawyers: the unhappy Marshall Manley and health specialist Sherwin Memel, who wanted to return to law after a bitter experience as a top executive with American Medicorp Inc., a company involved in the acquisition of hospitals that would later be taken over by Humana Inc.

Memel stayed at the firm for only two years, using the operation to get started in practice again. He then began what would eventually become the fastest-growing law firm in Los Angeles, Memel Jacobs Pierno Gersh and Ellsworth.

Marshall Manley was a different story. His damn-the-torpedoes style of law was more suitable to his new firm than it had been at McKenna and Fitting. Most important, Manatt and Rothenberg agreed with him that he should be rewarded not for hours spent on legal business, but for the amount of business he was able to refer to other lawyers in the firm. By the summer of 1978, with his $600,000-per-year City Investing portfolio, he had worked his way onto the letterhead of what was now Manatt Phelps Rothenberg Manley and Tunney. Around Century City Manley was generally credited with making the firm one of the busiest and most exciting law firms in Los Angeles. Here Manley didn't have to go far to find celebrity. Charles Manatt was one of the most politically connected lawyers in the country, about to become the chairman of the Democratic National Committee. Alan Rothenberg had one of the nation's best sports practices. His association with Jack Kent Cooke put him in the middle of the fast-paced world of professional basketball and hockey. He had nearly become commissioner of the National Basketball Association; he owned his own NBA team, the Los Angeles Clippers. And John Tunney was the former senator from California, the son of former heavyweight champion Gene Tunney. Lee Phillips, another Manatt partner, represented stars Barbra Streisand, Linda Ronstadt, and Joni Mitchell.

It was exactly the environment that Marshall Manley had always envisioned on those dreary days back east. He was making hundreds of thousands of dollars while hobnobbing with the rich and glamorous. In 1975 he divorced his psychologist wife, whom he had brought west, and married a beautiful blonde model, California style. His only regret was that his father hadn't lived long enough to see his success. But aside from that one disappointment, Marshall had everything any transplant from the east could have ever wanted. And then he met Steve Brill.

CHAPTER

8

HAD STEVEN BRILL been a licensed lawyer, he almost certainly would have been one of the scorpions or coral snakes inhabiting the Finley Kumble jungle. His Queens background, his explosive temper, and his boundless ambition might have made Brill a natural at the firm.

He had been brought up in the Far Rockaway section of Queens, like Kumble the son of a purveyor of spirits. But whereas Kumble's father ran clubs, Brill's father owned a liquor store in lower Manhattan. As a child, Brill's drill-sergeant qualities were noted by his playmates. At the age of nine, he had organized his neighborhood into snow-shoveling units and supplemented his allowance by negotiating contracts with home owners. Tom Sawyer style, Brill's weaker-willed friends did the shoveling while Brill supervised.

Steven eventually went to Deerfield Academy in Connecticut and was joyfully accepted at Yale University after cockily telling interviewers that Harvard was his backup school. In 1971, at the age of twenty, he had already sold his first piece, about a homeless person, to the *New York Times* Op-Ed page for $150. After graduation from Yale, he enrolled at Yale Law School, though he spent little time in class and a lot of time working as an aide to New York City mayor John V. Lindsay. Because Brill never took the bar examination, critics and angry targets of his often scathing pieces often insinuated that he had flunked out of law school. It wasn't true. Brill did graduate from Yale, but had never intended to become a lawyer. He just didn't want to leave New Haven. Classmates called him a "phantom" student, but that was all right because Brill was already in love with journalism.

By the age of twenty-five, the precocious young writer was selling free-lance articles to both *New York* magazine and *Harper's*. It seemed that nothing he did or wrote was without controversy. His first nationally recognized magazine piece, in *New York* magazine, was entitled "George Wallace Is Worse than You Think He Is." Wallace and his aides denied that Brill had even interviewed the governor for the story; Brill insisted that he had. Nobody quite knew whom to believe.

The Wallace article was followed by an even more controversial piece. "Jimmy Carter's Pathetic Lies" was published in the March 1976 issue of *Harper's*, early in Carter's presidential campaign, when the then little-known Georgia governor was crisscrossing the country spreading his political message. Carter was running primarily on a platform of honesty in government. He would look up at his audience with a kind of hangdog look and deliver the most memorable words of his pitch. "The one thing that I can promise," he would say in little more than a whisper, "is that I will never lie to you." After the presidency of Richard Nixon, that sounded pretty good to the American electorate, which later, of course, moved Carter's furniture to 1600 Pennsylvania Avenue.

To the already cynical Brill, such a statement was simply too much to believe. He was certain that Carter was as much a liar as any other American politician. So he decided to spend a few weeks with Carter and give the future president the Brill lie detector test. Brill would jot down each Carter statement and then attempt to document whether the president was telling the truth or not. Originally Brill tried to sell the idea for the piece to his journalistic mentor, editor Clay Felker of *New York* magazine. But not even Felker saw the potential, telling Brill, "By the time you finish, he'll be elected already." So Brill sold the idea to *Harper's* instead and on January 24, 1976, headed to Mississippi, where Carter was scheduled to address a group of high school students at a local hotel.

Carefully he took down Carter's every word. Carter told the group that he was a peanut farmer, that his house had no water or electricity, and that he had attended the U.S. Naval Academy and become a nuclear physicist. The jaded Brill had to stifle a gag when Carter issued his corny invitation to the students to come visit him in Washington. "When I am your president," Carter told the group. "I hope you'll come see me." Then Carter said something that compounded Brill's skepticism. Carter told the audience that if they had any questions, they should simply write him in Plains, Georgia. "I open every letter myself and read them all," Carter said. Brill smiled. No presidential candidate reads every letter, Brill knew. Even as Carter concluded his remarks with "If I ever lie to you, or if I ever mislead you, please don't vote for me," Brill knew that Carter was dead meat.

When Carter's press secretary, Jody Powell, acknowledged that Carter's mail wasn't always personally read but most often forwarded to Atlanta headquarters, Brill was forced to only one possible conclusion. "This is the paradox of Jimmy Carter," wrote Brill. "His campaign is the most sincerely insincere, politically antipolitical, and slickly unslick campaign of the year."

But the letter-bag revelation was only the first. Brill also discovered that Carter's naval academy degree was in engineering, not nuclear physics. Carter, of course, hadn't claimed to have such a degree. Nor did Brill approve of Carter's claim to be a peanut farmer. He wrote: "Carter is actually a wealthy agribusinessman. He does own and live on a peanut farm, but it is run by his brother." These were the pathetic lies.

Even though the article did not hit the newsstands until February 17, word of its allegations began reaching the Carter campaign staff on February 2. At a press conference on February 3, Carter himself called the piece "the most remarkable work of fiction I've ever read." Most of the reporters covering the Carter campaign agreed that Brill's broadside was a little overstated.

The overly dramatic title of the article, which Brill hadn't written, didn't help matters.

By February 9 the piece had created such a political uproar that *Time* magazine dispatched a photographer to Brill's apartment to get a picture of the controversial author. It didn't take him long to figure out what kind of a slant *Time*'s story would have. The photographer, Ted Thai, asked him to pose with a cigar in his mouth. When Brill looked puzzled, Thai explained, "They don't trust me to make a twenty-five-year-old look as mean and nasty as they want you to look."

Time's story was entitled "Doing a Job on Jimmy." *Time* had been an early promoter of Carter and was partly responsible for vaulting Carter to national prominence by putting him on the cover as representative of a new breed of southern governors several years earlier. (After Carter's election, *Time* editor Hedley Donovan was named a special White House adviser.) *Time* charged that few candidates for the presidency had been subjected to as much media vitriol as Carter and noted that Brill's piece was merely the latest example. Illustrated with equally sized pictures of politician and pundit, *Time*'s article said, "Many charges Carter has already rebutted. Several new accusations are absurdly trivial . . . most of the charges are open to serious question . . . a dozen other points are challenged."

Time hinted that Brill had set out to do a hatchet job on Carter as far back as November and concluded by quoting an unnamed Washington correspondent that Brill is "a hit man . . . the liberal enforcer."

Harper's editor Louis Lapham, in the May issue, responded with a zinging defense. Lapham clearly thought little of Carter. He wrote: "Carter is impressive, primarily for the ruthlessness of his self-interest. His grandiose claims for himself prove to be the pretentions of another used car salesman. To Governor Carter the plain statement of fact constitutes a monstrous distortion."

Lapham insisted that Brill had a reputation "as a careful reporter who enjoys the tedious work of searching the record and the archives."

As it turned out, no one cared much what twenty-five-year-old Steve Brill thought, and Carter was elected to the presidency anyway.

Brill also moved ahead. The controversy had only improved his reputation among the anti-Carter New York literati.

In 1977 Simon and Schuster editor Alice Mayhew asked Brill to write a book for her publishing house. He could choose the subject. Brill picked the corrupt Teamsters union. Former union president James Hoffa had recently disappeared, and it seemed that no journalist had really tackled the country's most dishonest union in an organized way. So at the age of twenty-seven, Brill sold an idea for a book on the Teamsters to one of the country's premier publishing houses. No one seemed to mind that, in his proposal, he had mistakenly called the president of the union Frank Fitzgibbons instead of Frank Fitzsimmons. The book was published in October 1978.

Investigating the Teamsters soon after Hoffa's mob-related disappearance was not, however, without perils. In the spring of 1978, Brill had joined *Esquire* magazine as its new columnist on legal matters. An early riser, Brill was in the office on Thursday morning, April 27, when the phone rang. The caller identified himself as Special Agent Brevard of the Federal Bureau of Investigation. "We'd like to talk to you about Jimmy Hoffa," Brevard announced.

Brill attempted to call his attorney, famed libel law expert Floyd Abrams, but Abrams was out of town. By the afternoon Brevard and a fellow gumshoe named Billowitz were standing in Brill's office. They had a two-part message. First, they told him that they had reliable information that he was in possession of FBI documents and memos pertaining to the Hoffa murder. If that was indeed the case, said the feds, Brill was breaking the law.

Second, and even more threatening, the agents claimed that they had information that Brill possessed a tape-recorded confession from someone involved in the Hoffa murder.

Brill listened in amazement. Not only was he not in possession of any sealed indictment or tape recording, but he was reasonably sure that no such documents or recordings existed. "I'm not going to comment at all on anything you've said," Brill responded unsurely.

The FBI's request for Brill's cooperation was not subtle. Observed one agent: "You may be in danger if people on the street think you have some of these materials like a taped confession. We want to protect you." Brill considered the comment a thinly veiled threat: if he didn't tell what he had learned now, word might be leaked to the street that Brill held such a tape. The agency's motive, Brill believed, was avoiding embarrassment. They had been investigating the crime for months and hadn't solved it. They didn't want some twenty-five-year-old sleuth showing them up.

By Monday morning Brill had convinced himself the agents were fishing for information that might be in the book. But then the phone rang again. This time it was agent Billowitz.

Brill recorded the call. His fears had not been the product of a paranoid imagination.

"Let me tell you basically what we are going to have to do," said Billowitz. "We're going to have to verify it in another manner—and if that means talking to people that you have dealt with in getting that information, we're going to have to do it." And just to make sure Brill got the point, Billowitz whispered the initials of a prominent underworld hit man who might not react passively to even a suggestion that Brill had some sort of taped confession from a conspirator.

The toughest young investigative reporter in the country literally quaked. He giggled. He stuttered and turned incoherent. "We definitely should have a talk," he sputtered.

But the FBI wasn't finished. "That's going to be the first person we talk to," Billowitz said. "I don't know what it's going to do to you or your position. I really don't."

Since he had begun writing about the Teamsters, Brill had been asked hundreds of times if his life had been threatened. Not seriously, he would reply, not from mob leaders or union members. But now, suddenly, he was scared. For the first time, Brill regretted ever having begun the book.

Finally gaining his wits, he called Robert Fiske, the U.S. attorney for the southern district of New York. Fiske was skeptical of Brill's story.

"Bob, you don't have to believe me. I taped the conversation," Brill said. Key parts of the tape were transcribed and given to Fiske's executive assistant, Barry Kingham. Kingham wasn't impressed. He told Brill that he didn't interpret the agent's statements as threats, although he did see how Brill might think they were.

Although Fiske had put the agents on hold, there seemed almost no way to get them to stop their investigation completely. Brill finally decided that the only way to deflate the crisis was to make public the FBI attempt to muscle him.

Kingham was aghast. "You mean you'd go to the press?" he exclaimed.

"Barry," Brill responded. "I am the press."

Within two days, Fiske and Abrams reached an agreement that basically ended the agents' witch-hunt. Brill assured Fiske orally that he had no tape-recorded confessions. In return Fiske ordered the agents not to question Hoffa suspects about anything involving Brill's research. But the lesson that the experience taught about the power of the press would never be lost on Steve Brill.

In April 1978 he had been offered the opportunity to write a column about the law for *Esquire.* He was, after all, a law school graduate, and to *Esquire* editor Clay Felker, the law seemed to be a potentially unexplored area. Two years earlier, when he and Felker had been at *New York* magazine, he had written a major piece about New York's two bursting merger-and-acquisition firms, Skadden Arps Slate Meagher and Flom and the smaller, newer, and ultimately richer Wachtell Lipton Rosen and Katz. Lots of people had written stories about the law. But no one, until Steve Brill took over the beat for *Esquire,* had ever attempted to peek behind the closed doors of the nation's powerful law firms. Behind every corporate president, every successful politician, every multimillion deal was a law firm. But their activities, their profits, their methods of operation were among the most secret in America, and everything about the so-called code of legal ethics was designed to insulate and protect them from public scrutiny. Many lawyers considered even answering a press call unethical. In many states lawyer-dominated legislatures gave bar organizations official power to license and discipline lawyers and to tax their members. Yet while these groups had the capacity to act officially, their actions, even the disciplinary proceedings, were always taken behind closed doors. It was that tightly locked door that self-assured and cocky Steve Brill planned to batter down.

There hardly seemed a more likely first subject for a fascinating glimpse of a law firm on the rise than Manatt Phelps Rothenberg Manley and Tunney. By the spring of 1978, the organization had expanded to sixty lawyers. Charles Manatt was on the verge of becoming the national chairman of the Democratic party. Rothenberg was the most famous sports lawyer in the country. And Manley, at the age of thirty-eight, was making so much money and bringing in so many new clients that he made the energetic Manatt and Rothenberg look lazy by comparison. They were, quite simply, the fastest-growing law firm in the country. On the other coast, their success made Steven Kumble, dejected by his inability to get an office in Miami off the ground, sick with envy.

Brill flew out to Los Angeles to meet the partners in Manatt Phelps. But before he arrived, the partners met in panic. Only one partner in the firm had ever heard of Brill, and he warned the others that the young journalist was dangerous and negative. Alan Rothenberg and Charles Manatt agreed that no one in the firm should cooperate with or talk to Brill.

Marshall didn't particularly care what the other partners thought. He decided to take his chances with the journalistic prodigy. Sitting in a mod-blue office with no desk, a ski-injured arm in a sling, Manley propped his feet up on a glass coffee table. Behind him was a personally autographed poster of a Winston cigarette girl. Manley proudly explained she was his gorgeous new wife, Tonya. Then they walked over to a Century City restaurant for the interview.

"We come up against older guys who interviewed us for jobs when we were coming out of school, and we kick the shit out of them," said Manley. "Our clients see that. They see we're goddam smarter than the old firms. They see our adrenaline."

As Brill excitedly scribbled, Manley went further, breaking with every tradition-bound canon of the legal brotherhood's vow of silence. "I have no qualms about stealing lawyers and clients from other firms," he said. "It's the keystone of our program."

This wasn't exactly something that lawyers in Los Angeles didn't know. Manley was not shy about calling clients after another firm had blown a case for them and suggesting that the client move its business to Manatt Phelps. But no one would ever dare publicly accuse another lawyer of such a despicable act. Here Manley was not just admitting that he stole clients—he was bragging about it.

Brill's article, subtitled "Manatt Phelps has no qualms about stealing clients or lawyers," appeared in the May 23 issue of *Esquire.* Wrote Brill:

> Manley and lately several other Manatt Phelps partners have pushed client hunting far beyond the coy country club, locker room haunts that have always typified partners at prosperous firms. Sources inside the firm claim that the prospects of certain clients switching over to Manatt Phelps after losing an important case are openly talked about. Manley, or whoever is assigned the task, is often not terribly subtle about enticing such clients into the fold; he calls them and/or makes contact through mutual associates, saying that he could have done better. New client accounts, such as Manley's landing of clothier and shirt maker Phillips–Van Heusen this spring, are announced around the firm as triumphantly as they are at an ad agency.

When Brill's article appeared, Manatt and Rothenberg could hardly believe their eyes. But this time the accuracy of Brill's research was unchallenged. No one who knew Marshall Manley, especially his partners, doubted for one minute that every syllable of every quote was real.

Manatt, the politician, was fairly calm. But Rothenberg, who had suffered sincere pangs of guilt when he carted Jack Kent Cooke's files out of O'Melveny and Myers, was beside himself. Nothing in the story made him more angry than an attack Manley had made on a rival Century City firm, Irell and Manella. Irell was a good firm with the same type of young, aggressive, eastern-educated lawyers that populated Manatt Phelps. But instead of insulting any of the many sleazy or bigoted Los Angeles firms, Manley chose to pick on Irell, telling Brill, "Firms like Irell and Manella grew up in the late sixties and early seventies when there was a business boom out here. But we've grown in the mid-seventies when the economy has flattened out. The reason is simple. We're better than Irell. We're more exciting and we're much more aggressive."

Try as Manatt did, he could not calm his partners. Manley was already unpopular with a majority of his colleagues. For several years Manatt and Rothenberg had been defending Manley, keeping his critics at bay. Rothenberg himself had never really understood Manley. The prep-school-educated son of a Detroit pharmacist, Rothenberg, though he liked Manley, looked at his friend with the same alarm that assimilated German Jews had expressed when great numbers of Russian and eastern Europe emigrants came to the United States. Manley was rough in tactics and in speech.

Professionally, there had always been a sharp rivalry between the two men. Rothenberg viewed himself as an aggressive, hard-working, and extremely talented and successful lawyer. Yet he retained a sharp sense of his humanity. He was courteous to the firm's employees. At picnics and outings, he was among the first to organize the touch-football game. Every year he took on the best of the summer law clerks in racquetball. He was an all around decent guy who liked to brag that at the University of Michigan he had majored in fooling around.

Rothenberg was happy with himself. He wasn't driven, and he would never be a hustler of Marshall's intensity. Manley, who coupled his natural brilliance and street smarts with an incredible ability to work, work, work and to produce fees at an absolutely astounding rate was a character unique to American law, but one extremely difficult to work for or with. Ultimately, he knew, Manley would have to go.

With the publication of the *Esquire* article, it was clear to Rothenberg that Marshall had finally overplayed his hand. When the article came out, Manley, who was in Hawaii on a business trip, told Rothenberg to relax and wait until he returned. Alan suggested he return immediately. But Manley stayed on. In Manley's absence, Rothenberg convened the twenty-three Manatt Phelps partners and asked for suggestions on what might be done. His colleagues were generally mortified. In 1978 no name partner in any respected American law firm had ever said the kinds of things that Manley had. The partnership was practically unanimous: they wanted Manley out.

Nobody in the Los Angeles legal community gave a damn about Marshall Manley anyway. Client stealing was considered to be genteel society's equivalent of cattle rustling. Two days later the partners reconvened and, with only two dissenting votes, decided to ask him to leave the firm. Rothenberg then led a delegation of his partners to the nearby offices of Irell and Manella to apologize for the incident.

When Manley returned from Hawaii, he was surprised at his partners' swift action. Initially distraught, he first denied that he had ever talked to Brill. That was obviously ridiculous. Then Manley claimed that he had made the damaging statements because he had been on drugs after his skiing accident. That was even more absurd. Nothing he could say would soothe Rothenberg. Manley was out. Frustrated, he called Brill with a passel of excuses. He claimed he was misquoted. When that didn't wash, Manley used the drug argument. "Listen," said Brill. "A couple of years ago I wrote an article like this about Herbert Wachtell. It made him famous, and this article is going to do the same for you." Manley was astounded. He had never come across a reporter as audacious as Brill.

Rothenberg's pique would cost the firm. It didn't take long for the Manatt partners to put pencil to paper and start calculating how much that cost would be.

Realizing that he couldn't persuade his partners to change their minds, Manley closed the door of his office and began calling clients. Almost all pledged to keep their business with him, no matter where he landed. And with the kind of business Manley controlled, he would undoubtedly land at a very good firm.

Suddenly, a panicked partnership began having second thoughts about their decision. Maybe Manley's remarks hadn't been so bad after all. When self-respect and honor were weighed against the possibility of declining income, the Manatt partners began to reconsider, and they decided to ask Manley to stay but give up his partnership in the firm. In exchange for keeping his business with the firm, the other partners offered him a more-than-generous offer. But it was too late. Manley was too deeply hurt. Oblivious to the envy his success brought and to the hatred that his tactics engendered, Manley had considered Rothenberg his friend. Unmoved by the appeals to reconsider the situation, Manley walked out on July 1, 1978. Within months, without the fees from Manley's clients, Manatt Phelps would begin losing partners. Its growth reversed, Manatt Phelps quickly dropped to lawyerdom's second rank. It was not a fate Marshall Manley would share. He was about to scale heights of power and wealth that few of his colleagues could even imagine.

CHAPTER

9

S TEVEN K UMBLE read Brill's story about Marshall Manley and the growth of Manatt Phelps with more than usual interest. If the names were changed, the same story might easily be about his own law firm. No firm, east or west of the Rockies, was meaner, and no one need take Kumble's word for it, either. All you had to do was follow the constant carping of the federal judiciary, which seemed to complain about Finley Kumble's conduct every few years. The latest had come in an episode involving longtime client Interstate Properties and a new client, Pyramid Company of Utica. Once competing firms, the two companies had decided to get together and jointly develop one big shopping center outside of Utica. When problems developed between the two corporations, Interstate sued Pyramid, and as usual, Finley Kumble was caught in the middle. Most law firms would have asked both parties to find new lawyers rather than sue a client. But Finley Kumble had no such thought. Underberg and Kumble informed Pyramid that they were ceasing their representation and would be representing Interstate in the suit. The partners in Pyramid howled, claiming that they had given confidential information about their company to Finley Kumble that now could be turned against them. Alan Gelb countered in court that Pyramid knew full well who the firm's more important client was, the larger Interstate Properties, and had signed a waiver confirming that fact. Federal judge Robert Carter reluctantly allowed Finley Kumble to continue in the case. But he observed, "Finley Kumble entrenched upon the limits of the Canon of Ethics prescriptions. Finley Kumble's zeal in its pursuit of expanding its roster of clients brought it close to, although not quite beyond, the limits of permissible conduct." No firm anywhere could come closer to the line and not get caught than Finley Kumble could.

Here it was, the tenth anniversary of Finley Kumble, and no firm in New York City was growing faster. It had moved from Madison to more fashionable Park Avenue. The acquisition of Heine had been a stroke of genius. He was a solid—more than solid—first-rate corporate lawyer known and respected in the city of New York.

In addition, Kumble had made major acquisitions in both bankruptcy and labor law. Gary Blum and Burton Lifland, who was later to become the chief bankruptcy judge for the southern district of New York, had succumbed to Kumble's pitch in 1975.

Two years later, Wagner and Kumble convinced the New York District Council of Carpenters that their politically connected firm would be just perfect to represent the union in labor negotiations and in creating a retirement plan for the members. When officials of the district council decided to accept Finley Kumble's solicitation, they had no idea that the firm not only didn't have a labor practice, it didn't have one specialist in labor law or retirement work. But Kumble was only momentarily nonplussed. Through a headhunter he contacted Carl Schwarz, a partner at a New York litigation boutique, Fellner and Rovins, whose lawyers were on the verge of splitting in different directions anyway.

"I'm in urgent need of a labor practice," Kumble pleaded. "I've got this client, but I don't have anyone to do the work."

Schwarz accepted Kumble's offer and quickly built up the firm's labor practice to include six partners and seven associates in New York. In addition to the carpenters, Schwarz added such clients as Long Island University, the Metropolitan Museum of Art, the Hyatt Corporation, Lerner Stores, and the Doral Country Club in Florida. For ten years the labor department would be an island of sanity in Finley Kumble. But like Snider and so many other capable, hard-working lawyers, Schwarz would never become an important part of the firm's management. And, like Snider, Schwarz would eventually make too much money, in his case nearly $500,000 per year, to even think of leaving. Schwarz and Snider were good, talented lawyers that Kumble believed were a dime a dozen.

Following the extremely successful Schwarz acquisition, Kumble and Wagner reached into the heart of New York's Shea Gould Climenko and Casey to snare name partner Robert Casey, a personable tax lawyer with an impressive roster of railroad and shipping industry clients. Casey had been having personality clashes with his crusty partners William Shea and Milton Gould. He had hoped to bring his friend and fellow Shea Gould lawyer Wilbur Mills with him to Finley Kumble. Mills, the former Arkansas congressman who had spent a lifetime studying the tax code, had become best known for chasing stripper Annabella Battistella, better known as Fannie Fox, into Washington's Tidal Basin. That was not exactly the image Kumble hoped to give his firm. Casey, told to leave Mills behind, did so, and his former firm became known as Shea and Gould after Jesse Climenko retired.

Kumble had always sneered at the tax practice but was smart enough to see that if the firm had any hopes of reaching the big time, it would need one. But that was not the only reason he wanted the Irish tax expert.

"Every firm should have a Casey," Kumble observed. "It's good from a marketing point of view." He was so taken with the idea that he insisted Casey's name be added to the firm's name to further balance the preponderance of Jewish-sounding names. And, like everything else that Kumble touched in those days, it seemed to work. Casey immediately brought his new and profitable clients to the firm.

More important, Kumble was beginning to realize that it was a lot easier to attract new clients by hiring their lawyers than by convincing them that Finley Kumble, with its checkered past, could do a better job.

But Kumble was not satisfied. He acknowledged that the firm

had dismally failed in attracting the kind of national press coverage that Manley had brought to Manatt Phelps. Even his hiring of Robert Wagner had turned sour from a public relations standpoint. More than sour, it was practically a disaster.

One of the major clients brought to the firm by Wagner was a French businessman named Willie Bouchara. On a visit to New York in 1974, Bouchara was astounded that the world's greatest city had no bus shelters. He told friends that he couldn't imagine Paris without them. So in 1975, Bouchara worked out a deal with the city of New York whereby he would build and maintain bus shelters on city sidewalks in the Bronx and Manhattan on a three-year experimental basis. In exchange, the city would receive a percentage of the revenues from the advertising that would adorn each shelter. In the next three years, Bouchara, operating under the name BusTop Shelters Inc., built some five hundred shelters. The flat-topped glass and steel shelters were enthusiastically received by the rained-on residents of New York and by advertisers.

In 1978 the franchise was due to expire. Early in 1977 Bouchara approached Robert Wagner, patron of the city's franchise director, Morris Tarshis, to negotiate a long-term extension of the shelter franchise. Wagner worked out a beautiful deal for Bouchara in which the contract would be extended to his client for twenty years, without any competitive bidding.

Wagner's representation of Bouchara might have gone smoothly, but that wouldn't have been the Finley Kumble way. There was at the time a partner in the rival law firm Rosenman, Colin, Freund, Lewis and Cohen who doubled as a member of the New York State Senate. Queens state senator Jack Bronston hated Robert Wagner with a passion that would prove self-destructive.

The feud had its origins in a state political battle that had taken place more than a decade earlier. In 1965 Bronston was known as the intellectual leader of New York's legislature. A graduate of Harvard and Harvard Law, Bronston was brilliant, witty, and charismatic. He also had a habit of irritating established politicians. Before moving to New York, he had been a

New Jersey state senator. After losing a challenge to the legislative leadership there, he moved across the river, ran for office in New York, and in 1958 narrowly upset an incumbent Republican. In 1961 Bronston lined up behind state controller Arthur Levitt in Levitt's unsuccessful bid to unseat Wagner as New York City mayor. In that campaign Bronston publicly referred to Wagner as "weak and inattentive."

Nonetheless, the talented Bronston moved in Albany, as he had in Trenton, to the brink of power. In 1965 he was considered a leading contender for the important post of senate majority leader, a position that would have made Bronston one of the most influential politicians in the state of New York, perhaps a potential candidate for governor.

But Robert Wagner, remembering the election of 1961, engineered an eleventh-hour maneuver giving the job to a rival state senator, Joseph Zaretski. Bronston was crushed and bitter.

When, twelve years later, Bronston saw that Wagner was trying to cook up what he quickly perceived to be one of the most incredible sweetheart deals ever made in the city franchise office, he decided to do everything he could to torpedo the arrangement. On his official state senate stationery, Jack began writing letters complaining about the awarding of the bid on a noncompetitive basis. The plot thickened when Kumble attempted to match Bouchara up with New York City investor Saul Steinberg. Bouchara didn't have enough money of his own to put up all nine hundred new shelters required by his agreement with the city, so outside investors were needed.

But after meeting the Frenchman, Steinberg decided that Bouchara didn't know anything about running a business. He let it be known that if he became an investor, he intended to run the show. Kumble continued his efforts to match Bouchara with Steinberg. But Heine sensed that the well-meaning and innocent Bouchara was about to be screwed. Taking Bouchara aside during a meeting, Heine told Bouchara that Steinberg would want control. "He is both a shrewd businessman and a shark," Heine said honestly.

Showing more than a bit of French intuition, Bouchara took Heine's advice as a warning that Steinberg, if he became a major investor in BusTop, would attempt to take over the company. The proud Frenchman consequently informed Kumble that he wanted nothing to do with such a partner.

Steinberg, who by now had convinced himself that he could operate a bus shelter business by himself, responded to the rebuff by forming his own company, the Convenience and Safety Company, which then became Bouchara's major competitor for the contract. To represent him in his bid to get the contract, Steinberg hired Rosenman Colin's Jack Bronston, the only man more determined than he to prevent Finley Kumble's client from receiving the extension. There was one big problem, however, another partner at Rosenman Colin had already agreed to represent Alan Patricof, an investor who was attempting to work out the terms of a $1.3 million loan that would capitalize BusTop. Bronston was told in no uncertain terms by his partners that his representation of Convenience and Safety represented a severe conflict of interest. On May 17, 1977, Bronston told one of his partners Steinberg wanted to retain the firm. Samuel Lindenbaum told Jack that it was impossible. Lindenbaum wanted to work with Patricof to ensure Bouchara won the conflict. The issue couldn't be more clear, he told Bronston.

But Bronston's lust for vengeance against the former New York City mayor was too great, and he refused to back off. By June 2, working with a Rosenman Colin associate, Bronston quietly had Steinberg's company registered in Delaware. He continued to attempt to convince the partners to accept his new client. In one memo sent on June 9, 1977, Bronston suggested that representation of the company "will serve as an investment vehicle for the erection of public bus shelters in New York City, Philadelphia, Chicago and Seattle."

The answer from executive committee member Murray Cohen was unequivocal: "We should not do anything on this. There is a definite conflict. If we were successful on behalf of Convenience and Safety, we would jeopardize the financial investment of the investors in BusTop." Nine days later, Bronston was elected to a one-year term as the Steinberg corporation's assistant secretary.

From June until October, Bronston met with Steinberg fifteen more times. On October 28, 1977, on his official stationery, Bronston wrote a letter to the executive assistant of the city comptroller, Harrison Goldin, stating that approval of the Bus-Top franchise "would not appear to be in the public interest." The letter from the state senator provided just the help Steinberg needed. Goldin intervened to defer approval of Bouchara's bid and to urge that Steinberg be given the franchise. In return, Bronston received a $12,500 check from Steinberg, of which, on July 11, 1978, $3,500 was donated to Goldin as a campaign contribution. The Patricof group, which ended up on the losing side of the transaction, paid $52,000 in legal fees to Rosenman Colin, completely unaware that a partner in that firm had undermined their efforts to win the contract.

The machinations resulted in a grand jury investigation into the awarding of the contract. Not even the representation of legendary defense lawyer Louis Nizer could prevent Bronston from being indicted and convicted for mail fraud. The prosecution charged that Bronston had used his state influence to help a client he was personally representing. He spent three and one-half years at the federal penitentiary at Allenwood, where Bob Persky had served his time. The conviction was based, in the words of the court, on Bronston's "breach of his duty of loyalty to his firm's clients," and his concealing from Rosenman clients that he was actually working behind the scenes to put the franchise into Steinberg's hands. Said the court, "His specific intent was to defraud his firm's client of the very economic value his firm had been retained to protect."

As Bronston would put it, "I tried to zing Wagner and I got zung."

But the bus shelter scandal was not without its effects on Wagner and Finley Kumble. At a time when the one thing Kumble wanted and needed most was a reversal of the firm's sleazy public image—the firm was once again enmeshed in scandal. But this was in some ways worse than past scandals because, unlike the others, it wasn't just grist for the bar's rumor mills. This one made the front page of the *New York Times.*

Bouchara, extremely unhappy when Steinberg went from potential investor to major competitor, switched attorneys and filed a fifty-five-page affidavit in the case, blasting Kumble and Heine for providing contradictory advice.

Bouchara said Kumble had introduced him to two men described as "potential investors." The Frenchman claimed that only after Steinberg and his partner were armed with confidential financial information did they decide to start their own company and pursue the franchise contract. The embarrassment to Finley Kumble was considerable. Roy Grutman, whose hatred of Kumble was actually growing more intense after his resignation, took the opportunity to file his own affidavit blasting Wagner and his former law firm. Wrote Grutman:

> During the time that I was a member of Finley Kumble, Robert F. Wagner, at the instigation of Kumble, was promoted onto the firm as a name partner over my strenuous objection. As I explicitly articulated to Mr. Wagner, my reservations related to the fact that name partners were either founding partners or had so distinguished themselves by their lawyering that the firm would want their name in its caption. . . . In attempting to persuade me to yield to his wishes Mr. Kumble argued that the Wagner name would be part of his intention to use and manipulate the Wagner name and association as an aid to getting things done and also attracting business which needed political connections. I protested that such a notion was not professional and utterly repugnant to me. Mr. Kumble could only see the dollar signs that the Wagner name could be used to attract.

The whole episode, in public relations terms, was a disaster. It was followed, four months after Brill's article on Manley, with a Brill mention in *Esquire.* But this wasn't exactly what Kumble had had in mind. It was the article about the Arlan's bankruptcy, skewering Finley Kumble for entering into the fee-splitting agreement. The details were just beginning to leak out seven years after the fact through some newly filed documents at the Securities and Exchange Commission.

"How do we know about this fee splitting agreement?" asked Brill. "Because, the SEC explains, it was all done in writing and because Finley Kumble had the audacity to sue." So not only was Finley Kumble corrupt, but they were stupid, Brill seemed to be saying.

When Kumble finally reached the end of the dreadful article, he saw the following miniheadline: "Manley Out at Manatt Phelps." In two long paragraphs, it briefly reported the news from California. The firm had asked Manley to leave, Manley had rounded up his clients, the firm had tried to change its mind, and Manley had left on July 1. The story ended, however, with a bit of news: "Now his friends report he's negotiating to move over to one of two Los Angeles firms eager to take him."

Kumble didn't have to think twice. A year earlier, a friend of Underberg's in California had already spotted and recommended Manley as the perfect Finley Kumble partner, and Underberg had unsuccessfully attempted to recruit Manley. At that time Marshall had had no interest in leaving. But despite the original rebuff, his controversial name had been echoing in Kumble's mind for months. Kumble's partners urged him not to hire Marshall. "This is no technical lawyer, this guy's going around California scaring the shit out of people," one told Kumble. But Kumble and Underberg brushed off the warnings. It was time to act—Brill's article warned that Manley was already having discussions with Los Angeles firms. They made contact, Manley flew to New York, and in October, for a price of some $226,000 and the promise that he had carte blanche to build a West Coast practice, Marshall Manley was hired as the newest partner at Finley Kumble.

CHAPTER

10

ALTHOUGH STEVEN KUMBLE had not enjoyed much success in building his Miami branch, his Florida trips had not been totally wasted.

By 1979 his marriage to Barbara was long over. But in Florida Kumble had found heaven in his marriage to Margaret "Peggy" VanderVoort, a Coral Gables divorcee with substantial interests in breeding and racing thoroughbreds. Although Kumble had absolutely no interest in horse racing, he found it a little more palatable than the theater because it provided an excellent setting to meet the rich and famous, any one of whom at some point might need the services of a savvy New York lawyer. He had become a regular guest at the annual Flamingo Ball held at Hialeah each year before its big race, the Flamingo Stakes.

So it was that on November 10, 1979, Kumble found himself in Laurel, Maryland, for the running of the Washington, D.C., International, one of the more unusual horse races run every year in the United States. Sort of an equine Olympic event, the invitees represent different countries. The 1979 race, featuring a $200,000 purse to the winning owner, was one of the more lackluster. It afforded Kumble even more than the usual opportunity to schmooze.

The object of his attentions that day, however, was neither client nor horse. This time a politician had caught Kumble's eye, former Maryland senator Joseph Tydings.

Like Wagner, Tydings was the son of a politician far more

famous than he. His father, Millard Tydings, had been the U.S. senator from Maryland. But the younger Tydings had himself been a U.S. attorney in Baltimore. In the LBJ landslide of 1964, he had won election to the U.S. Senate. In those post–JFK assassination days, Tydings seemed to fit the Camelot image, combining a patrician manner with idealistic liberal politics. He seemed sure to find his way onto a national ticket, probably as vice-president, possibly even as president, if he ever chose to run.

But Tydings's ambition clashed with one overriding reality of politics, stated by Theodore Roosevelt in a clash with muckraking reporter Jacob Riis some sixty years earlier. "You must never remind a man at work on a political job that he may be president," Roosevelt said. "Once that thought is put in someone's head they turn careful, calculating and cautious and beat themselves."

In 1970 Tydings faced a vicious primary challenge from George Wallace–style conservative Maryland Democrat George Mahoney, who campaigned on the simplistic platform "Your home is your castle." Tydings, who had been a close personal friend of Robert Kennedy, was also made vulnerable because of his staunch support of gun licensing and registration. He had personally steered a gun-control bill through the Senate Judiciary Committee and onto the floor of the Senate where it was finally beaten. Despite massive opposition to Tydings by such groups as the National Rifle Association, he managed to defeat Mahoney. But weakened by the fierce primary, Tydings then had to face a popular Republican congressman, J. Glenn Beall, Jr., in the general election. Beall continued to hammer on the gun-control theme and he used Tydings' opposition to Nixon Supreme Court nominees Clement Haynesworth and G. Harrold Carswell to make an argument that Tydings was weak on the crime issue. On election day, after just one dynamic term in office, Tydings was turned out by the narrowest of margins.

His Maryland connections made him a natural recruit for the D.C. firm of Danzansky Dickey Quint and Gordon which he joined after his defeat. Of all the firms based in Washington, Danzansky Dickey was by far the most political in a local sense.

Other firms, such as Covington and Burling and Arnold and Porter, were national powerhouses. But Joseph Baer Danzansky, through his presidency of the Giant Food Corporation, the area's biggest retailer, and his chairmanship of the powerful National Bank of Washington, was a regional and local power without peer. He had also been treasurer of Tydings' campaign. When Danzansky died on November 8, 1979, the *Washington Post* editorialized that if the District of Columbia ever had a city father, it was Joe Danzansky.

But by the late 1970s the firm had reached a crossroads. Washington, no longer a sleepy southern town, was about to embark on a drastic reclamation that would result in the destruction of thousands of cheap downtown town houses, to be replaced with thousands of expensive Yuppie dwellings. Real estate prices would skyrocket. New office buildings for practically every block were on the drawing board. The entire historic stretch of Pennsylvania Avenue between the White House and the U.S. Capitol was about to be redeveloped. Instead of being a strictly government town, Washington was evolving into a city of business and commerce as well. Almost overnight, it seemed, Washington had grown up. For Danzansky Dickey, that posed a challenge. The firm could not hope to keep pace with its competitors by appealing to a local clientele. They, like the city, had to broaden their client base, and the Danzansky Dickey partners had two ways they could go about it.

The choice favored by Danzansky's son, Steve, was, paradoxically, one of slow but aggressive growth. This was the route that had been taken by Covington and Burling and by Arnold and Porter, the two Washington law firms that had achieved greatness. It would be expensive. It would mean hiring expensive or promising practitioners in new specialties and bankrolling them until their practices developed and caught hold. It would mean competing with Covington and Burling and with Arnold and Porter for important national clients, something Danzansky Dickey had never done. During the growth period, partners' incomes would suffer. But Steve Danzansky was certain that, over the long haul, a short-term sacrifice would pay off and

Danzansky Dickey would ultimately move into the top tier of D.C. firms.

But Tydings was eager to find a quicker route to the big time. And that route meant a merger. Danzansky Dickey could leap to prominence by merging with another D.C. firm or by attempting to make themselves attractive to one of the many New York City firms that for the first time were thinking about Washington as a place for expansion.

Danzansky Dickey was in many ways old-fashioned. As one might expect from a firm that was founded on the principle that law is a high calling and often a public service, it was not very efficient in collecting its bills. It wasn't that the law firm didn't have the computers to churn out the bills. Lawyers in the firm weren't pushed to collect, and there was a fear that if the billing department was too aggressive, it would antagonize the client. Yet the firm spent fairly lavishly. When it recruited former Texas congressman Frank Ikard as a partner, it agreed to put Ikard's chauffeur on the payroll at a salary almost equal to that of some of the younger lawyers.

Firm leaders looked around D.C. for merger partners, but few rivals were interested. One serious possibility was Dickstein Shapiro and Morin, a firm led by three Brooklyn natives, including former Nixon aide and confidant Leonard Garment, who after leaving the White House had become the city legal establishment's most famous lawyer for politicians in trouble. Dickstein was the polar opposite of Danzansky. It had practically no interest in local affairs or politics but was dedicated to working the halls of government for its out-of-state clients. That was the arena in which Garment excelled. He worked the executive branch of government the way Darrow played a jury. It was a different kind of legal practice, one that had little to do with law and everything to do with power. In Tydings' eyes a merger between the two firms would be perfect. However, when partners at Dickstein saw how little revenue Danzansky Dickey partners generated, they hastily, and somewhat regretfully, called off the merger.

Other law firms saw Danzansky Dickey as simply a drain on

profits. Steven Kumble saw it as an opportunity. Kumble looked on Danzansky Dickey with the eye of a corporate raider who considers the parts to be more valuable than the whole. The problem with the firm, Kumble decided, was that it didn't market either itself or its famous lawyers, especially its former U.S. senator, Joe Tydings. It wasn't operating like a business. In the true spirit of marketing, Kumble hired a New York management consultant to analyze the firm. Through that management report, Kumble almost alone was able to see an untapped resource that could generate profits for his fast-growing New York group.

Tydings was impressed with Kumble's arguments. He had always had national aspirations—if he couldn't become a national figure as a politician, why not as a lawyer? Kumble was talking about an opportunity to enter the big time. Here was an organization that already had established a Los Angeles office and was on the move. And Kumble wasn't just offering Tydings a role in the firm—he was willing to put Tydings on the management committee immediately. Here was an opportunity that might come along only once in a lifetime.

Kumble also did a selling job on Danzansky partner Robert Washington, Jr., who through his friendships with D.C. government officials was starting to bring millions of dollars of city legal work to the firm. Washington, a friend of Steve Danzansky's, was initially skeptical. But Kumble gave Washington personal attention, telling him that he was the one lawyer Finley Kumble wanted the most. And in case Washington had any doubts about Kumble's sincerity, he was promised a place on the firm's national management committee. Washington, still a relatively junior partner, was impressed and decided to support the merger.

One slight snag developed in the negotiations, a snag Kumble and Tydings simply decided to ignore for as long as they could. This was an extremely important and potentially lucrative class action antitrust case pitting the National Sugar Refining Company against a number of grocery store chains, including Pantry Pride, Burlington Food Stores, and the Frankford Quaker Grocery Company. Finley Kumble was representing the National

Sugar Refining Company; Tydings was co–lead counsel for the grocery store plaintiffs. Neither he nor Kumble, naturally, bothered to tell or inform his cocounsel that he was negotiating a merger with the opposition.

But that wasn't the only problem. Steve Danzansky was dead set against the merger and had persuaded two of his partners to oppose it as well. Repeatedly throughout the spring and summer of 1980, as merger talks continued, Danzansky warned that something was wrong with the merger proposal. He had taken it upon himself to call former Finley Kumble partners and was convinced that Kumble and friends were bad news.

But Tydings relentlessly pushed through the merger, promising the firm's partners that the Danzansky Dickey name would remain (in parentheses) on the firm's stationery. They would therefore retain their identity. Tydings assured the lawyers that they would not become simply a branch of a New York firm. Perhaps more important, Kumble had agreed that the bigger firm would take over the $1 million in debt that Danzansky Dickey owed to its primary lender, the National Bank of Washington. With that burden about to be lifted from their shoulders, on October 16 the vote was taken. With only three dissenting votes out of twenty, Danzansky Dickey agreed to the merger. On October 31, 1980, the *Washington Post* announced the marriage of the two firms. "One of Washington's most politically influential firms will merge with a large New York law firm that counts former Mayor Robert Wagner among its partners." The article predicted that the merger would catapult "the smaller D.C. firm into a full national presence and the merger would make Finley Kumble one of the 25 largest law firms in the country." After Wagner, Kumble didn't have too many big names to brag about. The article cited Kumble's former mentor Nathaniel Goldstein, who had since come to work for Kumble, and Sheldon Lytton, a former chief of staff to the lieutenant governor of California, as its other prominent partners. That wouldn't be a problem for Kumble in the future. Tydings would be marketed. He would be used to attract both new lawyers and new clients. Steve was beside himself with glee. Oscar Kumble's son now owned a former U.S. senator, one with a name more patrician than and just as glittery as Wagner's. "Tydings's father had a bridge named after him," Kumble gushed. "The only bridge my father had was in his mouth."

Among those not so thrilled at the revelation was Harold Kohn, the attorney in Philadelphia representing several of the grocery store plaintiffs in the antitrust suit. Kohn rubbed his eyes in disbelief when he discovered that for the last year his cocounsel had been secretly negotiating a merger with the counsel for the opposition. When he stopped rubbing, Kohn filed a motion in court asking that $195,000 of nearly $1,000,000 that Tydings had been paid be returned to the plaintiffs. The sum represented the fees and costs awarded to Tydings for work performed between November 1979 and February 1981. Forced into court to defend his honor, Tydings denied that he had shared any information about the sugar case with Kumble. Kumble thought it was "ridiculous" that anybody should have to tell the judge. "What was Tydings supposed to do?" he said. "Run to the judge and say I met this guy at the race track?"

A federal appeals court judge decided that was almost exactly what Tydings should have done on June 27, 1980, the date the talks became substantive. After that point, wrote the judge, it was reasonable to assume that there might be an appearance that the two firms were exchanging confidential information, and he ordered Tydings to return the fees that were earned after that date.

Ironically, Danzansky was meanwhile looking everywhere to find a good example of Finley Kumble corruption to quash the merger. It never occurred to him to look right under his own partner's feet. Few in the firm believed Danzansky's predictions of doom. What they did see were the projection sheets that Kumble had offered to each partner, demonstrating how much more money each would earn under the Finley Kumble umbrella. The numbers were big, in some cases almost double. Other promises were just as big. When one antitrust lawyer asked Kumble if he would be able to get more help on his cases, Steve responded, "Just give me a note with what you need. You'll have it."

Only Danzansky and two other partners didn't buy it. They refused to participate in the merger and instead formed the D.C. office of another New York firm, Willkie Farr and Gallagher. By the effective date of the merger, February 1, 1981, Danzansky's skepticism was already being borne out. Wrote the *Post,* "When the first announcement was made last fall, it was reported that the Danzansky Dickey name would remain and get second billing. But there will be no second billing. Danzansky Dickey has dissolved."

On the night before the merger took effect, the partners, associates, and staff of Danzansky Dickey met for the last time in the tenth-floor conference room of their downtown Washington office building. They toasted the forty years of service the firm had given the city of Washington. Tydings went around the room and asked each partner to give a toast. The final partner to speak was the antitrust lawyer, Ken Kudon. "There are those who think bigness is badness," he said. "But this is the wave of the future." The party over, the tottering lawyers made their way to the reception area. At the elevator, a uniformed guard had been stationed. He demanded that each attorney sign for any files being removed.

The Finley Kumble era in Washington had begun.

CHAPTER

11

THE LOS ANGELES OFFICE immediately began a period of rapid growth under the miraculous Manley. But the fast start was not without bumps. Marshall's first hire, former assistant U.S. attorney Leonard Sharenow, angrily quit after a difference of opinion about how to handle a divorce case. Conscientious men like Sharenow who wouldn't compromise their principles were, however, in the minority. Having acquired what he considered a blank check to spend and hire, Manley began hiring politicians and former judges and using their names to sell the firm to other top lawyers. Manley and Kumble, who had practiced on opposite coasts, were truly men of one mind. "My God," said the wife of one partner after meeting Manley, "It's as if a twin had sprung up on the other coast."

"There's only one difference between them," observed another partner. "Manley wants riches. Kumble wants acceptance."

Even their court battles had a strikingly similar cast. When Manley's client, City Investing, became a majority stockholder in the bankrupt Sambo's restaurant chain, Manley quickly worked out an arrangement whereby he could represent both the management of Sambo's and the parent board, though the restaurant shareholders and Scharffenberger's City Investing had divergent interests. The results were eerily similar to early Finley Kumble history. The firm was castigated and its role was disallowed by a federal bankruptcy court judge, Calvin Ashland.

Manley's rough-and-tumble image hardly needed tarnishing, and the results of the Sambo's case reinforced what every lawyer who followed such things already knew—he would pursue any edge he could find to satisfy his client, especially when that client was George Scharffenberger.

If Manley's style of practice was applauded in New York, his free-spending ways weren't as admired. He purchased plush office space in Beverly Hills, and his own office had a private hideaway. Kumble listened to the complaints from his New York partners, cramped into tiny offices without windows and served by erratic air conditioners. "If you want a Xerox machine, you've got to pay for it," he would say. That was Kumble's explanation whenever a partner in another city, of often lesser status, was awarded a higher salary than his New York City compatriot. It did little to assuage the complaints. From the very beginning, almost everything about Manley's style and practice bugged the lawyers in New York.

Washington was certainly less annoying. Unlike the L.A. office, the Washington branch was a preexisting unit. It didn't drain the firm's capital nearly as much as Manley's operation. But neither was the D.C. office as productive as Kumble had hoped. His efforts to intimidate them into greater productivity only antagonized Joe Tydings, whose friendship with Kumble proved to be extremely short-lived. Tydings had also clashed with Heine, who didn't want the firm representing plaintiffs in class actions anymore. That smacked too much of legal-aid work. Finley Kumble defended and received large fees from big companies; it didn't attack them. But suits against big business were the bread and butter of Tydings's law practice. Without them he was a legal eunuch. The New York office seemed unreasonable in telling him not to try his kind of cases and then blasting him for not producing. But that was exactly the box Tydings was in.

Although it wasn't so profitable, the Washington office was at least prestigious and certainly stable. Kumble was able, once again, to turn his attention to Miami.

For all its beauty, Miami was neither a center of commerce

like Los Angeles nor a center of government like Washington. Miami wasn't even the center of Florida. By the vast majority of state legislators from elsewhere in Florida, Miami was viewed as a foreign outpost rightly belonging to either Long Island or Cuba, depending on the politician's particular bigotry.

In almost every way, Miami seemed an odd place for a New York law firm. New York lawyers certainly wouldn't be welcome in Florida courts. The appearance of a northern attorney in cracker-dominated Tallahassee on a lobbying assignment would mean instant death to whatever cause the lawyer was espousing. Transplants were hardly welcome; six-month-a-year snowbirds, even less so.

But Kumble was determined to succeed in Miami for the same reasons that he had had when he put Bob Mallow and Burt Hartman there in the first place. Within months after concluding the Washington merger, it appeared that he had succeeded in luring Miami's forty-lawyer firm of Rudin Barnett McClosky Schuster and Russell. Intense and difficult negotiations ensued, and Tydings was trotted down to Miami to clinch the deal. But while the formal papers approving the merger sat on a Miami partner's desk, Rudin Barnett, in November 1981, suddenly called off the merger. Unlike Steve Danzansky, Donald McClosky was successful in a last-minute effort to stop what he told his partners was "a runaway freight train." Almost a year's worth of Kumble's effort had gone down the drain. Fortunately, however, he had a second choice that he thought might be interested. Kumble introduced himself to Martin Fine of Miami's Fine Jacobson Block Goldberg and Semet. The firm seemed sold on the merger, and once again a contract was prepared. But at the last minute, a large faction of partners voted against the merger. Fine acceded to the wisdom of his fellow partners and informed Kumble that the merger was off.

For three unhappy members of the Fine firm, that was an interesting development. J. Arthur Goldberg (no relation to the former U.S. Supreme Court justice), an extremely accomplished tax expert, and two younger partners, Barry Semet and Fred Lickstein, were feuding with Fine over firm policy. When they realized that the merger had fallen through, Goldberg asked Kumble if he might consider taking just the three of them.

The offer couldn't have been more welcome. Kumble had just about exhausted the lawyer listings in the Miami phone book, and this latest rejection had been totally unexpected. But suddenly his luck was changing. The Miami office was back.

Not long after Goldberg, Semet, and Lickstein set up shop under the Finley Kumble name, Washington partner Mitch Cutler recommended that Kumble hire Philip Bloom, a well-known Miami litigator who had been practicing alone. While vacationing at his wife's Golden Isles estate, Kumble called Bloom and asked if he could come up to his house at 9 A.M. on Sunday for a talk. Bloom attempted to point out that normal people generally don't have business meetings at that hour on Sundays. Besides, Bloom told Kumble, "I'll be playing tennis." Attempting then to cut the conversation short, Bloom finally said, "Look, I really would not be interested."

"All signs point to you," Kumble replied.

The cryptic response made Bloom realize it was useless to resist.

"Okay," said Kumble. "Make it 10:30 then."

When Bloom arrived at Kumble's house, he found the firm's financial information and spread sheets scattered on a table. "We have no secrets," said Kumble. Bloom pretended to look over the material while Kumble continued his pitch. Bloom would be in charge of all litigation in Miami and would be trying cases all over the country.

Bloom agreed that it sounded like a fantastic opportunity. "That's great," said Kumble. "Now let me take you to meet Arthur Goldberg." Kumble had never bothered to tell the head of the Miami office that it might have a new partner.

When Bloom arrived to begin work at the firm, he could hardly believe his eyes. Although a brilliant lawyer, Goldberg was something of an eccentric. He often walked around the office without socks; he kept clients waiting endlessly and never kept appointments; and he rarely returned Kumble's or Heine's phone calls. Goldberg and his two partners just did their work and ignored the New York office. Goldberg and Lickstein's casual style was often more than the stiff Heine could bear. The feeling was mutual. After one rather stormy meeting with Heine in Miami, Lickstein had refused to take Heine to the airport. "Let him take a cab," Lickstein had stormed. Bloom, who remained loyal to the New York office, was offended.

"You can't let a partner take a cab," Bloom said, "not in Miami." Bloom offered to drive the New Yorker himself.

Disillusioned with the constant bickering, Bloom began looking for work elsewhere. But Kumble flew Bloom to New York for a pep talk, and he stopped looking.

But Bloom began to realize that, though he wasn't leaving, Goldberg, Lickstein, and Semet certainly were. The behavior of his three colleagues was daily becoming more and more secretive. They began making extra copies of all their client files. Bloom decided it was time to warn Kumble that something serious was about to happen.

"Steve, I think we're about to have a problem," Bloom told Kumble. "I think Goldberg, Lickstein, and Semet are leaving."

"That's ridiculous," said Kumble. "Let me tell you something. There are three reasons why they aren't leaving. One: They're too well paid. Two: They could never get another position of this caliber. Three: They are making too much money."

Bloom could have said, "I think that's two," but he didn't. If Joseph Pulitzer once said that the three most important things in journalism are accuracy, accuracy, and accuracy, Kumble could certainly be forgiven for describing the three most important things in life as money, money, and money.

Unable to convince Kumble of impending disaster, Bloom went about his business and said no more.

But on a bright August 1982 Saturday morning in Miami, Bloom surprised his co-workers by appearing in the office to work on a trial brief. In their offices Lickstein and Semet were removing everything from the walls and stuffing things in boxes.

"We're redecorating," sneered Lickstein.

"What kind of bullshit is that," Bloom exploded. "You're leaving."

Semet and Lickstein stuck to their story, but Goldberg called Bloom in to talk. Yes, we are leaving, he admitted. "But please don't tell Kumble until we're gone."

"I'm not going to jump in with a shotgun," Bloom said disgustedly.

A flustered Bloom agreed to postpone calling Kumble until he had finished his brief. When he did call, Kumble was playing tennis with Heine at a management committee meeting in Sun Valley, California. Bloom had talked so fast that Steven could only guess he had gotten the message right.

"What was it?" Heine asked.

Replied Kumble, "They're either redecorating or they're gone."

The following Monday it became clear that they were gone. When Kumble dialed the number of his Miami office, the answering service referred calls to the number of Goldberg's new firm in Coral Gables, Goldberg Semet and Lickstein. In addition to their clients, they had taken the firm's five associates, the receptionist, all the secretaries, and the bookkeeper.

Kumble threatened to sue the three for the damage done to the firm's business and the theft of what he claimed were Finley Kumble clients. Eventually, in an arbitration proceeding, the Goldberg group settled with Kumble, agreeing to pay $200,000 for the business interruption and the loss of clients.

The Miami office was now reduced to Bloom, who found himself more amused than frustrated by Kumble's antics. Once, Kumble's aunt asked him to help her on an $1,800 redecorating problem; Bloom quickly agreed to come to her aid. It just so happened that later in the day Bloom had occasion to talk to Kumble and mentioned that he had talked to Steve's aunt. Kumble asked what she had wanted, and Bloom explained.

"You tell her that the minimum retainer is $2,500," Kumble replied.

"But Steve, she's your aunt. We can't charge her $2,500 for an $1,800 problem."

"Aunt, schmant," said Kumble. "If she can't pay her retainer, she can go elsewhere."

A guy who could be suckered by a sweet-talking aunt was clearly not destined for greatness at Finley Kumble. Bloom would eventually leave the firm and become a Dade County circuit court judge in Miami. Just eight months after everything had seemed calm, the Miami office was once more in turmoil. Kumble again had to do a quick study of the Miami lawyers' directory. And he was determined not to fail.

CHAPTER

12

STEVE BRILL was nothing if not precocious. He had taken on a future president at the age of twenty-six and tackled a seemingly impossible literary project at twenty-seven. And in 1978, at the age of twenty-eight, he was about to become a magazine publisher.

Brill's articles on the inside workings of law firms were not just new but almost revolutionary. The impact of his piece on Manatt Phelps and those that followed seemed cataclysmic to a profession that had structured its entire canon of ethics and practices to shield itself and its activities from public view. It hardly seems possible in 1989, when journalists often can't get lawyers off the phone, but in 1979 most corporate lawyers wouldn't even return a phone call from a reporter. If a call was returned, it was to explain that the rules of the court or the bar prohibited the attorney from publicly discussing the case without the permission of the client. A few, invariably talking off the record, might provide some background information. Lawyers who engaged in even modest off-the-record chatter were often chastised by their more established colleagues. The extreme minority, mostly the flamboyant trial lawyers, might hold an occasional press conference. But in the view of the American Bar Association, a group controlled by the powerful corporate lawyers, the trial lawyers were little more than glorified ambulance chasers who brought ill repute to their honorable profession.

The indiscretions of the trial lawyers were tolerated because somebody had to represent unpopular clients.

Trial lawyers were often the subject of a double-standard type of snobbery. After every airplane crash, for example, personal injury lawyers would be branded "masters of disaster," accused of taking advantage of relatives in a time of grief. The truth was (and is) that the quiet insurance company lawyers wanted to get to the families first, to convince them to sign away their losses for a fraction of what they could get with one of the top "masters of disaster" at their side. The plaintiff's bar, known as trial lawyers, was the subject of other criticism as well. Their fees for one-third of a settlement were often made a part of the public record and condemned as exorbitant, although without their help the victim would have received much less. But the fees of the insurance companies and the big corporations who were usually the objects of the trial lawyers' attacks were cloaked in mystery. Presumably paid by the hour, these lawyers at big New York City and Century City firms were making unknown salaries. As private partnerships, their income remained undisclosed. The top salaries of law partners, unlike those of *Fortune* 500 executives, was one of the most tightly held secrets in American business. Nor did anyone have a clue about the profits of the top firms. Structured on an almost feudal system of barony, law partners made their money off the sweat of their serfs, politely called associates.

A typical large law firm might have the following arrangement. A group with fifty partners employs 100 associates. Each associate might earn a salary of $50,000 a year (1979 dollars). But he would be expected to expend a minimum of two thousand hours of work per year for the clients of the partners. The partners might typically bill the clients at a rate of $100 per hour for the associates' time, with each associate generating $150,000 per year in profit for the partners. If there are two associates for every partner, each partner would be making $300,000 in profit per year. In addition to that income, the partner is billing his own time at around $250 per hour. So if the partner works just one thousand hours per year, half of the time put in by the associate, he would be pulling in another $250,000. With overhead for expenses and office rent and secretaries at around 50 percent, any partner in such a firm should be bringing in a profit of $275,000 a year, while only working twenty hours a week. But that figure could go even higher. Associates could sometimes be whipped into working up to three thousand hours per year. If for every partner there are three associates instead of two and the partner can create enough business for all of them to stay at the two-thousand-hour level, even more money would roll in. Business-getting partners such as Marshall Manley—rainmakers—would reach a point where all their legal work was done by associates and they themselves never directly billed a client. That freed Manley to spend his time chasing clients or making private business deals or traveling the world if he so desired.

It was the pursuit of the exalted status of partner, with its huge rewards, that drove the associates to work sixty, seventy, eighty hours a week. At one big national law firm, Los Angeles–based Gibson Dunn and Crutcher, it was said that a senior partner drove by every night at midnight to see which lights were on in which windows. The life of an associate was not easy. There were no guarantees of partnership, no matter how hard one worked. Female lawyers, fooled into thinking that with hard work they could make partner, found out that the big firms could almost always find a way to dump them, rather than admit them to the most exclusive club. The associates who actually had the best chance of making partnership were those who showed rainmaking potential of their own. But at such firms as Finley Kumble, where the reputation wasn't so savory and client gathering was done at the very top, becoming a partner was difficult. Few associates at Finley Kumble made partner. They were worked to death and then discarded. At humane firms, associates—who ordinarily must labor seven years to make partner—are told by the fifth year whether or not they will make it. At the Finley Kumbles of the profession, they are left holding a thread of hope until the end, when they are brutally let go and told to start their careers all over again. For those unlucky ones, the world of high-powered corporate law is then closed. Many join smaller firms. Some become teachers. Almost all eventually end up being happier people.

In the world that existed before Steve Brill appeared on the scene, prospective associates had little way of knowing which law firms promoted associates and which ran roughshod over their hopes. Law school graduates could only rely on word of mouth to determine how much business the partners could generate and how stable a potential employer might be. It was not unusual for a young lawyer to arrive at a law firm only to find that a major client had just defected and that there wasn't enough work to support the staff of associates.

Information about clients was also a closely kept secret. Unless a case had made its way to the newspapers, client rosters were never revealed. A lawyer asked whom he represented might well respond with indignation. One might as well ask for the names of the women with whom he had slept.

All business affairs were held closely under wraps, and that was how the senior partners in large law firms wanted it. Clients liked stability, and the internal problems of large firms were not an appropriate matter for public discussion. Furthermore, once one became a partner in a firm, he was a partner for life. Knowing that lawyers down the street were making twice the profit off their associates could only disrupt things. The last thing the legal profession needed was lawyers jumping around, moving from firm to firm. Manley and Kumble had already come to believe that they could build a coast-to-coast organization by stealing other firms' clients. But, because clients don't generally like switching lawyers, they had to steal the attorneys at rival firms who controlled the work of the big corporate clients. As late as 1979, lawyers were still reluctant to switch. No one really knew what the other guy was making, how many associates he had for every partner, or who the other firm's clients were. For Kumble and Manley's grandiose strategy to succeed, there had to be a journal to provide that information. Luckily for them, Steve Brill had come up with exactly that idea.

The reception that his articles on the legal profession had received convinced Brill that lawyers would pay to find out what their colleagues were making and how they were making it. Along with his friend and one-time boss Jay Kriegel, who had been John Lindsay's chief of staff when Brill worked for the mayor's office, he hit upon the idea of devoting an entire magazine to the subject. They discussed the plan with *Esquire*'s Clay Felker, who agreed it was a good idea. He discussed it with the then-owners of *Esquire,* the British newspaper conglomerate Associated Newspapers Ltd., and they asked to talk it over with Brill and Kriegel. Felker didn't have to say much. They also had been impressed with the reception to Brill's unusual work and were looking to invest their money in the United States anyway. Hearing that the top men at ANG would talk to him, Brill raced over to the Hotel Pierre. There, without even listening to his pitch, the Brits promised to put the first $3 million of what would eventually be a total investment of $35 million into the proposed magazine for lawyers. Brill's total expense in extracting the investment had been $50, the cost of the ticket he got for double parking, plus the cost of getting his towed car out of the police lot.

In February 1979 the first issue of *American Lawyer* was mailed to attorneys across the country. Obtaining mailing lists of lawyers hadn't been as easy as Brill had expected. The American Bar Association, keeper of the best lists, refused to give or even to sell names to Brill because of the scandal that his past articles had provoked.

"We set out to pursue a vision," wrote Kriegel in that first issue. "That news of our society's most challenging profession can be lively and provocative." The first issue went right to the heart of what *American Lawyer* would emphasize: money.

The lead story, written by Brill, was entitled "Flom Takes Over as Top Money Maker in '78." The artwork featured Joseph Flom, leader of Skadden Arps Slate Meagher and Flom, ensconced in a dollar bill. Where the words United States of America were supposed to be, the name of the firm appeared. The motto on the bill was In Flom We Trust.

Skadden Arps had, of course, been the firm once retained by Herman Weisman to stop the Finley Kumble train from ever leaving the station. Skadden Arps had failed in that effort but in little else.

Despite the position of his name, Skadden Arps was Flom's law firm. A graduate of Harvard Law School, he had joined the obscure five-lawyer firm as an associate in 1948. In the late 1960s, the firm was still relatively unknown, picking up whatever work and clients it could. But slowly Flom began developing expertise in helping shareholders challenge the management of the companies they owned. The firm's turning point occurred in 1974 when Flom represented International Nickel Corporation and successfully won control of a target company, ESB Inc. He had also represented Chicago's Marshall Field and saved it from a takeover effort by Carter Hawley Hale in 1975. His advice to Marshall Field was to start building stores in towns where Carter Hawley Hale already had outlets. The strategy so complicated the antitrust aspects of the proposed takeover that it was simply dropped.

By 1983 Flom and Skadden Arps were party to almost every major deal. Flom became so knowledgeable about the intricacies of takeover acquisition and defense that many large firms paid him an annual retainer simply to make sure that a potential corporate raider couldn't use his skills against them. Invariably Flom's opponent in these battles was Wachtell Lipton Rosen and Katz, the firm Brill had written about for *New York* magazine in 1976.

The success and profitability of Skadden and of Wachtell Lipton left old-line corporate firms such as Sullivan and Cromwell and Cravath Swaine and Moore wondering what had hit them. Average earnings at Skadden were $350,000 per year, almost double the New York City average. Of the twenty-two major takeover fights in 1978, Skadden had represented one side or the other in twenty-one of them. In most of those battles, the other side had chosen to be represented by Wachtell.

Skadden and Wachtell's success was exactly what Kumble had always dreamed of. Like other aggressive Jewish lawyers,

Kumble would never be welcome at many of the Wasp-domi-
nated Wall Street firms. Ironically, the lawyers at these new
successful firms didn't think much of Kumble either.

When Kumble read Brill's new magazine, he saw the Manatt
Phelps fiasco all over again. He simply couldn't understand how
to attract Brill's attention. Whenever Finley Kumble was mentioned, it was in the context of the BusTop shelter mess. On
another occasion Brill brushed off the firm in a brief reference
with the adjective "notorious." Since the new magazine was
most popular in law schools (sort of the journalistic equivalent
of "Saturday Night Live") where the best and most potentially
profitable hard-working young associates of the future resided,
such references were considered disastrous.

In one report on the summer programs that Finley Kumble
offered prospective recruits, Brill wrote that the recurring complaint of participants in his survey "was the seeming lack of
concern among lawyers at the firm. Lunches are few and far
between. Partners are unresponsive. Their attitude toward people is terrible. What was lacking was a basic human concern for
other people."

The article revealed that many Finley Kumble summer in-
terns, from whom permanent associates would likely be chosen,
were not even given telephones and that only partners were
allowed to use the firm's circular staircase connecting two of its
floors. Everyone else had to trudge up the fire stairs.

How could Kumble hope to recruit more Don Sniders when
the firm was subjected to humiliation from Brill each month?

So Kumble did what he had always done best. He decided to
turn on the charm, inviting the twenty-nine-year-old Brill to
fancy dinners at his Westchester County home. He introduced
Brill to the rich and powerful, many of them Kumble's connections from his firm's real estate practice. At one party Brill was
seated next to Leona Helmsley, wife of hotel magnate and occasional client Harry Helmsley.

Finally, Kumble began to get some attention that wasn't all
negative. Brill had begun writing a series of articles on law firm
management. He had never practiced law and had little aptitude

for many of the management aspects of running a company. He himself was an intimidating boss. Too often, by his own admission, Brill berated and humiliated employees. For example, a reporter had once said he had tried and tried to learn if a certain out-of-state firm was opening a New York branch. No one at the firm would comment. Brill picked up the phone and got the information from the phone operator. While the reporter stared red-faced, Brill rubbed it in. "It's called reporting," he bellowed so everyone could hear.

He fired or threatened to fire staffers constantly and made often impossible demands on his reporters. Like Kumble, he was alternately charming and fearsome, capable of imperious behavior. Then, in moments of largesse, Brill would bestow friendship and gifts on his employees. In one such episode, he decided to take his entire magazine staff to a baseball game at Yankee Stadium. He bought tickets and had a bus pick everybody up in front of the office. Brill, however, rode to the game in a limousine.

But Brill was also a charismatic leader who worked himself as hard as his staff, which lived and died by his praise, and in the office watched his every move. He was totally dedicated to his magazine. In addition to running the business, Brill each month penned the longest story in the magazine. His journalistic instincts and talents, and especially the ease with which he wrote, were the subject of awe in his newsroom. It certainly seemed a more natural side of Brill than did the business side, which often seemed chaotic.

But neither his own difficulty in managing a struggling business nor his lack of experience in practicing law deterred Brill from going into a law firm, snooping around for a while, and then writing a "memo" in *American Lawyer* about how their management was doing. In November 1980, Brill featured Finley Kumble in one of those management memos. He wrote:

Identifying problems at Finley Kumble is like breaking up a good party. Having more than tripled in size since 1979 (mostly because of the L.A. and Washington, D.C., offices) yours is by far the fastest-growing large firm in the nation. It is also one of the most profitable. Several members of the management committee draw more than $600,000 per year.

Yet the firm has problems, severe ones, in areas ranging from rent to treatment of associates to the overriding question of whether any national full service firm can succeed and whether the firm's structure and compensation schedule fatally undermine its institutional staying power.

With equal pomposity, Brill proceeded to advise the firm on its long-range planning, billing principles and rates, billing enforcement and accounting, equipment space and rent, governance, partner compensation, press relations, recruiting, and client development.

Any manager of a large business would just love to have some young know-it-all walk in the door and tell the whole world what he is doing wrong. Of course. In the next issue of the magazine, Kumble wrote an almost sychophantic letter to the editor praising Brill's article as "objective and fair" and describing his criticisms as "both instructive and constructive."

In the following months, the critical articles and the pejorative adjectives seemed to lessen. Partners at the firm jokingly began referring to one section of the *American Lawyer*, the gossipy "Bar Talk" section, as "Kumble's Corner" because of the frequency with which the firm was mentioned.

American Lawyer itself continued to struggle financially, the strain finally causing an irreparable split between Kriegel and Brill. Kriegel wanted to give up on the magazine. He thought the task of selling the renegade publication to its targeted audience of elite lawyers was too difficult. Instead, Kriegel joined a group that was trying to buy the *New York Daily News*. When he informed Brill of his intentions, there was an explosion. Brill desperately wanted to make *American Lawyer* succeed. Kriegel, who later became an executive at CBS, argued it was a lost cause. "I'm sticking with it," Brill said. "Get out now." They are not known to have spoken since.

Kriegel's departure made Brill both publisher and editor,

which for him may have meant that the whole fight had been worthwhile.

In legal circles, everyone wanted to read the magazine, but few would admit it. It was a little bit like a porn magazine—if a lawyer were going to read it, he might hide it between the pages of the *Racing Form.* Many lawyers refused to subscribe, hurting the publication's circulation base. But it survived because the pass-along rate was so high. Almost every big firm in the country got at least one copy, and it was usually circulated to all the offices. Brill compensated for this lack of circulation by boosting the subscription rate to more than $200 per year for just ten issues. Since total readership was much higher than circulation figures, he was also able to attract steady advertising from companies wishing to tap a lucrative market. *American Lawyer* was soon joined by two other publications, both of which were considered more respectable and mainstream: the *National Law Journal* and the Washington, D.C.–based *Legal Times.*

The articles in these publications on firm profitability and the movement of attorneys and clients had exactly the impact that Kumble and Manley expected. Lawyers, seeing what their colleagues were making, began to move around. A new era in law practice had begun. Almost overnight, a lawyer no longer planned to spend his entire life with one firm. That was true as much in Miami as in New York.

Although Brill's coverage of Finley Kumble had improved, Kumble felt there were still plenty of stories the firm could have lived without. That included one "Bar Talk" article entitled "Cleaned Out in Miami."

The story recounted in brief how Goldberg, Semet, and Lickstein had suddenly departed, although inaccurately leaving the notion that Kumble had actually wished them away.

"Arthur missed too many partnership meetings," the story quoted Kumble. "The other lawyers could sense his lack of enthusiasm."

Wrote Brill: "Undeterred by the latest wave of infidelity, Kumble is looking at fresh merger prospects. 'We're on the verge of doing something very dynamic, we're down here to stay,' says Kumble." In fact, Kumble didn't know what he was going to do. But once again Brill was inadvertently about to help.

In early 1982 the editor/publisher had marshaled his small band of about a dozen reporters to do a feature article on the twenty hottest law firms in America. One of the reporters assigned to the project was Jill Abramson, a talented graduate of Harvard who had previously spent some time working in the south for NBC's elections unit. Abramson had a friend, Michael Nifong, who was an associate at the Miami office of Squire Sanders and Dempsey, a large Cleveland-based firm that had already smoothly and successfully moved into Florida. She asked him if he knew of any firms that might qualify in the Miami area. Nifong thought for a moment and then suggested Tew Critchlow Sonberg Traum and Friedbauer.

Tew Critchlow was hardly a hot new firm. Swamped by larger competitors and on the brink of financial collapse, Tew Critchlow was desperately searching for a way out of trouble when Abramson called asking if she might include the firm in her story. It was as if God himself had sent an angel to Miami. About all the firm had going were one-shot business deals. It had been unable to snare a single large steady client. In the hopes of luring a particular local bank as a client, the firm had moved to an office building in a remote section of North Miami. But the bank business failed to develop, and the firm was stuck in the boondocks, far from the center of action. Thomas Tew, the leader of the firm, who had once worked for the Securities and Exchange Commission, wanted nothing more than to be noticed by a large out-of-state firm. Indeed, a merger would not only return the firm to respectable practice, but it marked the only hope of getting out of its disastrous lease and back into downtown Miami. Furthermore, his firm's narrow securities practice wasn't really marketable in and of itself. Tew was the first to realize that they should be part of a larger operation. *American Lawyer* was the perfect vehicle for Tew to use to get out that message.

Midway through the preparation for her article, Abramson began to realize that the firm wasn't so hot after all. But Brill and the other editors were counting on her piece as one of the twenty. Cutting Tew Critchlow would mean finding somebody else. And Tew was so enthusiastic—he couldn't do enough to help her. The story was published.

Tew gave himself credit for a famous case that had actually been handled by another partner who had since moved to Atlanta. And, playing coy, he told Abramson that the last thing he wanted was a merger partner. On the contrary, his firm comprised a bunch of hotshots who were going to grow up on their own and challenge the big boys. If he had telexed Kumble personally, Tew couldn't have sent a more seductive message.

On September 9, 1982, Tew was flying back to Miami from New York with his two partners, Richard Critchlow and Steve Sonberg. He casually mentioned that he had been contacted by a big-time New York lawyer by the name of Kumble. And on the following day, his forty-second birthday, Tew would be meeting with Kumble. Critchlow and Sonberg immediately noted that they hadn't been invited to participate. They also noticed that, while the firm had received offers before, Tew seemed especially excited about this meeting. "This is the chance for us to do the sophisticated kind of work we've always wanted," Tew said. "This is our chance to become competitive with the other big Miami firms."

Tew's enthusiasm before the meeting couldn't compare with his excitement after the meeting at the Doral in Miami Beach. Tew, it turned out, had been a high school classmate of Kumble's second wife, Peggy, and he and Steve had gotten along famously. Everything about Kumble was first class, from his Gucci shoes to his red suspenders. In addition, Tew had been highly recommended by Washington partner Mitchell Cutler, who had worked with him on SEC matters.

Every other firm with which Tew had met had viewed his Miami office as a place to baby-sit a particular client. But Kumble offered much more. Here was a chance to build, with the New York firm's capital, a full-service office that would be part of a large national law firm. They would work with lawyers in Los

Angeles, New York, and Washington. Here was Tew's ticket to the big time. He simply couldn't believe his good fortune.

Back at the office on Monday with his partners, Tew had stars in his eyes. "This was a man with vision," he told his partners. Not all were convinced. Several had friends who knew firsthand of Finley Kumble's practices and, like Steve Danzansky in Washington a few years earlier, urged caution. Others knew lawyers in the Goldberg Semet group. They knew Kumble had tried to meddle and that he pushed the lawyers to produce. They might make a lot of money, Tew's partners worried, but they might lose the good life.

Tew made it clear that anybody who wanted out could get out; the merger was going to move forward. His partners begged him to slow down. But Tew was gone, overwhelmed by the Kumble charm. Sign on the dotted line, and legal glory and riches will be yours. At firm meetings in October and November, Kumble assured the Tew Critchlow partnership that the Miami office, like the one in Washington, would remain autonomous. They would not become slaves to the headquarters in New York. Tew would be placed on the national management committee and be Miami's spokesman in the firm. Nothing would change, Kumble assured the nervous partners, "except the name on the door and that you will all make a lot more money."

In late November a majority of the partnership agreed to join Tew in setting up the new firm. Several partners, including name partner Sid Traum, refused to participate and went elsewhere.

In December Kumble invited Tew, Critchlow, and Sonberg to New York for the press conference at which the merger would be announced to the legal and business press. The evening before the conference, Kumble arranged a small cocktail party at the firm's Park Avenue offices. As the partners came into the conference room, Critchlow and Sonberg huddled to one side. No one had said much to them, and none of the New York partners seemed particularly friendly. It was clear that Tom Tew was the star of the show. But he was, after all, their leader. So

Critchlow and Sonberg were content to stand back and watch the show. If Tew did well, they would do well.

Kumble tapped his glass to quiet the murmur. "I want to introduce our new partners from Miami," Kumble said. "John Schulte, Harry Durant, and Tom Tew. Let's all welcome John, Harry, and Tom."

The jaws of Critchlow and Sonberg hit the floor. Sonberg began to experience immediate and severe nausea. They didn't know John Schulte or Harry Durant, but they knew who they were. Schulte and Durant were two banking partners from the Miami firm of Smathers and Thompson. Nobody had ever said a word about John and Harry. Tom was going to be the Miami spokesman on the national management committee. Here they were, the two partners whose job it had been to sell the merger to others, and nobody had known a damn thing about John and Harry. Kumble had pledged that nothing would change except the name on the door. But here was Kumble on a first-name basis with John and Harry, not knowing Critchlow or Sonberg from Adam. And now, as Sonberg listened with increasing alarm, Kumble was announcing that all three men would be serving on the firm's national management committee. Their firm was already outvoted by the Smathers and Thompson group, and they hadn't even opened for business yet.

"Rick," Sonberg whispered to his friend and partner, "I think we've been fucked."

Dinner at 21 was a repeat performance of the cocktail party. The press conference came and went, and then the group headed to Washington to make the announcement to *Legal Times* and the Washington, D.C., business press. Nothing could change because Sonberg had been right. Their friend and leader, Tom Tew, had known for weeks that the Smathers and Thompson group was merging with them. But he hadn't told his partners, fearing it would scotch the deal.

In Washington's Mayflower Hotel, Critchlow stormed into Tew's hotel room. "Tom, we've been fucked," Critchlow exploded. "Did you know that Schulte and Durant were going to be on the management committee?"

"Don't worry," Tew said. "I've got it under control."

But Critchlow continued to worry, and Sonberg was even sicker. Sensing that they were causing trouble, Kumble asked the two to fly back to Miami ahead of the group. He would talk to them down there. What made the situation even more confusing was the realization that Durant and Schulte had no idea that Tew hadn't told the whole story to his partners. A final tortuous press conference was held in Miami on Friday. On Saturday morning, Tew came into the office to meet with his irate partners. They couldn't believe that he hadn't been straight with them.

"I didn't know until the very end that they were coming," Tew insisted. "Kumble was negotiating with both groups. He didn't know which one would come, and he wanted it to be kept a secret."

Tew's explanations were met with more angry accusations. He had lied to his own partners. He had fucked them over. The merger, a consensus of the partnership determined, was off. Tew had never endured a session as grueling and difficult. He broke down and cried.

But on Monday morning the merger was announced in the *Miami Herald.* The sign painters came in and changed the name on the door. Schulte and Durant appeared with several other lawyers they were bringing over to the new firm. Despite the meeting on Saturday morning, Finley Kumble's takeover was a fait accompli.

With the coup accomplished, Kumble appeared once again to give the restless troops their first lecture as members of the nation's fastest-growing law firm. He complained that during the past month billings and collections had been "totally unacceptable." One of the partners attempted to interject that between Christmas and the merger, things hadn't been exactly normal. "I don't want to be interrupted," Kumble snapped. The marriage had been consummated, and there would be no honeymoon.

Ironically, the lawyer who fared most poorly in the merger was neither Critchlow nor Sonberg nor any member of the Tew

Critchlow group. It was Harry Durant, a southern good old boy who had been included in the deal only because he controlled the business of several foreign banks, including the important Algemene Bank Nederland. Just as Tew had kept the full details of the merger from his partners, so Schulte hadn't been completely forthcoming with his partner. Durant learned of the Tew Critchlow merger through a phone call from Schulte while Durant and his wife were attending an international bar association convention in New Delhi. Durant wasn't pleased with the news but was hardly in a position to do anything about it. That he and Schulte were leaving was an open secret at Smathers and Thompson, and Durant had no avenue for retreat. Nor was there any way Durant's reservations about joining with Tew could be registered. Schulte was not asking Durant for advice on the merger; he was telling him it was a done deal. "We could both absolutely say no," Schulte said. "But we'd be missing the golden opportunity of our lives." Halfway across the world, Durant acquiesced.

Durant had never worked with screaming, bickering New Yorkers. In one three-way phone call with Kumble and Heine, the two men, whose offices were adjacent, began yelling at each other, apparently forgetting that Durant was even on the line. As quiet Harry hung up the phone, Heine and Kumble continued their spat. Finally, in July 1983, Durant decided to pack it in. His partnership agreement asked that he give three months' notice before resigning, and Durant, being a gentleman, sent a letter by Federal Express announcing that, as of October 15, he would be leaving. The next day he received a call from Underberg.

"We think it would be best if you vacate immediately," Underberg said.

Durant was not surprised. Little that the New Yorkers did surprised him after nine months in what he considered the Finley Kumble hellhole. He hung up the phone and went over to the records room to pick up his client files. They'd been locked and the custodian ordered not to yield them. From that time on, whenever Durant wanted the files of one of his clients,

Schulte had to stand over him and give explicit permission for him to be given the papers. Over each client, a heated battle would erupt. Most unhappy lawyers elected to stay with Finley Kumble rather than disappear into the uncertain professional future that awaited Durant. It was, without doubt, the most humiliating experience of Harry Durant's professional life.

In the same turbulent month of July, both Sonberg and Critchlow also attempted to quit. After personal appeals from Kumble and Tew, Critchlow relented and decided to stay. But he would never again be viewed as a major partner. Sonberg joined another Miami firm, but just as Durant's relationship with Schulte was shattered, so his close friendship with Tew was destroyed. With the malcontents gone, Tew and Schulte began to build what would soon become the largest out-of-state law office in Florida history.

And all it had cost was a few lifelong friendships.

CHAPTER

13

HARRY DURANT'S nine-month nightmare was over, and he returned home to lick his wounds and contemplate the next step in his professional life. Eventually Durant would wind up in a small Texas firm comfortably surrounded by family members. After his ordeal at Finley Kumble, only one partner called to offer sympathy. That partner was Marshall Manley.

But to the New York partners, Manley out-Kumbled Kumble. From afar he seemed more ruthless and more uncontrollably ambitious. Just as he had left two good lawyers, Manatt and Rothenberg, in the dust, Manley was now outsprinting Kumble himself.

When Marshall Manley was admitted to the partnership, several firm partners had been concerned enough to ask Kumble to call off the deal. "Don't worry," Kumble said. "Within five years, we'll have a 100-lawyer office in Los Angeles." Later he was forced to admit that his projections had been way off. Kumble, considered a management genius by his partners, badly missed on that prediction. It wouldn't take Marshall nearly that long.

Manley's experience at McKenna and Fitting had taught him that a law firm should be run as a business. The people who brought in the clients should be rewarded. Like Kumble, Manley believed that any half-decent law school graduate could draft documents, take depositions, even argue before a judge in court. The real talent, the one that separated the leaders from the drones, was in attracting and dealing with those Kumble termed the "true enemy." That was, of course, the client. Never in the history of the legal profession had anyone been more adept at that than Marshall Manley. In coming to Finley Kumble, he had, with very few exceptions, minimized his participation in what is popularly considered to be the practice of law. He'd become, according to some of his partners, an "account executive." Manley brought in the clients, and then he brought in the lawyers to work for those clients. Following an address to an antitrust conference in Idaho, Marshall announced to a surprised colleague, "I think I'll go work the crowd now."

Observed the partner, "For Manley, getting business was the same as picking pockets."

Within what seemed to be an incredibly short period of time, Manley's recruits had built a financial practice that was the envy of Los Angeles. The firm represented twelve banks, seventeen savings and loan associations, and numerous real estate limited partnerships including the $130 million University Group.

The Los Angeles office almost immediately gave Finley Kumble practically a license to print money. Few in L.A. had ever heard of the firm. Fewer still had any idea of Finley Kumble's reputation. West of the Rockies (at least to those who hadn't read *Esquire*), the firm appeared to be a shiny jewel. Manley had no trouble bringing in top-drawer talent, including Sheldon Lytton, a former chief of staff to the state's lieutenant governor, Mike Curb. He hired former judges and prosecutors. Eventually he raided the L.A. branch of Philadelphia's Pepper Hamilton and Sheetz, bringing into the firm Richard Brown, one of the country's top sports and broadcasting lawyers.

Manley, who was nothing if not direct, later revealed to Brown exactly why he was wanted at Finley Kumble. Brown was the attorney for Gene Autry and his California Angels. "When people find out we have Gene Autry as a client," said Manley, "everybody will want to bring their work here."

New York Mets fan Manley was excited about building a sports practice at Finley Kumble. He also began creating an entertainment practice and brought in noted lawyers from the movie industry. The firm began representing such high-profile companies as Geffen Records, Tri-Star Pictures, and movie producer Dino DeLaurentiis. Manley hired attorney Alan Schwartz, who brought clients such as producer Mel Brooks, and writers Alexander Solzhenitsyn and Truman Capote to the roster. They made the firm look even more respectable. When Manley heard former Olympic sprinter Wilma Rudolph complain at a party that she couldn't get any endorsement money, Manley brought her to the office and gave her business to Brown. Within a year he had her under contract to Wonder Bread, and her endorsement fees jumped to $300,000 in one year.

In California Manley was unstoppable. But when his client-hunting journeys brought him to potentially lucrative clients in New York, he was met with puzzling rejections. At first Marshall didn't understand why the magic wasn't working in the east. This was, after all, his native turf.

Slowly it began to sink in that something was wrong with the Finley Kumble name—blue-chip clients wanted nothing to do with the firm. Finley Kumble frequently sued clients for unpaid fees. The New York office was full of rude, belligerent men. Fistfights in the office may not have been common, but they weren't unheard of. The friendship between Kumble and Heine had, over the years, become an uneasy one. Wagner, the politician, had learned to stay out of the way.

Comparing the New York operation with what he had created in Los Angeles, Marshall Manley grew annoyed. Partnership compensation was determined in New York, and Manley incessantly complained that L.A. partners weren't getting their fair share. Although supposedly a member of the management committee, he was often left out of the decision-making process.

On some issues he seemed to be making progress. Heine and Underberg agreed to distribute more of the firm's income to the California partners, and they persuaded Kumble to go along.

But in the midst of Manley's professional success came personal trauma. As the poster he had framed in his office indicated, he at first adored his beautiful second wife, Tonya. Tonya had

told Manley that she had been a successful model, that she had
been a Winston cigarette girl and a model for Breck hair sprays,
and that she had attended UCLA. He was flattered by her attention and proud to have such a luscious ornament on his arm.
They moved to a million-dollar mansion in Beverly Hills. Manley got her a job as a management trainee with one of his savings-
and-loan clients.

But by September 24, 1981, she was driving Manley crazy.
According to court documents, she was spending Manley's
$22,000-per-month draw at a prodigious rate. She suspected her
husband of hiring private detectives to watch her. One day on
an airplane, she sat down next to a young man who told her he
was a lawyer. "Oh, my husband's a lawyer," she said. "What
firm are you with?"

"Finley Kumble," the young lawyer replied.

Tonya freaked. She accused the unsuspecting associate of
being put on the plane by Manley to follow her, and she caused
a scene. Finally, Manley did hire private investigators. According to Manley, he learned that Tonya didn't exactly have the
biography she claimed. He filed for an annulment, claiming
fraud. The case was settled.

It became one of the stickiest, nastiest divorce and custody
fights in Los Angeles history. The Manleys fought bitterly over
custody of their child and over the division of Marshall's considerable assets and his expensive California houses, Maui con-
dominiums, and his film interests. Among the movies in which
Manley had invested were *Midnight Express, Flash Gordon,*
and *California Suite.* He was particularly concerned about the
court's handling of his investment in Peggy Kumble's Vermont
horse farm. Manley described the investment to the court as "a
very sensitive and valuable relationship that needs to be pre-
served."

As part of the settlement, the marriage was dissolved on October 3, 1983, and Manley agreed to pay $2,000 a month in child
support and $6,000 a month to Tonya. In addition, he had to
pay $119,000 for her attorney's fees. His own legal bill was up

in the $400,000 range. But he figured he had saved that fee by using lawyers from his office.

A few weeks after the judgment, Manley was still extremely edgy. He nearly went over the edge when he received a bill from Finley Kumble in New York demanding the payment of $400,000 in legal fees.

Marshall picked up the phone and demanded to know what this was all about. "Partners don't bill partners," he said.

"I paid for my divorce," said Kumble.

"That's not the practice here in California," Manley responded.

But Kumble was unmoved. Heine, however, told Manley to forget about the bill. Though, irate, Manley filed the papers away.

A few weeks later, Manley received another bill from Kumble. And when he didn't pay that one, he received a third.

Marshall stewed. Each day became worse than the one before. This was Manatt Phelps all over again. Rothenberg had pushed him out without ever giving him a chance to tell his side of the story. Now Kumble was pushing him, yet had never had the courtesy to call Manley and discuss the bill with him as a partner should. In conversations with Heine, Manley made no secret of the strain he felt the situation was creating. "Kumble's pushing me right down to the ground," he said.

The nerve that had been struck during the Manatt Phelps expulsion was reexposed. Manley had built a tremendous institution at Manatt Phelps, and it had been ripped from him in what he felt was the most unfair and arbitrary fashion. Now, despite the fact that he was the primary earner at Finley Kumble, it was happening again. Manley, who should have been the unchallenged leader of the firm, was being muscled.

Manley felt he had no choice. He decided to leave Finley Kumble and began negotiating with New York's Shea and Gould, itself looking to open a West Coast office. Through a partner in the Washington, D.C., office, Heine discovered that Manley had been offered $1 million a year to become partners with William Shea and Milton Gould. Just as panic had ensued at Manatt Phelps when partners realized how much money Manley brought in, a similar concern pervaded Finley Kumble's new offices at 425 Park Avenue.

The following morning Manley arrived at his office to find Kumble, Underberg, Heine, and Alan Gelb sitting around his desk. They had already spoken to the other L.A. partners to find out how many would stay at Finley Kumble if Manley left. The answer was, simply, not many. This could easily be the Florida fiasco all over again, and that helped Manley's bargaining position considerably.

Manley recited his litany of complaints. He was tired of the L.A. office being treated like a colony. "Stop treating the L.A. lawyers like servants," he demanded. This was a national firm, and the L.A. office was not just the jewel in terms of quality, it was the gold mine in terms of profitability. Manley insisted that if he were to stay at the firm, it would only be as the co–managing partner with Kumble. In addition, his name would be added to the firm's letterhead.

On the issue of naming Manley a co–managing partner, Underberg objected.

"What's going to happen to me?" he asked. "I'm not going to have a title."

But Heine persisted. Manley was too valuable to lose, and meeting his terms was the only alternative. Manley had to become the national comanager. Kumble and Underberg swallowed hard. Steve sat in stony silence throughout Manley's diatribe. If the decision were his alone, Manley would be gone. He had put Miami together three times; he could rebuild Los Angeles. But Heine insisted that Manley's demands be met, and Underberg basically agreed. The firm agreed to eat the divorce bill and to stop dunning Manley. That night, after dinner at La Scala and margaritas at the Beverly Hills Hotel, which Manley did not attend, a distraught Kumble threw up in the back of a cab.

On his return to New York, Kumble didn't hide his annoyance with Heine siding against him. Worse, from a professional point of view, Kumble thought that his ace corporate lawyer had been outnegotiated.

It was the beginning of the end of Heine and Kumble's friendship. Nor would Kumble ever have much to say to Manley again. Although all three men would travel around the country together on recruiting trips, the personal tensions created by the episode were hardly conducive to smooth management. Manley had agreed to stay, but he felt only marginally better about the firm. He was well aware that the domineering Kumble had little interest in comanaging anything. And as long as he was three thousand miles away, little could be done about it.

CHAPTER
14

ALTHOUGH HEINE'S LOYALTY had become a serious question to Steven Kumble, there was no denying that, at the Finley Kumble zoo, Heine was one of the few inhabitants with a top reputation as a practicing attorney. This was more than Kumble would admit about many of his other characters, especially the politicians who had been brought into the firm because of their names or reputations. Kumble and Heine considered the exalted former senator Joe Tydings to be a "lightweight," because he had a small inclination to bring in clients. Hugh Carey, who had joined the firm after stepping down as New York's governor to be with his close friend Robert Wagner, in Kumble's view was there for one purpose and one purpose only—to use his famous name to bring clients in the door.

Robert Casey, the new tax lawyer, was openly derided, mostly because of the firm leader's long-standing antipathy to tax attorneys. Kumble constantly threatened to replace Casey as head of the tax department, but he always balked for fear of losing Casey's loyal clients. The Irishman himself began hating the New York office and started spending most of his time in Washington, working with congressmen and senators on changes in the federal government's tax code. He had become more of a lobbyist than a lawyer.

The litigation section, usually one of the crown jewels of any law firm, had never recovered from the loss of Roy Grutman ten years earlier. Alan Gelb, who had been with Kumble from the beginning, was not considered a star. Kumble and Heine refused even to acknowledge that he was litigation chief. For nearly ten years, Gelb had been the "acting chairman" of litigation.

Kumble and Manley, the two stars of the firm, didn't practice law. Manley scoured the country searching for new clients and partners. Kumble moved from office to office with his long yellow pad, trying to keep the revenue coming in. The two managing partners could not even mention each other's name without spitting. Manley derided Kumble as a "collections clerk." Manley was put down as an "account executive."

But Heine was a lawyer. He had clients, and he performed work for those clients. In 1983, Heine landed a client that offered Finley Kumble the opportunity to at last enter the legal big time in law's hottest area: mergers and acquisitions.

In 1981 millionaire Connecticut investor Samuel Heyman saw what he considered a terrific opportunity in the GAF Corporation, the large chemical and roofing company. The origins of GAF were fairly exotic. The company had once been part of Nazi Germany's I. G. Farben empire. But in 1942, shortly after the advent of World War II, it was seized as enemy property. In 1965 the U.S. government sold GAF, and it became a publicly traded company.

The company was operated rather loosely by Jesse Werner, a chemist whose days with the company went back to its German beginnings. Werner, however, was more scientist than businessman, and to Heyman's annoyance, he used his position to purchase for GAF WNCN, a New York City classical music radio station, which Werner wanted because he loved classical music.

Heyman believed the company to be a good investment target because Werner was expected to retire in 1981. Heyman expected this news to be so well received on Wall Street that he invested $4 million in GAF stock, at just over $12 per share. But Werner didn't resign. Instead, he fired the man securities analysts expected to replace him and signed a contract that kept him in his position for five more years. Wall Street was not pleased. The price of the stock quickly sank to just over $8 per share. Heyman's $4 million investment was quickly disappearing. Heyman was a graduate of Harvard Law School and a former assistant U.S. attorney in Hartford who had quit practicing law after his father's death in 1968 to run the family's real estate and investment business. He was not the kind of man to take that kind of loss quietly. If Werner wouldn't quit, maybe he'd be willing to listen to advice. So Heyman invited Werner to his home for dinner and outlined some steps that he thought the management of GAF could take to make it a better-run, more efficient company. Werner, however, was not interested in being told how to run his company. Although he accepted the dinner invitation, he didn't understand what right Heyman, a mere stockholder, had to make these suggestions. Among the most repugnant of Heyman's notions was that Werner should sell his beloved radio station.

The relationship between the two nose-dived further several weeks later, when Werner told a reporter for the *Wall Street Journal* that Heyman's children appeared as if "they were rented for the evening."

To Samuel Heyman, a devoted family man, that meant war, a proxy war for control of the company.

To fight the battle, Heyman enlisted Kenneth Bialkin, a senior partner at the old-line New York City firm of Willkie, Farr and Gallagher. Bialkin was not exactly out to make a name for himself, and Willkie Farr itself was secure in what it was and whom it represented. Bialkin warned Heyman of the difficulties and viciousness a takeover fight could involve. In addition, he pointed out, at that time few such attempts by stockholders had ever succeeded.

The determined former prosecutor was not about to be discouraged. Heyman put together an insurgent slate of directors and girded for the 1982 annual meeting at which he would challenge Werner's control.

To fight off the insurgent, Werner had retained the best in the field, Joseph Flom, the senior partner at Skadden Arps. Like Bialkin, Flom urged a settlement of the dispute. He offered terms that sounded to Heyman's inexperienced ears like a total victory for the stockholders. In exchange for Heyman not challenging

Werner's leadership, GAF would sell off its unprofitable roofing division as Heyman wanted and reimburse Heyman $250,000 for expenses and attorneys' fees. On March 22, 1982, GAF issued a press release stating that it had retained Morgan Stanley and Company to study three separate merger or sale proposals "with a view towards maximizing near term benefits to shareholders." With the release of that statement, the price of GAF stock shot up by $5. Heyman was happy. Bialkin was relieved.

But as time passed, it seemed that Werner was either unable or unwilling to keep the promises made in the settlement agreement. The unprofitable divisions were not sold. A merger apparently was not seriously contemplated. The stock began drifting downward. Worst of all, Werner's board attempted to renege on its promise to pay Heyman's expenses by suing Sam in federal court for misrepresentation and breach of contract. The lawsuit claimed Heyman had incurred nowhere near the amount of money in expenses that he had claimed. Flom's Skadden Arps, known for its aggressive defense of takeover targets, complicated Heyman's legal situation by asking for $5 million in punitive damages.

Stunned, Heyman went back to Bialkin and declared the settlement a failure. He wanted to go ahead with the proxy fight. But Bialkin told Heyman that he had no stomach for the fight. Privately, he viewed Heyman's quest to take over GAF as quixotic and futile. Bialkin and most of Heyman's financial backers told him that his stake in the company was too small. They urged him to align himself with a more experienced and more amply financed corporate raider. But Heyman wanted nothing to do with raiders. He was the shareholder in a white hat, and he planned to march against bad management with a couple of trusty sidekicks, not at the head of scruffy posse of investors armed with junk bonds.

Bialkin knew that few experienced corporate lawyers would want any part of the GAF takeover battle. No shareholder had ever succeeded in taking over a company as large as this target. But one firm, Bialkin suggested, might be interested. They didn't have much experience in mergers and acquisitions, and this case might give them a chance to make a name for themselves. That firm was Finley Kumble.

Heyman already knew Andrew Heine. His wife, Ronnie, was, like Heine, a graduate of Yale Law School. The suggestion sounded reasonable to Heyman. Nor was Heine a complete novice in M&A work, having handled some smaller mergers, notably that of Interstate Stores with Vornado Corporation. Heyman decided to ask Heine about Finley Kumble's interest.

Heine assured Heyman that Finley Kumble was more than willing to go to the mat with Skadden Arps, its old nemesis. In addition, Heine said that Finley Kumble's litigation department would take over defense of the GAF suit.

"This is an area in which we want to make a name for ourselves," Heine told his client. But Heine was not promising any miracles. Nor was Heyman placing blind faith in a firm that, he had quickly discovered, lacked a sterling reputation. From outside the firm, Heyman hired Columbia University Law School professor Harvey Goldschmid, a corporate law expert, just to keep an eye on things.

Yet Heine had not become a Finley Kumble partner for nothing. Shortly after taking on the case, viewed as one of the most important in the firm's fourteen-year history, Heine called Robert Smith, a young lawyer in the twenty-five-lawyer New Jersey firm of Hannoch Weisman (no relation to Herman), and offered him a substantial pay raise to join Finley Kumble. The young associate was delighted at the opportunity, moved over to Finley Kumble, and was immediately put to work on Heyman's proxy fight.

GAF and Skadden Arps were not amused. Robert Smith's job at Hannoch Weisman involved coordinating GAF's product liability cases. GAF's roofing business, which accounted for 20 percent of the company's sales, had been hit with a flood of cases relating to claims that the company had sold defective products. In addition, GAF was involved in a massive nationwide litigation effort involving asbestos products.

The disposition and potential loss from these suits could play an important part in takeover negotiations and maneuvering. No one had a better understanding of GAF's situation in these matters than Smith, who on behalf of his client had spent nearly half of his working hours on GAF motions, dispositions, and research.

GAF claimed that Smith had more than merely a good understanding of their affairs. They said he had been exposed to confidential information regarding the company's financial and technical history. Unfamiliar with Finley Kumble's pattern of conduct in such matters, a federal judge refused to disqualify the firm. Wrote the judge: "A cynical observer would believe perhaps that this has been done deliberately with a view toward utilizing confidential information obtained by Smith during his prior employment. However the appearance of impropriety, standing alone, does not warrant attorney disqualification."

Having dodged that bullet, Heine, Heyman, and Goldschmid forged ahead with their plan to take over the GAF management and, in the process, to beat Joe Flom.

The fight turned out to be everything Kenneth Bialkin had predicted and more. It was, at the time, quite simply the most vicious proxy battle that had ever been fought.

Heyman and GAF took turns buying full-page advertisements blasting each other. GAF's ads even accused Heyman of failing to pay his legal fees to Willkie Farr, implying wrongly that he had switched to Finley Kumble for that reason. Werner didn't stop at placing anti-Heyman ads in the *Wall Street Journal* and the *New York Times*. He ran them in Heyman's hometown Greenwich, Connecticut, papers, hoping to embarrass Heyman on his home turf, in front of the neighbors.

In addition, GAF put out the word that any banker or proxy solicitation organization found working with Heyman would never again do any work for GAF. As a result of the threat, Heyman lost his investment banking firm of Salomon Brothers.

But Samuel Heyman was dynamic and persuasive. His ads trumpeted the fact that GAF shares had lost 80 percent of their value, and that while dividends had been slashed by 75 percent, Werner had been rewarded with increasingly lucrative compensation packages. He quoted from the publication *Adweek* that

Werner was one of the seven "most overpaid people in America." Heyman also charged that Werner had acquired the unprofitable radio station merely "to indulge a personal hobby."

He approached institutional investors in GAF, and they were willing to listen. GAF was a poorly run company. Salomon Brothers might have backed out, but he was able to win the support of Morgan Guaranty, Chemical Bank, Lehman Brothers, and Prudential Bache. The unthinkable was about to happen. Heyman began to realize that he might just have the votes to oust Werner and to elect his own slate of directors, which included Joe Tydings, at the April 28, 1983, shareholders' meeting at the Radisson Plaza Hotel in Charlotte, North Carolina.

But Flom could also count. On April 10, in an effort to bring the dissident shareholders back into the fold, Werner announced at last that he had agreed to sell the building materials division. Then, on April 22, he entered into a contract to sell the chemical division to Allied Corporation. Heyman, in an effort to hold his troops in line, warned that if Werner's GAF board was reelected, both deals would be canceled.

The April 28 board meeting was one of the most chaotic in corporate history. While Heyman worked the telephones outside the hall, getting his supporters to telex in their proxies, Werner, who could see that he was beaten, announced that the polls would not close until May 13. Customarily, polls close at the end of a shareholders' meeting. Heine became livid and called Flom into a conference room to argue the point. While the two lawyers were gone and Heyman was still on the phone, Werner called for a motion to adjourn.

Only Heyman's wife, Ronnie, had the presence of mind to attempt to prolong the meeting. "This is Russian justice," she declared. "If you see you are going to lose, you keep the polls open and try to contain the thing. You want to keep this thing open for two more weeks so Mr. Flom can do some more arm-twisting, so you can pressure and cajole."

It was a bravura performance, but to no avail. Werner adjourned the meeting.

Heine had mapped out a nearly perfect strategy. He had come to the brink of engineering a victory that few had thought was even remotely possible and in doing so had brought Finley Kumble, at long last, to the top rank of firms. When word got out of their accomplishments on behalf of Sam Heyman, Steve Kumble wouldn't ever have to worry about finding clients. They would come flocking to Finley Kumble.

But Heine had left Werner an opening to challenge his victory. On February 18, 1983, Heyman's GAF Shareholders Committee for New Management had been required to file its proxy application with the Securities and Exchange Commission. Among the questions that Heyman was required to answer was one asking if he was involved in any lawsuits that might reflect on his ability to manage a company. And there was one little suit that Heine's team decided was irrelevant.

Nearly a year earlier, on May 17, 1982, Heyman's sister, Abigail, had filed suit against her brother alleging mismanagement of the trust fund that she had inherited from their father. Her twenty-eight-page complaint alleged that Samuel had diverted assets, used the trust fund money for his own personal benefit, and made contributions of Abigail's money, without her permission, to various charities.

The problems between the siblings stemmed from Abigail's marriage to a psychiatrist who was twenty years older than she was. Prior to her relationship with the psychiatrist, Abigail had become pregnant while unmarried. According to court documents, Abigail "had an abortion performed, photographed her own abortion while the operation was in progress, published the photos in a nationally circulated book, and discussed the matter in a television interview."

Heyman and his mother were convinced that Abigail was being manipulated by the psychiatrist, who they believed was interested only in her money. As Heyman was later to testify. "She had lost all grasp of reality. I feared for the preservation of her assets."

Alarmed by Abigail's erratic behavior, Heyman and his

mother transferred all of her liquid assets, about $850,000, to a joint venture for which Heyman would have signing power until 1990.

Because of the personal nature of the suit, its contents were placed under seal by the Connecticut courts. But though the suit was sealed, the docket sheet listing it was not. As a result, private investigators hired by Werner, at a cost of $341,600, discovered the lawsuit. About a month before the shareholders' meeting, GAF asked the Connecticut court to give it access to the information contained in the court file. At the same time, GAF issued a press release saying, "When a person such as Heyman asks stockholders of a public corporation to vote him into a position of trust in that corporation, all matters which may bear on his integrity and character should be made available to such stockholders."

After losing the April 28 vote—Heyman's slate of directors had received 58 percent of the votes from the shareholders— GAF asked the federal court in New York City to issue an order delaying certification of the results. GAF's papers said information in the Connecticut lawsuit might cast doubt on Heyman's "integrity and fitness."

With the case in the courts, Heine assigned it to Finley's litigation department, still headed by Alan Gelb. Gelb turned principal responsibility for the matter over to litigator Jeffrey Fillman, a former Kumble classmate at Harvard who had been with the firm since its earliest days. Heine had done well but hadn't closed the deal. Now it was up to the Finley litigators to hang onto the victory.

But they weren't up to the task. The litigation team made numerous mistakes, the most serious of which was antagonizing the federal magistrate assigned to hear nonurgent motions in the case. Unfortunately for Fillman and Gelb, the magistrate had once been the judge's law clerk, and by alienating the younger jurist, they angered Judge Edward McMahon. On June 8, McMahon ruled that the allegations should have been disclosed to the stockholders. Certification of the shareholders' vote was permanently enjoined, and a new proxy vote was ordered by the court.

Heyman vowed to appeal the district court ruling to the U.S. Court of Appeals. But before he did so, Goldschmid urged that Heyman fire his lawyers. A former partner at the distinguished white-shoe firm of Debevoise Plimpton Lyons and Gates, Goldschmid had lost all confidence in Finley Kumble. Although Heyman was satisfied with Heine's work, he agreed with the assessment of the litigation department; moreover, Heyman felt that Finley Kumble's billing were far too high. "To do what we need done," said Goldschmid, "we need an Arthur Liman," the ace litigator from Paul Weiss Rifkind Wharton and Garrison. Heine didn't argue; he knew Heyman and Goldschmid were right.

The decision was a bitter blow to Steven Kumble. The firm had never been closer to respectability than on that day in September when Heine had masterminded one of the greatest upset victories in corporate history. But now fellow lawyers would remember only that when the crunch time came, Finley Kumble couldn't deliver the goods. Arthur Liman was a heavy hitter; Alan Gelb was not.

Making matters worse, Liman won the appeal. Heyman took over GAF and made it one of the great stories in American business. It could have been the institutional client that the New York office of Finley Kumble had never before been able to attract. But now GAF was Arthur Liman's client. Over the next few years, Liman's firm would reap millions in fees from Heyman's attempted takeover of Union Carbide and other dramatic ventures. Finley Kumble had once had those fees within its grasp. It was another humiliation, but one Kumble vowed to fix. The firm would hire a litigator who could hold onto clients like Sam Heyman.

In the midst of the finger pointing over the disaster, Kumble needed little convincing that it was time to replace one other department head. It didn't seem fair to him that Gelb should shoulder all the blame. The firm's corporate department was equally at fault. Heine had been outmanuevered by Joe Flom and Skadden Arps: he shouldn't have been out of the ballroom at the fateful moment. Tom Tew, who knew securities law, complained about Heine's performance to his friend Kumble. "We need people in our corporate department who are involved in the number one legal issue of our time, M&A work," Tew emphasized. Remembering Heine's performance in Los Angeles, Kumble couldn't agree more. But getting rid of his fellow "scorpion" would prove to be every bit as perilous as Roy Grutman had once predicted.

CHAPTER

15

HARVEY DANIEL MYERSON had come a long way since being asked as a young associate at New York's Webster and Sheffield to draft some letters in the complicated Newberger Loeb case. A native Philadelphian and a graduate of Columbia University Law School, Myerson had slowly but surely climbed to the top rank of New York City litigators.

Myerson's big score had come in 1976, when he was asked to take over the defense work for Houston's McRae Consolidated Oil and Gas Company. McRae, operating under the name Petrofunds, was in the business of raising money from investors to finance its oil- and gas-drilling program. On May 26, 1976, after a two-year investigation, the Securities and Exchange Commission charged that the company had not been truthful in disclosing to investors that some of the money was being diverted for other purposes. More serious, the SEC alleged that company executives were skimming off profits that should have been paid to investors. The charges were considered important enough to warrant major press coverage in the *Wall Street Journal.* For McRae, the prospects looked bleak. At worst the company would be lost. At best, it seemed, the SEC could keep them tied up in expensive litigation for years. As the judge in the case acknowledged, "The record fairly bristles with inferences of wrongful conduct in instance after instance." To fight the SEC action, which was filed in New York, McRae turned to Webster and Sheffield's litigation department. With the most experienced litigators in the firm busy with the defense of tobacco giant Liggett and Myers in several antitrust actions, Myerson was handed the case. Crucial to the SEC's prosecution was its request that the company be put in the hands of a court-appointed receiver and enjoined from doing business during the proceedings. Since the proceedings could drag on for years, the SEC's motion would have put McRae out of business. Harvey Myerson immediately began his counterattack, taking voluminous depositions and flooding the court with motions vigorously fighting the SEC allegations. Most important, Myerson marshaled a band of satisfied investors and had them write letters of support to the court. Such letters ordinarily have little effect on a judge, but Myerson had calculated correctly that his case was different. What they proved to federal judge Edward Weinfeld was that "this is not a typical fraud case. Whether or not the Petrofunds investors should have received more than they did, as the Commission contends, many of them appear to be satisfied with their return."

By June 22, less than a month after the filing of the complaint, Weinfeld pulled the rug from under the SEC's case. "The fact that the Commission has compiled a massive record of testimony and exhibits over its 25 month investigation does not relieve it of the burden of proving its claim," Weinfeld declared. In record time Myerson had brought the SEC to its knees. Just a year later, the SEC announced that it was settling all of its claims against Petrofunds in exchange for the company's promise to establish an audit department that would review all of its operations in light of SEC rules. In other words, it was a total rout of the powerful government agency. McRae was so delighted with Myerson's performance that Myerson continued to represent the firm in defense of a $200 million lawsuit brought by unhappy investors, which he also won.

Fueled by his millionaire Houston oil clients, Harvey Myerson had become a star, and he wasn't about to let anyone forget it. He began racing Ferraris, driving around New York in a Rolls Royce, smoking $10 Cuban cigars, imported through Switzerland, and wearing ridiculous-looking raccoon coats. The father of five girls from two separate marriages, Myerson played tennis at a home in Martha's Vineyard and enjoyed golf in the West Indies.

He was rewarded by his partners with a place on the firm's management committee. Personally, however, many of them were appalled by Myerson's gruff manner, his huge ego, his large expense account claims, and what was reputed to be his $2,500-a-month cigar habit. During smoky partnership meetings, it was no surprise that he expressed an ardent desire to be the top earner at the firm. It was a view not shared by his fellow litigators, most of whom, although extremely wealthy by normal standards, were living far more humbly.

But in 1982 Myerson's legal reputation suffered a blow. He had been hired by Allegheny Beverage Company, which controlled the franchise for Pepsi-Cola in eastern Virginia. Allegheny's chairman, controversial investor Morton Lapides, wanted Myerson to break the stranglehold that he claimed a competing Coca-Cola bottler seemed to have on the area. On November 25, 1980, Myerson filed suit charging that the Mid-Atlantic Coca-Cola Bottling Company was engaging in predatory pricing policies and had conspired with other smaller soft-drink manufacturers to drive Lapides's company out of business. But this time Myerson's opponent wasn't some government lawyer. Mid-Atlantic Coca-Cola turned to Richard Wertheimer of Washington's illustrious Arnold and Porter, a lawyer as well versed in unfair trade practice laws as anybody in the country. At the trial in Norfolk, Virginia, Myerson was beaten. On appeal, he sought not only a reversal but an award of triple damages to punish Mid-Atlantic for their conduct. But this time he was flailing in the dark. Myerson, the court ruled, had failed to show that Coke's actions had caused Pepsi any injury. The case was lost, and Lapides, who himself was later indicted and sent to prison for price fixing, fired Myerson in disgust.

Despite the setback, Myerson still acted like the top banana, still carped about increasing his partnership draw, still continued to annoy his colleagues. Shortly before Christmas in 1983, perhaps to their relief, Myerson decided that he would take his oil-patch clients and start his own law firm. His best friend at Webster and Sheffield, Richard DeScherer, had a good tax practice, with the investment firm of Shearson Lehman as a major client. Between the two of them, Myerson figured, they had the nucleus of a hot new firm, one free of the stuffy litigators they were cursed to endure at Webster and Sheffield. Quietly DeScherer began making the rounds of the firm, querying other lawyers about an interest in bolting with the two of them to start a new venture. Eventually DeScherer came up with a list of ten lawyers who could be counted upon to join them. Undertaken with the greatest secrecy, the code name for the project was "the Frog." But no matter how Myerson and DeScherer juggled the figures, with all the start-up expenses, it seemed the Frog could never generate the money they were already making at Webster and Sheffield. Clients generally like the stability of a large, established firm, and there was no way to ensure that, in a defection, some of them wouldn't stick with the older group.

In May 1984, word of the Frog's existence finally leaked out to Webster and Sheffield partner Theodore Lynn. When he confronted Myerson, the Frog still wasn't ready. But Lynn made it clear that in view of Myerson's intentions, he should think about leaving immediately.

Myerson and DeScherer were forced into action. Instead of forming their own firm, Myerson enlisted the services of a headhunter and began negotiating for his group with three prominent New York City firms. The most exciting was Wachtell Lipton Rosen and Katz, which, through its expertise in takeover work, had become the most profitable law firm on a per-partner basis in the country. Wachtell was willing to give Myerson $1 million a year, but they had no interest in Myerson's ten-lawyer group. Myerson explained to Wachtell that he had put together the group and had to be loyal to it. Wachtell said he simply didn't want to absorb ten lawyers. So the deal was off.

The other two firms were Donovan Leisure and Finley Kumble, code-named "the Bee." When Myerson reported back to his group with Wachtell's decision, there was general disappointment. Donovan Leisure, a firm famous for its antitrust practice, was in general decline, largely because the Justice Department had gone to sleep during the Reagan administration. Businesses weren't being harassed and that meant lower fees for Donovan Leisure, accustomed to representing businesses with governmental problems. Finley Kumble had money but was considered a horrible place to work. The ten lawyers, most of them young, had agreed to defect thinking they were about to start their own exciting new firm. When Finley Kumble began to emerge as the likeliest salvation for Myerson's windblown Frog, three of the ten dropped out, deciding to stay with Webster and Sheffield. But for the seven others, Myerson insisted that Finley Kumble offered the most promise. It was a jungle, Myerson acknowledged. But he had extracted certain promises in his negotiations with Steven Kumble. DeScherer would soon replace Robert Casey as the head of the firm's tax department. The young lawyers in the group would be guaranteed partnerships in just a couple of years. Myerson himself was promised a draw that would approach $900,000 a year, and he would get a spot on the firm's management committee. Most important, Myerson had already proved his loyalty to them by declining the Wachtell offer. He promised to continue to be their guardian and would personally make sure that all Kumble's guarantees were kept.

When one of the associates in the group, Atlanta native Kenneth Henderson, paid a visit to Finley Kumble, he was appalled at the working conditions. Fifth- and sixth-year associates were working in interior offices without so much as a window. Discussions with associates there revealed that 70-hour work weeks were common. When Henderson returned to Webster and Sheffield, he told Myerson that the deal was off. Finley Kumble was simply too horrible. "The place is a sleazy, third-rate sweat shop," he complained.

But Myerson assured Henderson that he shouldn't worry: things would change at Finley Kumble—maybe not immediately, but Myerson had plans. The "Bee" might not be under his control now, he hinted, but it would be. It was just a matter of time.

In addition to coming into the firm as a member of its management committee, Myerson had extracted from Kumble a promise that he would be director of national litigation. That was news, of course, to Alan Gelb.

Gelb had always viewed himself as the most unappreciated lawyer at Finley Kumble. He was blamed for every litigation screw-up. Ever since Grutman had left, he lived constantly with the fear of once again being superseded. After the GAF debacle, the talk of bringing in a litigation heavy hitter was more prevalent than ever. Needless to say, Kumble maintained the greatest secrecy in his talks with Myerson. When Gelb was told of the deal with Myerson, he was given the impression it was a fait accompli. Gelb was so furious that he put his foot through Neil Underberg's glass coffee table.

But this time the litigation department at Finley Kumble decided to fight. To a man, they asked Kumble to reconsider bringing Harvey Myerson into the firm. Jeffrey Fillman, who had worked closely with Gelb on GAF, led the opposition. Hadn't the firm had enough of big shots from the outside? Hadn't Kumble learned anything from his experience with Marshall Manley? On almost every acquisition, the partnership by consensus had gone along with Kumble. This time Fillman was asking him not to do it. Kumble was unmoved and was on the verge of putting the Myerson acquisition to a vote. But Carl Schwarz, the in-house expert on labor relations, warned Kumble off. "I wouldn't put this one to a vote, Steve," he said.

The unusual message from Schwarz opened Kumble's eyes. He agreed to postpone the vote and went into huddled meetings with Heine and Gelb. When those sessions were over, Gelb was pacified. He would remain head of the litigation department in New York. Myerson would become overall head of a national litigation section. More important, Gelb would be named to the national management committee. At long last, Gelb felt, he had won the recognition he deserved.

For many of the young partners and associates at Finley Kumble, Myerson's arrival was viewed as a sign of hope. The feuding among Manley, Kumble, and Heine seemed only to be getting worse, and the firm had become balkanized and turf conscious. Rivalries existed not only between the offices themselves, but between cliques in the New York office. Like street-gang members, each Finley Kumble faction took care of its own.

If anyone could change things at Finley Kumble, it seemed to be Harvey Myerson. If nothing else, he was new, and he had an aura of success.

But by 1985 the reality at Finley Kumble proved to be even more absurd than its reputation. In the midst of a massive renovation of the firm's offices one summer, workmen had covered the entire area with tentlike tarpaulin. Sawdust was everywhere, and carpenters stood on paint-splotched ladders drilling holes in the ceiling. Steve strolled through one afternoon, eyeing the electric fans that the young associates in the interior offices had placed near their desks for relief from the summer heat. "I want these fans out of here," Kumble shouted. "It looks unprofessional."

Another Kumble obsession was that lawyers in the firm not walk down the hallway without lids on their coffee cups. Among the clients that Myerson had brought to the firm was the Houston-based Kelley Oil Corporation. One afternoon Kelley's president, Joe Bridges, was using the office of Myerson associate Arthur Ruegger. He had walked down to the canteen and was returning to Ruegger's office when Kumble accosted the Texan.

"Where the fuck is the top of your coffee cup?" Kumble yelled. "How many times do I have to tell you people! If I see you one more time in here without a lid on your cup, you are out of here—fired!"

Bridges froze in a state of shock as Kumble brushed past him. The oilman returned to the coffee room to get his lid, and there found Kumble slumped disconsolately in a chair in the corner.

"Let me introduce myself," Bridges said. "I'm the president of the Kelley Oil Corporation."

"I'm sorry, I thought you worked here," said Kumble. "It's just that I have spent $300,000 on these carpets, and people walk down the hall without the lids on their coffee cups. I think you can understand."

"Have you considered putting a sign up here in the canteen, reminding people to put lids on their cups?" Bridges asked.

"That wouldn't work with this crew," Kumble said. "I think I'm just going to have take the coffee away from them."

But while Kumble was almost universally disliked by the firm's younger lawyers, he still controlled the purse strings and had more say than anyone about how partnership money was apportioned. And while he was almost irrational in his harangues about collecting money, in one-on-one sessions with lawyers in his office, he often made associates and young partners feel like they would be future stars. But, because the young lawyers had been encouraged to borrow and live beyond their means and because Finley Kumble salaries were extremely high, few lawyers in the firm could afford to leave.

In addition to the success Kumble was having in attracting new lawyers and their clients, his attempts to get good press seemed at last to be paying off.

In the summer of 1983, Steve Brill assigned his top reporter, Connie Bruck, to profile Kumble in the *American Lawyer*'s "Heavy Hitter" section. While many of the *American Lawyer*'s feature stories tended to accentuate law firm screw-ups or misconduct, "Heavy Hitter" was a compartment laudatory in itself. In the amoral world of the large law firm, there was no greater compliment than to be a heavy hitter, a term that Brill modestly claimed to have added to the legal jargon.

Throughout 1983 Brill had taken to chronicling the advances of Kumble and Manley. In May, for example, Brill reported Kumble's acquisition of one of California's top energy experts, Robert Krueger; the acquisition of a top aviation disaster expert in Washington; and the possibility that Kumble was exploring opening an office in Cleveland.

Just four months later, Bruck's article appeared on Kumble entitled "Steve Kumble and the Art of Empire Building." In many ways, Kumble gave *American Lawyer* the same pitch he had used on Tydings, Tew, and even Manley. Turning on the now-legendary Kumble charm, he disarmed the author with his admission that the firm had made mistakes and drew a line between the old firm and a nonexistent new one.

Appearing a few months before their climactic disagreement over Marshall Manley, the article described how hard Steve worked to keep Heine happy. "Not long after Andrew came," he said, "he decided that we should serve tea at 3 P.M., so I went out and bought a teacart and a silver tea service—silver-plated to go with the firm's image—and we had this guy wheel it around, tea and cookies. Then the wheel fell off, so we nailed it on and it was stationary, you had to go to it. After a while it began to look really tarnished, so I told the guy to clean it up. He used steel wool and all the silver came off. That was the end of Andrew's innovation."

The firm's greatest achievement, boasted Kumble, was respectability. Finley, the "papa of the candy store," was even trotted out for the occasion to say, "What the firm has achieved today is beyond my fondest dreams—not the size but the acceptance. People tell me, 'God you've gotten white collar in a hurry.'"

Of particular amusement to his colleagues was Steve's comment that the most enjoyable job in his professional life was "working on a transaction where the documents are as close to perfect as they can be and the result for a client is as perfect as possible."

The piece increased the stature of the firm in the legal community and was used to support Kumble's spiel to new recruits. Like the acquisition of such names as Wagner and Tydings, the Bruck article seemed to prove that a new "good Finley Kumble" had arrived. It had an immediate and positive impact on hiring and client-getting.

The article spawned one of the warmest moments between Heine and Kumble. Just after the piece was released, on July 3, 1983, at Kumble's fiftieth-birthday party at the Helmsley Palace Hotel, Heine wheeled out a new silver cart and presented it to Kumble as a birthday present. The two men smiled and hugged. But it was one of the last such times that the two friends would share.

The following summer, Brill had decided that it was time to give the law firm the magazine's full treatment—a front-page cover story. Fortuitously, for Brill at least, the young journalist ran into Manley, Kumble, Heine, Washington, and Underberg on a flight from Chicago to New York. Brill, who by now had become so influential within the profession that the American Bar Association invited him to speak, was returning from an ABA convention. The Finley Kumble quintet had been talking to Don Reuben of one-hundred-lawyer Reuben and Proctor about a merger and, before boarding the plane, had stopped at the airport lounge.

As Brill later wrote:

> It is about seven on an evening in August and the five men chiefly responsible for running the fastest-growing and second largest law firm in America are waiting to board a New York bound jet at O'Hare airport. They have spent the afternoon in downtown Chicago trying to negotiate yet another in the series of mergers and acquisitions—this one involving a firm of more than 100 lawyers—that has made the firm of Finley Kumble Wagner Heine Underberg, Manley & Casey the most interesting and to some the most reviled law partnership of the new age.
>
> As they're about to take their first class seats, the Tiffany cufflinked and perfectly tanned Andrew Heine, one of the big five and the firm's lead corporate securities partner, yells an obscenity having to do with a supposed sexual exploit to one of his partners. A half dozen strangers turn to eyeball their coarse fellow passenger but not before lead real estate partner Neil Underberg, a tiny courtly looking man in a three piece suit, bellows just as loudly to this reporter, "Don't write any of what he said in any goddamn article." Whereupon Steven Kumble deadpans. "You ought to put it in Ripley's Believe It or Not."
>
> A fourth partner, the elegantly tailored Robert Washington, Jr., of the firm's Washington D.C. office winces at the vaudeville act unfolding in front of him. The fifth member

of the roadshow, L.A.-based Marshall Manley, a man who at 44 is probably the best single client enticer in the history of the law business, seems oblivious or numb to the episode.

If there had been any possibility that these five men could continue as partners and somehow restore old friendships, it was shattered with the publication of Brill's front-page article, "Should You Sign On When the Finleyman Calls?" There, as big as life on the cover, was the Finleyman himself—Marshall Manley—identified in the caption as the firm's top client getter and premier recruiter.

But the article inside seemed even worse to Kumble. If nothing else, he complained, the firm should have been called Kumbleland, not Finleyland. But there it was, "Finleyland," of all things. And there he was in all his glory, Marshall Manley.

Brill had adopted Manley's notion that the L.A. office was the crown jewel of the Finleyland empire. His Beverly Hills outpost was described as "elegant" and subdued. New York headquarters, on the other hand, "is a row of windowless tiger cages, each holding two or more lawyers in the 177-lawyer New York outpost where on the tenth floor a young partner could recently be heard screaming at a secretary for not moving enough folding chairs into a makeshift conference room."

But what really angered Kumble were two remarks about him from colleagues, one from Heine and another from Robert Washington. Even Brill was flabbergasted by "how freely the partners dumped on each other." In one of the most painful comments, Heine was quoted as saying "We keep ethical problems like conflict questions away from Steve." Heine tried to explain to Kumble that Brill had taken the comment out of context. He claimed he had been asked if the firm had a committee that looked at potential conflicts of interest. Heine said he replied that the firm did have such a committee, adding that Kumble wasn't on it—thus, the comment to Brill. His labored explanation did little to assuage Steve Kumble.

Bob Washington assaulted Kumble's role in the distribution of partnership income, calling the figures "Kumble's bullshit."

Added Washington, "We hope to get Steve back to practicing law and away from all those numbers that he keeps: any administrator can do that." He then took a swipe at the New York office, claiming that the D.C. and L.A. partners could probably do better without New York. Washington, like Heine, claimed that he was misunderstood, but he couldn't deny that he had talked to Brill.

"I speak for the firm," Kumble angrily told Washington at a breakfast one morning at Manhattan's Regency Hotel. "You and Andy shouldn't have talked to him."

But if Kumble was the target of most of the article's fire, newcomer Harvey Myerson was not immune. Jeffrey Fillman, who hadn't been as quick as Gelb to accept the new star litigator, had remarked, "Let's face it, Harvey just isn't the kind of star that people think he is. He's been a plus. But he's no Arthur Liman."

For fifteen years, Kumble had longed for big-time press treatment. He had hired and fired public relations men. He had entertained Brill at his home. He had seated him next to the rich and famous. He had cooperated with reporters. He had returned calls. But it had all come down to one monumental and mighty insult. Marshall Manley on the cover. "Finleyland." A row of tiger cages. Open assaults on his leadership of the firm, not just from the colonies in Washington and L.A., but from Heine, just twenty feet away. That was what had stung Kumble the most— Heine. He had brought Heine into the firm before anybody. He had put his name on the letterhead. Anywhere you want it, Kumble had told him. He had even given him a silver teacart. They had been through thick and thin. He had given Heine the reins of power, and Heine had again stabbed him in his gut. There was nothing about which Kumble was more sensitive than ethics, perhaps because it was the area in which the firm was most vulnerable. Their ethics had always been a problem, and Kumble had been able to diffuse it with the new recruits by bringing it up first. That was the old Finley Kumble, he would tell the new hirees. That was prehistory. That was Persky. He served time. He's long gone. We are respectable. We are white collar. We are a sophisticated national practice. But there, hidden in parentheses, Heine had dared to tell the world the truth, even if he hadn't meant to, about his partner. Even so, they managed to keep the feud out of the public eye, until the American Bakeries mess.

In March 1981, a thirty-two-year-old commodities trader from New York, Neil S. Leist, began purchasing shares of Chicago-based American Bakeries, the country's third-largest bread maker. Their two biggest brands were Taystee and Merita.

Within a year Leist had managed to purchase 16 percent of the company's 2.2 million shares, and he was able to win control of four seats on the company's twelve-member board.

He had been directed in his takeover effort by Leonard Toboroff, a New York City attorney with his own small law firm. Leist was a longtime client of Leonard's. Toboroff had taken on Neil's representation in a major challenge to the New York Mercantile Exchange regarding the constitutionality of the country's commodities laws. The case involved potatoes futures contracts, and at the time of Leist's successful takeover, it was before the U.S. Supreme Court.

On November 2, 1981, Toboroff had argued Leist's case before the nation's highest court. When he walked down the steps and looked across at the Capitol, Toboroff knew his legal career had reached its peak. He decided to come to an arrangement with a big firm, hand over his clients, and get involved in business activities. His first choice had been to join Joe Flom at Skadden Arps. When Flom expressed no interest, Toboroff sought out Steve Kumble. Kumble agreed that they could come to an understanding, and Leonard became what is called "of counsel" to Finley Kumble. He wasn't a partner, but he did move into the offices and become an important member of the firm. Among the clients picked up from Toboroff was Neil Leist.

By March 1982, a slate of directors headed by Leist finally took four seats on the company's board. The other directors finally caved in to Leist's relentless pressure, agreeing to make the young executive both company president and chief executive officer at a salary of $275,000 per year. Coincidental to

Leist's takeover, H. Garrett Bewkes, a former senior vice-president at Norton Simon Corporation, owner of Canada Dry and Hunt Foods, had taken early retirement and put out the word that he was looking for a company to manage. Heine, an old friend from Yale, promised to keep an eye out.

"I'm tired of being a number two guy," Bewkes told friends.

At 1:16 A.M. on May 24, on the Montauk Highway on Long Island, Leist's car jumped the center line and careened into a parked truck. A twenty-two-year-old passenger in his car was killed. Leist himself was taken in critical condition to Southampton Hospital, where, brain dead, he lay in a coma. Toboroff arranged to have a helicopter transport Leist to experts at New York's Bellevue Hospital.

But where others saw only tragedy, the lawyers at Finley Kumble recognized opportunity. Following the accident, Toboroff was named acting CEO of American Bakeries. But by June 15, Finley Kumble didn't need such direct control. Kumble ran into a relative of Bewkes at a Waldorf Astoria dinner party and passed the word back to the retiree that a great position had opened up. Toboroff and Heine then successfully convinced the other members of the board to hire Bewkes as Leist's successor. Bewkes was also allowed to name three new directors, one of which was Andy Heine, who put together a deal in which a group controlled by Bewkes purchased all the stock from poor Leist. Among the shareholders in the new group were both Heine and Kumble.

Almost immediately after seizing control, Bewkes began undoing everything Leist had started, including canceling a new plant that had been ordered. Most remarkably, Bewkes moved to cut off company benefits to the stricken Leist, notifying the attorneys tending to the comatose man's estate that his salary and benefits would cease. If that wasn't bad enough, Bewkes bad-mouthed Leist to the *Wall Street Journal*, saying "I don't think Neil really understood paybacks and analyses and things like that." It would probably make a better story if an angry Leist had recovered from his coma, reclaimed his company, and boxed

Bewkes's ears. Unfortunately, after lingering in the coma for two years, Leist, then thirty-five, died.

Never enamored of the baking business, Bewkes decided to use the company, the fourth-largest bakery in the nation, as an investment vehicle. Bewkes had his sights set on five hundred luxury campgrounds, called Camp Coast to Coast. His idea was to buy the campgrounds and then sell memberships to them. To finance the acquisition, Bewkes had asked Heine to help in selling 550,000 shares of common stock to European investors.

Much more so than under Leist, American Bakeries under Bewkes became an important Finley Kumble client.

In early 1985, Heine received a call from a distraught and excited Bewkes. In the midst of his own takeover frenzy, he had just found out that a group had purchased 5 percent of his company's stock.

"Who the hell is that?" Heine grumbled.

"Why don't you go down the hall and ask your partner Steve Kumble?" Bewkes replied.

Heine claims to then have learned that Kumble had bought a sizable stake in American Bakeries, which, when added to director Heine's stake and that of a few other corporate department lawyers, totaled more than 5 percent interest in the company. Such a large percentage of ownership seemed to require that Finley Kumble register its holdings with the Securities and Exchange Commission. Furious, Heine stormed into Kumble's office, then marched back down the hall to his own office, and wrote a memo.

In the memo, Heine expressed shock at Bewkes's disclosure to him that Kumble had purchased so much stock in American Bakeries that it required the filing of a potentially controversial public disclosure statement with the SEC.

Calling it "obvious" that such a filing was required by the securities laws, Heine bemoaned being reduced to writing a memo saying that in view of his and Kumble's present state of communications, or lack thereof, he considered it "the least provocative." Far preferable, he concluded, than raising the issue "in front of others."

Heine warned that Kumble was not aware of the possible "legal and personal problems" his stock purchase presented and he complained about having been put in the embarrassing position of having to tell a client that the firm had acquired a stock position so strong that, according to the SEC, it had been put in the position of being construed as a potential hostile owner.

As both the attorneys and owners of American Bakeries, Finley Kumble's position as counsel would, in Heine's view, be badly compromised. How could a law firm give honest advice to a client, if it had a stake in the client's bottom line? But from the days of Microthermal, Finley Kumble lawyers, like many others in that era, had often seemed indifferent to such concerns. But the public climate was much different now and there were concerns. One big one was that the legal press, especially Steve Brill, might subscribe to SEC reporting services that would quickly pick up the stock purchase. Another concern was that, since lawyers always have access to inside information, their stock purchases could be deemed suspect.

Heine stewed that the whole situation had jeopardized the partnership and raised questions that he hoped would not get outside firm walls.

But no partner had been more jeopardized in a legal sense than Andy, since on January 13, 1985, Heine himself had unknowingly sworn to an SEC document that had not listed Kumble or the firm as owning 5 percent of American Bakeries.

Filing false statements with the Securities and Exchange Commission was part of what Kumble had always passed off as the old Finley Kumble. Heine was determined it not be part of the new.

Kumble was livid at being lectured to by Heine. He first made a show in front of Leonard Toboroff of tearing up the memo and dropping it in the wastebasket. Then he sat down and wrote his reply, calling Heine's version of events "pure baloney."

Kumble insisted that his purchases should not be considered part of the law firm's. Kumble announced that he had no intention of voting his shares in concert with his partners, therefore he argued, no filing with the SEC was required.

Kumble assured Heine that he had not acted on the basis of inside information.

He insisted that even a "cursory examination" of his stock purchases in American Bakeries would establish that.

In words so formal to a friend and colleague that they clearly revealed a concern that Heine himself might make an allegation to the press, Kumble continued his denial of anything improper. He reiterated formally that he had not received any inside information from Heine or any other director. He made clear that he had never solicited any such information in making his stock purchases.

Then Kumble's tone changed. He added a personal note, beseeching Heine to face him directly, and not write notes.

No more letters, Kumble pleaded. "Our offices are only 20 feet apart."

But Heine was only getting warmed up. Six days later another memo landed on the flustered Kumble's always neatly kept desk.

He would go ahead and file the required statement with the SEC regardless of what Kumble thought. Legally, we don't have "any choice," Heine said.

With the feud between Heine and Kumble escalating, Myerson, who had initially tried to work with Kumble, was forced to choose sides. The decision was not a difficult one. Kumble was following through on few of the promises made to the members of Myerson's group. Most significant, Myerson, although promised an important role on the management committee, like so many before him sometimes wasn't even told when a meeting was scheduled. DeScherer, promised the leadership of the national tax department, was told that this was impossible. Kumble didn't want to antagonize Robert Casey, who was a Kumble supporter. The younger lawyers, such as Kenneth Henderson, were still stuck in their tiger cages, despite pledges of offices with windows.

From the first, Myerson knew that one day he would take over the firm. But now things were happening much faster than he had anticipated, with management problems and morale far worse than anyone on the outside could have guessed. Then in the fall of 1985, Manley announced that he was becoming the chief executive officer of his major client, Scharffenberger's Home Group. Although Manley would continue on as a partner and move to New York, it cleared another potential opponent in the firm's management. Encouraged by the impatient members of his team to do something quickly, Myerson decided to take action. But before he did, Harvey Myerson would move to center stage in the most highly publicized trial of his career—the United States Football League's antitrust suit against Pete Rozelle and the National Football League. It was a case that could make Myerson a legend and at last vault Finley Kumble to the top of the legal mountain.

CHAPTER

16

IN 1980 New Orleans advertising executive David Dixon had the idea of setting up a new football league that would compete for players with the National Football League but would play its games in the spring rather than in the fall. The beauty of the concept was that it seemed to get around the television contract problem. His leagues would play their games in those few months each year when the NFL was dormant. Dixon's prospectus was read with interest by potential owners in football-hungry cities that had been unable to win NFL franchises.

Dixon turned out to be almost a genius. On May 11, 1982, a group of owners representing twelve teams and eight of the country's biggest television markets announced the formation of the United States Football League. George Allen, the almost legendary coach of the Washington Redskins, purchased a franchise for Chicago, which he would himself coach. Chuck Fairbanks, the former coach of the NCAA national champion Oklahoma Sooners, was hired to coach the New Jersey Generals. With the news that big-name coaches were signing on with the new league, the American Broadcasting Company signed a two-year $18 million contract to broadcast USFL games in 1983 and 1984, with options for the succeeding two seasons. By comparison, the network had agreed to pay the NFL $681.5 million just two months earlier for the right to broadcast a five-year package that included one Super Bowl, five conference championships, and its Monday night games. On February 23, 1983, the stature of the upstart league was further bolstered when Heisman Trophy winner Herschel Walker, the nation's best college football player, decided to forgo his final year at the University of Georgia and play for the Generals. The new league's first season began on March 6, 1983, with the Generals losing to the Los Angeles Express 20–15. Although Walker played only sparingly in that initial game, the interest his signing had generated in the new league brought the game a 35 percent share of the national television audience, three times what had been predicted by ABC executives.

The first season was something of a mixed bag. To the public it looked like a reasonable start. The league certainly seemed more interesting than the previous attempt at competition with the NFL, the ill-fated World Football League. The WFL had lost national interest by placing its franchises in non-NFL cities such as Memphis, Birmingham, and Orlando and then competing against the NFL juggernaut. It was a dismal failure.

Nonetheless, the USFL owners lost a total of $40 million after the first season, and five owners bailed out. Among them was Oklahoma oilman Walter Duncan, who sold his New Jersey Generals franchise and Herschel Walker to New York City real estate mogul Donald Trump. Immediately other owners in the league began to suspect that Trump had a none-too-hidden agenda for USFL ownership. Men such as John Bassett, the millionaire owner of the Tampa Bay Bandits, were genuinely committed to building a spring football institution. The Dixon prospectus had never said anything about competing with the NFL. The idea, which Bassett subscribed to, had been to complement the older league. Nor was Bassett obsessed with the concept of forcing a merger with the NFL, as the American Football League had two decades earlier. But Bassett's desire to keep the league fiscally sound by holding down salaries and avoiding salary wars with the bigger league wasn't shared by his fellow owners, especially Trump. First Trump began dangling a million dollars in front of NFL coach Don Shula to jump to his team and replace Fairbanks. When that didn't work, Trump hired Walt Michaels, former coach of the NFL's New York Jets. Trump continued to wave a red flag in the face of the NFL owners by stealing away Cleveland Browns' star quarterback Brian Sipe.

A war with the NFL was not exactly what Bassett had in mind. Few of the other USFL owners, though all wealthy men, had Trump's bankroll. It was a war most knew they could never win.

But to compete with Trump, several of the other USFL owners also began raiding the competition. Complained Bassett of his fellow owners, "Their wallets are bigger than their management skills." The peak of the lunacy came when the Los Angeles Express signed Brigham Young quarterback Steve Young for a record $40 million, the most money ever promised to a professional athlete.

Bassett, however, was proven correct. The teams in the league continued to lose money. Franchises moved from city to city. Owners appeared and disappeared. Unfortunately, Bassett, father of woman's tennis star Carling Bassett-Seguso, didn't have much time to gloat about being right. In 1986 he died of cancer.

After just two spring seasons, the USFL owners began to consider the possibility of abandoning their spring format and moving to a fall season. It was clear that the real money would come only from eventually forcing a merger with the NFL. If that occurred, the value of the football teams would soar, and the investments that each owner had made would prove worthwhile.

But Trump's hopes for a fall season were dashed when none of the national television networks showed an interest in carrying the USFL opposite the older, established league. Each of the three major networks had its own package with the NFL.

Frustrated in his effort to force a merger with the NFL in that way, Trump threatened a lawsuit. The NFL still wouldn't budge. So on October 17, 1984, the USFL filed suit in New York federal court, seeking $1.3 billion in damages against the NFL for alleged antitrust violations.

Trump originally retained the notorious New York City lawyer and power broker Roy Cohn for the job. But Cohn was in ill health and when it became apparent that the suit was more than a ploy, Trump needed a real litigator. Few of the big New

York firms wanted anything to do with it. The power of the NFL and its owners was enormous. They included Jack Kent Cooke and Edward Bennett Williams of the Washington Redskins and Lamar Hunt of the Kansas City Chiefs. The NFL owners were not exactly the kind of people you want to sue, unless you are a law firm with a death wish. For such a maverick job, Trump needed a maverick attorney. He chose Harvey Myerson.

Myerson had suffered nothing but disbelieving sniggers since he had arrived on the scene at Finley Kumble. He had claimed to control some $3 million in business. But his group's biggest client, Shearson Lehman, was dividing its work among several firms, and could hardly be said to be under Myerson's "control," although Shearson's CEO Peter A. Cohen had asked Myerson to lead its defense against $500 million in damage claims filed by investors whom the firm had steered to several disastrous investments, notably the defaulted bonds of WPPSS (Whoops), the Washington Public Power Supply System. Myerson had actually lost one of his other big clients before arriving at Finley Kumble. Morton Lapides, the Maryland businessman who had built Allegheny Beverage into a diversified company with $526 million in revenues, had fired him after losing the cola case in Norfolk.

It would take balls to sue the NFL, and lawyers are bred to be cautious. Moreover, not too many serious lawyers gave the USFL owners even a slight chance of winning the case. The problem was in the transparency of what Trump was trying to do: blackmail the NFL into admitting his team into its league. If Trump and the other owners had been genuinely sincere in attempting to establish a rival football league, they might have had a chance. But Donald Trump was not very subtle, and neither was Myerson, who saw the case as an opportunity both to quiet the guffaws and to ingratiate himself with the fabulously wealthy Trump.

Originally it appeared Myerson would be opposing Finley Kumble nemesis Arthur Liman. But in April 1985 Judge Peter Leisure ruled that the NFL couldn't hire Liman because he had represented some of the USFL owners at an early stage in the league's development. Instead, the league turned to Los Angeles attorney Frank Rothman, the dapper former president of MGM, who had recently become a partner in the Los Angeles office of Skadden Arps. Rothman was joined by Davis Polk and Wardwell's Robert Fiske, the former U.S. attorney who had played a role earlier in freeing Brill from the FBI's threats.

For the first time, the eyes of the nation were focused on Myerson. For Kumble too, the case was important. It had the highest profile of any litigation in which Finley Kumble had ever been involved. The consequences of victory would be enormous. Not since the GAF case had an opportunity like this presented itself. But the GAF battle had been fought behind the closed doors of a corporate boardroom. Now the television cameras would be on the courtroom steps every morning, and the Finley Kumble name would be dropped with the morning paper on every dewy doorstep.

The trial began on May 13, 1986, with opening arguments. Two days later Myerson called as his first witness Pete Rozelle, the commissioner of the National Football League.

For three days Myerson pounded away at Rozelle. One of the most powerful men in the United States, Rozelle remained quiet and controlled. As hour after hour of interrogation passed, many in the courtroom began to realize that Rozelle, head of the giant NFL, was coming off as the underdog. Myerson was so overbearing, so caught up in his own South Philadelphia tough-guy persona, that he didn't recognize all he had to do was ease up and let Pete Rozelle look like the arrogant one.

But though Myerson didn't trash Rozelle, the situation still looked good for the USFL. Myerson had uncovered a slew of embarrassing disclosures, including the fact that NFL employees had been sent to a Harvard Business School seminar on "How to Crush the USFL." There seemed little doubt that the power of the NFL had played a part in the television networks' decisions not to air the USFL's fall games. Suddenly a case that had appeared totally unwinnable seemed within reach. On June 18, spirits on the Finley Kumble team soared when Judge Peter Leisure accepted the league's damage estimate of $565 million.

Under antitrust laws, in which damage awards are tripled, that meant they could collect $1.69 billion in damages.

Although the USFL—Trump primarily—had been paying Finley Kumble's legal fees right along, they would eventually total some $2 million, a judgment in the billion-dollar range would almost certainly mean a major premium for the firm. And if the NFL agreed to settle and as part of the settlement allow Trump into the big league, Myerson would also score. Myerson had a habit, not that unusual in a big law firm, of adding premiums to bills when he achieved good results. According to one associate with whom he worked, Myerson had, after one victory, turned a $600,000 bill into $900,000. When the clients win, Myerson had learned, they rarely quibble over fees. Although at the beginning of the case no one had really expected to pay a premium, hopes were being raised by the strong case Myerson seemed to be developing. Maybe, just maybe, Myerson hadn't been puffing. Maybe he was a heavy-hitting litigator. Myerson, like most trial attorneys, including Roy Grutman in the Newberger Loeb case, never for a moment thought that he could lose. Not with all those television cameras on the steps and all those *New York Times* reporters in the press gallery.

On July 23, after sixty-four days of trial, Myerson and Rothman finally rose to give their summations to the jury. It was clash of legal titans, and a standing-room-only crowd of more than 320 persons packed the courtroom, filling both the pews and the aisles, as the bailiff locked the doors. Neither lawyer disappointed. Rothman, dressed in a gray suit and red tie, moved deftly from overhead projector to video camera and back to the jury. The USFL's lawsuit was nothing more than part of Donald Trump's master plan to force his way into the big league, Rothman claimed. And that was true. The USFL died, he argued, not because of the actions of Rozelle and the NFL but because of the incompetence of its owners and management.

After a break for lunch, Myerson took center stage and performed for over three hours. He begged and pleaded with the jury to grant justice to his little client, wronged by "the most powerful monopoly in the country."

By the end of his speech, Myerson's voice was nearly gone. "Please God, find for us. God bless you," he concluded.

For the next five days, the six jurors spent thirty-one hours trying to come to a verdict. Judge Leisure's instructions to the jury had consumed 155 pages.

"Just because you may have found the fact of some damage," Leisure concluded, " 'that does not mean that you are required to award a dollar amount. You may find that you are unable to compute the monetary damages, or that you cannot separate out the amount of the losses; or you may find the plaintiff failed to prove an amount of damages. You may decline to award damages under such circumstances, or you may award a nominal amount, say $1."

With those words fresh in their minds, the jurors left the courtroom and began deliberating. Only three of the six jurors, however, had been swayed by Myerson's arguments. Myerson had tried to make the case one of David versus Goliath. But Ira Berkow in the *New York Times* had more correctly characterized the nature of the contest when he wrote, "It's more like Donald versus Goliath."

Margaret Lilienfeld, one of the more influential jurors, hammered home the point that this wasn't the little guy versus the big guy. "It's billionaires versus billionaires," she said. "The big guys versus the big guys." The jurors deadlocked 3–3. Then, to avoid a hung jury, they apparently reached a compromise and announced they had a verdict.

At 3:55 P.M. on July 29, the jurors emerged and in open court announced a surprising decision. The impossible, the implausible had happened. They had concluded unanimously that Myerson had proven his case. The powerful National Football League, the jury decided, had in fact used its power to stamp out the young competitor.

That said, the jurors announced the damage award. For the wrongs that the new football league had suffered, the United States Football League was awarded $1. Under the laws governing antitrust actions, the verdict would be tripled. The USFL had won $3. It wasn't an award from which Myerson could squeeze much of a premium. Myerson's natural reaction normally would have been to claim victory or foul. But this verdict was too weird. Confused, suddenly uncertain whether he had won or lost, Myerson forgot to ask that the jury be polled. Judge Leisure turned to Myerson and asked, "Is there any application with respect to the verdict?"

Myerson replied, "No application, Your Honor."

It was a fatal error. Had Myerson taken the judge's hint and polled the jury to ensure they agreed and understood their decision, he would have learned that not all the jurors agreed with the damage award, and the verdict almost certainly would been thrown out or recalculated. But the jury wasn't polled, and no one realized until later that one of the jurors, Miriam Sanchez, was as confused as everyone else by what her jury had done. She had wanted to award the USFL $300 million in damages. But not until she was outside the courtroom, discharged from her duties as a juror, did she confess her confusion to a television reporter.

All Myerson could do was swallow his disappointment. He had won his case. Against all odds, he had proven his point. But he had only won thirty dimes for his client. "I would have been happy with $100 million," Myerson said. He had to admit that the damages were more important than the principle. "Without damages the USFL dies," said Myerson. And if the verdict wasn't bad enough, Myerson had to endure the public scorn of eminent *New York Times* sportswriter Dave Anderson. "Throughout the trial," Anderson wrote, "Myerson attempted to influence the jury with theatrics instead of truth, or with emotion instead of evidence."

Either way, the case became yet another humiliation. Though this was a high-profile embarrassment, only Steve Kumble knew how serious the defeat actually was. Myerson had said that without damages the USFL dies. What he didn't know was that, without his hoped-for premium, his own law firm would soon be gasping for breath.

CHAPTER

17

UNTIL THE SIX-MEMBER JURY in the USFL case returned its
$1 verdict, Steven Kumble had never worried much about ex-
penses. The law firm that had been created to mirror his own
life, personality, and philosophy was revenue driven. The theme
had always been "get the fee," not "save the money." Top-level
Park Avenue lawyers fly only first-class. On transatlantic flights,
that usually meant the Concorde. Nights were spent in only the
very best hotels. Secretaries and office workers were driven hard
but paid well, most receiving amenities such as car service, even
when regular taxis would have sufficed. When newly hired lawyers demanded exorbitant salaries, they almost always got them,
much to the dismay of those with greater seniority. Steve was
philosophical. "If you want a Xerox, you've got to pay for a
Xerox" was his explanation for almost everything.

Indeed, by early 1986 each of the offices seemed to be growing
logarithmically.

In January 1986 Finley Kumble took one of its biggest leaps
toward respectability: it began building a London office. Once
again it was mostly a Manley operation. The lawyer he wanted
to open the firm's first foreign division was Bruce Lilliston, resi-
dent managing partner in London for the entertainment-ori-
ented Los Angeles firm Mitchell Silberberg and Knupp. In recent
years more and more films were being funded by British entre-
preneurs, Alexander Salkind's *Superman* series being a prime
example.

Meanwhile, Manley stole four lawyers from the five-lawyer London office of Chicago-based Sidley and Austin, a move that brought the U.K. operations of Motown Records under the Finley umbrella. Although the office centered mostly around entertainment, Manley pledged to the new recruits that they were getting in on the ground floor of what would be one of the most exciting practices in history. In wooing Lilliston, Manley claimed that when President Reagan's term of office was over, Reagan would travel Europe as a pitchman for the firm. Although there apparently was no truth to Manley's statement, Lilliston saw no reason to disbelieve it. Law partners just don't expect to be looked in the eye and lied to. Manley claimed to Lilliston that, after Reagan had been shot, he had visited President and Mrs. Reagan in the hospital, "walking in with flowers and walking out with the president's tax and real estate business." Manley had never met with President Reagan and had met Governor Reagan only once. But there was a kernel of truth in those grandiose statements. Through presidential friend George Scharffenberger, Manley had picked up the real estate work that needed to be done for Wall Management, the consortium of Reagan's friends who were buying and donating a new house for the Reagans in Bel Air.

The London office became a nice toy for the Finley Kumble partners, especially Myerson, who jetted over on the Concorde numerous times, often billing the firm rather than a client for the trip. In August Manley asked Lilliston if Bruce would replace a resigned partner and move his entertainment practice back to Los Angeles. To ease Lilliston's move, Manley agreed to attempt to provide the thirty-three-year-old lawyer with $300,000 in home financing and an $80,000 personal loan from California's Merchant Bank, a financial institution that had included Manley and several other Finley Kumble partners on its board.

The day before Lilliston was to leave London for America, L.A. partner Alan Schwartz informed him that the firm was unable to arrange the $300,000 loan. It was too late for Lilliston to change his plans, so he flew to the States anyway and straightened out his financial situation later.

In Florida, meanwhile, Tew's operation merged with a Tallahassee firm to give Finley Kumble a presence in the state capital. He was attracting top lawyers from the most old-line competitive firms in Miami. No new partner symbolized Finley Kumble better than Herb Suskin, who came aboard after five years in the real estate department of Miami's top home-grown firm, Greenberg Traurig Askew Hoffman Lipoff Rosen and Quentel. Suskin had little interest in law but admitted a lot of interest in money and sailing. No firm in the country offered the opportunity to make a lot of money quickly, and Suskin's goal was to make so much that he could spend the rest of his life at sea.

Manley added lawyers in San Diego, and he culled the law corridors of San Francisco, looking to add an office there as well. Another state capital office was opened in Sacramento to serve Hugh Carey and partner William Normile's burgeoning municipal bond practice. Incredibly, no one in the Los Angeles office knew what Carey and Normile were doing.

D.C. partner Paul Perito was representing the Hunt Brothers' international mining subsidiary in a silver manipulation case. Eager to attract more of their lucrative work, he opened a fourteen-lawyer office in Dallas. Unfortunately for Perito and Finley Kumble, the Hunt family then informed the firm that, because of Lamar Hunt's ownership of the NFL's Kansas City Chiefs and Myerson's involvement in the suit against the league, it wouldn't be giving the firm any additional billings.

The bills were piling up for the new leases, salaries, and other start-up expenses. But no one was concerned. Finley Kumble partner draws were high and going higher. There was no better sign of a firm's financial health than high draws, paid on schedule. The business seemed robust, and with the revenue-conscious Kumble at the helm, no one worried. The firm was his life, and if there was one thing he was good at, it was business. The new acquisitions and offices made Finley Kumble the second-largest law firm in the United States, behind Chicago's Baker and McKenzie. Each major acquisition gave Steve another opportunity to brag to the national business and legal press about the class operation Finley Kumble had become. It was made up of governors, senators, congressmen, mayors, heavy hitters of all types. Among the clients were such blue-chippers as Shearson–Lehman Brothers, Donald Trump, the city of Washington, D.C., several foreign governments, and even President and Mrs. Reagan. The atmosphere had never been headier, not in New York, and certainly not in Washington.

But numbers jugglers who looked at the expense side of the Finley Kumble ledger shuddered when they heard Kumble outline his plan for the redecoration of the New York offices. Little in Steve Brill's "Finleyman" article hadn't stung him. Kumble couldn't do anything about most of it. The disloyalty of Heine and Washington wouldn't change. Heine could be dealt with later and Washington was proving to be a prodigious client getter. But one thing could be fixed: the problem of the tiger cages. The Beverly Hills office, Brill had told the law world, was a jewel. Manley's own office was adorned by two living–room sized Oriental rugs. Discreet folding wooden panels in a wall concealed a built-in television and a complete wet bar. Kumble's New York headquarters consisted of "a row of windowless tiger cages," inviting comparisons with the prison camps run by the North Vietnamese during the war. Such an image wouldn't exactly beckon either new recruits or new clients. But this was something over which Kumble, still the unquestioned head of the New York office, could control. Manley's Los Angeles office was not going to be the only interior designer's dream.

Kumble decided to redecorate his four floors at 425 Park Avenue in the style of the Palm Beach Polo Club. Just as he fussed over coffee cup lids, so he closely supervised the carpenters' work to make sure every detail was as perfect as it could be. Imperfections resulted in wholesale changes, and cost was not a factor. Incredibly, the price for the renovations came to more than $11 million. Included in the expense was a $500,000 art collection. When a couple of paintings Kumble wanted seemed beyond his reach, a New York artist was hired to dash off copies.

In late 1985 Kumble's nightmares seemed to be abating. Marshall Manley suddenly announced that he would be leaving his post as co–managing partner of the firm to become the chief executive officer of Scharffenberger's Home Group, a large insurance company.

From his earliest days, Kumble had believed in testing himself against the best. That was why he had chosen to go to Harvard Law instead of Yale. Yale was harder to get into, Kumble knew, but Harvard was tougher once you got there. Neither he nor his firm had ever shrunk from a fight. They had never been afraid to mix it up with Dewey Ballantine or any of the white-shoe firms. You couldn't become the biggest, and thus the best, by not taking on the champs. And that's what his life had been about. With his incredible charm and ruthlessness, Steven Kumble could dominate and control men of huge ego and intellect. He would become the biggest lawyer in New York and thus, everyone would believe, the best lawyer in New York.

Over and over again Kumble had proved his superiority. Heine, a fine corporate lawyer, would have loved to take over the firm. But Heine was too emotional. He lacked the charm. Kumble had sent Grutman packing. The former mayor of New York, Robert Wagner, and the former governor of the state, Hugh Carey, sat obediently in their offices, doing his bidding. Most satisfying of all, Nathaniel Goldstein, Kumble's first boss, as well as Burton Abrams, his first mentor, now worked for their former associate. Every man had a price, Kumble had learned. Every man had an ego, and he had become the master at finding the price and massaging the ego.

But with Marshall Manley, things had gone horribly wrong. He couldn't be controlled and certainly wasn't dependent on Kumble for his partnership draw. Manley could dictate his price. The partners said of Manley: "He's more Kumble than Kumble." He was not only more ruthless, but much more likeable. Manley had managed to become the master of his Los Angeles base, and practically every lawyer in the L.A. outpost admired him. People feared Steve Kumble, but few liked him, and his headquarters was beset with factions and battles. Worse, Manley had managed to forge an alliance with the D.C. office, where Bob Washington was beginning to believe that Kumble's presence blocked the firm's advance to true greatness. In the view of many non–New York partners, Kumble's real estate–oriented practice, his ties to real estate operators such as the Helmsleys, was an embarrassing anachronism in a sophisticated national law firm, just as Leon Finley's old wills and trusts practice had been an embarrassing anachronism to Kumble. Kumble had always known how to divide and conquer. But he had not conquered Marshall Manley. Manley had, by the authority vested in Steven Brill, become the personification of the "Finleyman."

Bob Washington agreed completely with Manley's derisive assessment of Kumble as nothing more than a collection clerk. Steve's only true support was in the Florida office, where Tom Tew had never lost his admiration for Kumble. The Miami partners actually came to welcome his harangues on fee collecting. Kumble liked giving them there, because he wasn't particularly welcome in either the L.A. or D.C. offices.

Manley's plans were not exactly clear to anybody. He announced that he planned to continue operating the Los Angeles office from his corporate suite in lower Manhattan. Kumble hoped that Manley would simply resign from the partnership altogether, but it wouldn't be that simple. In mid-1986 Manley finally did withdraw from his post as co–managing partner, but he used his influence to create a three-man national management team, replacing himself with Myerson and Washington. If nothing else, they were practicing law, which was more than could be said for Kumble. Washington had spoken for many of the partners in his interview with Steve Brill when he expressed his desire to retire Kumble from firm management and "get Steve back to practicing law."

CHAPTER

18

IT WAS OFTEN SAID in the nation's capital that few men were more difficult to get on the phone than Robert Washington, the imperious forty-four-year-old head of what had become the 150-lawyer D.C. outpost. His career had been meteoric, even in a city where political fortunes could rise and fall seemingly overnight. Had the egotistical Washington been a politician instead of a powerful behind-the-scenes operator (he had never been inside a courtroom), he might indeed have had his comeuppance. For on several occasions in his career, his wheeler-dealer mishmash of law and politics had landed embarrassingly on the front page of the powerful *Washington Post*.

He had been born on October 11, 1942, in the southwest Georgia farming town of Blakely, about midway between Albany, Georgia, and Dothan, Alabama. His mother had been a nursery school teacher, his father had owned a small cleaning company. Like many black families in the Deep South, the Washingtons moved north in 1945, to Newark, New Jersey. Bob was graduated from St. Peter's College at the age of twenty-five and in 1970 was graduated from Howard University Law School.

Connections at the then all-black university landed Washington a job on the U.S. Senate District Committee. In 1973, after taking time out to teach at Harvard Law School, Washington returned to become senior staff member on the House District Committee at a time when home rule for the District of Columbia was a burning issue. Michigan congressman Charles Diggs recognized Washington's intellect and ambition and asked him to become staff director and chief counsel. In that job Washington became the primary author of the legislation that eventually granted home rule to the district. His efforts brought him to the attention of numerous D.C. law firms, all of which courted him zealously. Linowes and Blocher, a D.C. real estate firm, was so sure it had Washington's hire sewn up that it threw a party to celebrate the new acquisition. But at the last minute, Washington changed his mind and decided to join Danzansky Dickey Quint Tydings and Gordon, a firm with higher visibility and a more diversified practice.

Washington's efforts on behalf of local government in the district had gone neither unnoticed nor unappreciated by local Washington politicians. He was named chairman of the district's Democratic party, and in 1978 he served as chief adviser and fund raiser for mayoral candidate Sterling Tucker. The job shot Bob Washington into prominence, though not necessarily as he might have liked.

Danzansky Dickey had long had links to one of the city's largest banks, the National Bank of Washington. Joseph Danzansky, founder of the firm, had served as chairman of the bank, and it had always been fairly free with loans both to the firm and to its individual partners. In 1978 Washington arranged a scheme with NBW, entirely legal but nonetheless controversial, whereby partners in the firm could make contributions to Tucker simply by signing a note to the bank. In this almost Kumblesque plan, the bank made loans to the partners who signed notes guaranteeing the loans and then contributed the money to Tucker's campaign.

But Washington was nothing if not adept. After Tucker lost the mayor's race to roguish, radical school board member Marion Barry, Washington quickly ingratiated himself with the Mississippi-born victor by hosting a lavish party in Barry's honor at his home. Later Washington accompanied Barry on a fact-finding trip to Africa.

The mayor, who had come into office promising to put city

business into the hands of black contractors, handed nearly all of the city's complicated outside legal work, especially its bond work, to his newfound friend. The business was said to be worth some $1.3 million to Danzansky Dickey, and it confirmed Washington's stardom. Lest anyone doubt his privileged position as the mayor's close friend and confidant, Washington was handed District of Columbia license plate 2 for his Mercedes. Only Barry had a lower number. Eventually Washington found himself presiding over such events as Barry's inaugural dinner. In return, the mayor addressed a firm partners' meeting and officially declared March 16, 1986, to be Finley Kumble Day in the district.

In another episode, Bob Washington was acting as counsel for the D.C. Investment Company, a local investment vehicle for minority enterprise operating with funds provided by the federal Small Business Administration. He raised eyebrows when a wine-exporting company in which he owned one-fifth of the stock was awarded a $450,000 loan, one of the largest DCIC had ever given. Asked by reporters to justify how such a wealthy lawyer could cash in on a government program for the disadvantaged, Washington replied simply, "I'm black, aren't I?"

After Finley Kumble took over Danzansky Dickey in 1980, Washington was put on the firm's fast track. It was hard for the New York partners not to be impressed by his slickness. Like Kumble and Manley, he had not been born wealthy, but he had a fierce determination to become filthy rich. Washington needed no lectures from Kumble on how to dress. He smoked $5 cigars and wore only the most expensive tailored suits, and moved into a $1 million home on D.C.'s exclusive Foxhall Road. From his days on Capitol Hill, Washington had learned the importance of cozying up to power. It was as if he had been born with the Finley Kumble ethic. When Kumble had taken over Danzansky Dickey, the jewel in the crown was thought to be Tydings. But like many out-of-office politicians, he had overstated his importance. Tydings's political influence paled in comparison to Washington's. In tribute to the hustling partner's prodigious ability to generate clients and fees, Washington, at Heine's suggestion, was made secretary of the firm's national management committee.

In 1985 Washington's closeness to Mayor Barry became an item of interest to New York banking giant Citicorp, which had come to the firm to avail itself of former governor Hugh Carey's friendship with Fernand St Germain, chairman of the House Banking Committee. Earlier in the year, the D.C. council's banking committee headed by Councilwoman Charlene Drew Jarvis had blocked a local interstate banking bill that would have allowed Citicorp to take over a D.C.-based savings and loan. In an effort to get that vote overturned, Citicorp enlisted Bob Washington. Washington agreed to use Finley Kumble to funnel a $21,000 payment to the boyfriend of Jarvis by hiring him as a Citicorp "consultant." The $21,000 was then billed back to Citicorp by Finley Kumble as part of the firm's fee. Shortly thereafter, both Barry and Jarvis withdrew their opposition to the Citicorp acquisition, and it went forward. At most law firms—those concerned about propriety—such a deal might have been considered embarrassing, especially after being loudly criticized on the editorial page of the *Washington Post.* But not at Finley Kumble. All that mattered was that Washington had achieved what Citicorp hired him to do—he'd closed the deal. In the world of 425 Park Avenue, partners drank a toast to Washington's savvy. He was, most certainly, one of them.

But Washington's savvy and hustle were only part of the reason for his rise to the top tier of Finley Kumble. There was also the matter of his directorship on the National Bank of Washington, an association that Manley, Myerson, and Heine saw as essential to breaking Kumble's control of the firm.

The National Bank of Washington had experienced a long and troubled history. In the late 1970s, owned by the then corrupt United Mine Workers, the bank caught the eye of federal regulators after granting a series of questionable loans. Investors in the bank turned to Luther Hodges, Jr., an assistant secretary of commerce, to take over the institution. One of Hodges's first acts was to ask Washington, as one of the most visible and bright black lawyers in town, to serve with him on the board. Washington's links to Mayor Barry were also a factor. Whatever the initial motivations, Hodges and Washington became close friends and tennis partners.

From 1983 to 1985, Hodges raised $70 million to buy out the interests of the UMW, a step that would free the bank from controls placed on it by the comptroller of the currency and the Federal Reserve Board. Bob Washington had put together two groups of investors for Hodges, one composed of personal friends, another of Finley Kumble partners. Together they gave Washington control of over 5.45 percent of the bank holding company's stock. To finance the investment in NBW, Washington and his partners borrowed from Citibank, which had already retained the firm to help with the interstate banking laws. Washington himself made a $1 million investment in the bank, putting up only $20,000 of his own money and borrowing the remaining $980,000 from Citibank. And to complete the web of spiraling interests, the D.C. office of Finley Kumble did all of NBW's legal work during the restructuring period.

Manley couldn't have been more impressed. If there was one lesson he tried to impress on his younger partners in Los Angeles, it was to own a bank. Manley, in fact, had his own bank, the Beverly Hills–based Merchant Bank of California. From its inception in 1982 until he moved east in late 1985, Manley, who owned 11.4 percent of the stock, had served as the chairman of Merchant Bank. But in early 1986, Merchant Bank had fallen on hard times, losing $5 million in bad loans. The California state banking superintendent ordered it to increase its capitalization, and Manley needed to quickly raise $3 million. Bob Washington was more than willing to help. Although Manley denied that anyone was pressured in the Los Angeles office, partners claimed to have been strong-armed into investing in the failing institution. In New York Harvey Myerson put the bite on partners loyal to him. And Bob Washington, through his good friend Luther Hodges, worked out the financing. It wasn't unlike the old Sterling Tucker loans. All Finley Kumble partners had to do was sign a note to NBW. Then the money was turned over to Manley's Merchant Bank. Eventually NBW loaned $2.2

million to over eighty Finley Kumble partners. Only Kumble's loyal forces in Miami refused to participate. Tom Tew looked askance at the deal and decided no one in Miami would be involved. Heine, Myerson, Manley, and Washington were now linked by something thicker than blood. They were linked by money. Harvey Myerson, who had already nearly exhausted his borrowing limits at New York banks, borrowed an additional $700,000 from NBW to redecorate his Manhattan apartment. Bob Washington had once again proven his mettle. He was, in the parlance of Manley and Heine, a "stand-up guy." More important, if the National Bank of Washington could emerge as a primary lender to the firm, Kumble's tight links to Manufacturers Hanover might become irrelevant. The last reason for paying obeisance to Kumble would be obliterated. Bob Washington had become one of the most important people in Marshall Manley's universe.

But Washington planned to dazzle his New York partners even more. After becoming head of the D.C. office in 1985, he was the unquestioned leader of the outpost. In early 1985 Bob masterminded a merger of his own, taking over the twenty-one-lawyer D.C. practice Perito, Duerk and Pinco. The acquisition pushed the number of lawyers in the Washington office over one hundred and at last made Finley Kumble the second biggest in the world.

At his Connecticut Avenue quarters, Washington couldn't find room for all his lawyers. He had to rent space in a nearby office building to house them. Perito had worked in the White House during the Nixon administration, and his Republican connections helped him land the representation of embattled administration figures such as Lyn Nofziger. Perito's potentially most profitable clients were the fabulously wealthy Hunt brothers, Nelson, Herbert, and Lamar, whose International Metals Investment subsidiary Perito was representing in connection with alleged manipulation of the silver markets. In addition to criminal practice, Perito's group had one of the largest and most important food-and-drug groups in the city. Most of the clients were foreign drug manufacturers seeking to gain permission to do research and sell their products in the United States.

But acquisitions such as Perito Duerk and Pinco were small potatoes compared to what Bob Washington had in mind. Paul Perito may have been a fine lawyer with paying clients, but he wasn't likely to be president.

In 1983 Washington read that Senate Majority Leader Howard Baker would be retiring, with the idea of plotting a bid for the presidency either in 1984, if Reagan chose not to seek reelection, or in 1988. Washington could think of no greater coup than to present as a gift to his demanding friends on the management committee the partnership of Howard Baker. Washington had already proved himself to be their equal in client gathering. Now he would establish himself in the other field that made a Finley Kumble lawyer—recruitment. Kumble was extremely proud of adding Hugh Carey to the roster a year earlier. But that had been easy. Carey and Wagner were best friends, and it hadn't been that hard to lure him aboard. In addition, Carey's political career was at a dead end. A controversial second marriage had doomed Carey's national political aspirations. But Howard Baker looked like a future president, and Bob Washington was determined to make him Finley Kumble's president.

For months Washington wined and dined the principled Tennessean, who was definitely in the market for a national law firm from which an exploratory presidential bid might be launched. Finley Kumble had as many offices as almost any other firm, and it seemed to be adding new ones every six months. Washington dangled a promised draw of $1 million in front of Baker. Who could resist?

Finally, Baker called Washington to his Capitol Hill office to tell him, in person, that he would be joining Houston-based megafirm Vinson and Elkins. It was a long limousine ride for Washington back to his Connecticut Avenue offices. The big fish had slipped away.

No firm leader or management committee member, however, was more determined than Bob Washington to launch the equivalent of a tactical nuclear strike on the firm's competitors. He had lost a chance to put the business on the international map in the Howard Baker fiasco. But in 1986, Washington turned his attention to two other retiring senators, Louisiana's Russell Long and Nevada's Paul Laxalt.

The addition of either to Finley Kumble would have a major impact. Long, son of Kingfish Huey Long himself, had been the longtime head of the Senate Finance Committee. No man in Washington was more familiar with the new changes that had taken place in the tax code, and no specialty seemed potentially more lucrative as corporations scrambled for exemptions and alterations in the law. But that was only half of Long's lure. He had also authored the federal legislation on ESOPs, Employee Stock Ownership Plans, which were soaring in popularity in corporate America. The big blue-chip corporations that had ignored Finley Kumble for so long would pay dearly to be able to call up Russell Long on a moment's notice and get advice on structuring their ESOP packages.

Paul Laxalt's value lay not so much in Senate experience or expertise. His nickname in the Senate, even among fellow Republicans, was "No Heavy Lifting." He had, however, one enormous asset. Laxalt was one of Ronald and Nancy Reagan's favorite people, known in the capital as "the first friend." In a firm that seemed top-heavy with former Democrats Tydings, Wagner, and Carey, Laxalt would provide balance. Like Baker before him, he was also exploring the possibility of a presidential race. His acquisition would give the firm a second shot at the White House. The questioning partners in New York were told, "At best we'll get a president. At worst a justice on the Supreme Court."

Washington's task would not be easy. Among those interested in Long was the Dallas firm of Akin, Gump, Strauss, Hauer and Feld, the operating base of Democratic party bigwig Robert Strauss. On the surface Strauss seemed to be the perfect partner for Long. Both were from the southwest, both were old-fashioned conservative Democrats. Texas-based Akin Gump had many clients who could benefit from Louisianian Long's exper-

tise in oil and gas. But a marriage of Russell Long to Robert
Strauss would have been like a wedding between first cousins.
Exactly because of their closeness, they would stay apart. All the
expertise that Long could add to Akin Gump already resided
there. Firms were generally looking to broaden their practices,
not heap expertise into a field in which they were already accomplished. In addition, Long had a demand that Akin Gump
wasn't prepared to meet.

"I've been talking to other firms," Long told Bob Washington.
"But there is something that they won't give me." Washington
listened intently as Long dropped his bombshell.

"You see, Bob," said Long. "The firm I go to will have to open
an office for me in Baton Rouge, and I want Kris Kirkpatrick to
head it up."

Kirkpatrick was Long's longtime aide on the Senate Finance
Committee, and Long was making it clear that whoever took care
of him would have to take care of his staffer. Forced to fend for
himself, Kirkpatrick would have been lucky to get a junior partnership of $150,000 per year. But Long wanted much more for
Kirkpatrick and was demanding that he be given responsibility
for an entire office.

Bob Washington didn't blink.

"Whatever you need, Russell," he said. "We will do it."

While his negotiations with Long were proceeding, Washington continued his pursuit of Laxalt. The Nevada senator was not
demanding the extensive home-state office that made Long so
expensive. But he didn't want to work in the same Connecticut
Avenue offices as the rest of the firm. He expected Finley Kumble to pick up the tab for new offices in the Willard Hotel,
within easier walking distance of the Oval Office. He elicited a
promise from Washington that, if he should run for president
or be called into the administration, the firm would support him
and promise him a job on his return.

As he had with Long, Washington assured Laxalt that there
would be no problem.

Although the negotiations seemed to be going well, even at
his most optimistic, Washington never expected to get both

men. He believed that Laxalt was being pursued by L.A.'s Gibson Dunn and Crutcher, which was home to such other presidential friends as William French Smith, former attorney general. But Gibson Dunn had undertaken the representation of the *Sacramento Bee* in defending a libel suit brought against the paper by Laxalt, and its recruiters had been warned to steer clear of the Nevada senator. That being the case, Laxalt decided on Finley Kumble, and after much soul-searching, so did Russell Long. Nobody had offered Long as much money as Finley Kumble had. Each man was promised an annual draw of $800,000, plus an expense account that would push their compensation to over $1 million per year. Kirkpatrick would get a salary of $225,000 per year, plus his Baton Rouge office. In addition, both Long and Laxalt would reside in the luxurious and plushly redecorated Willard. Long would be closer to the Capitol, Laxalt closer to the White House. Washington, again in true Kumble form, had never told each man about the other, and he worried about the reaction. To Washington's relief, the two were good friends and neighbors in Virginia.

Bob Washington had accommodated the senators' every demand and requested only one thing in return. Long and Laxalt were asked to sign a $400,000 note from a New York City bank. It was high, Washington acknowledged, but they would never feel the loan payments. They would be taken out of their draw over time and paid off just like rent. In the meantime, the new capital contributions were made immediately accessible to the firm to help defray the additional costs of adding partners, offices, and leases. No one knew how long it would be before the new partners began generating revenue.

After nearly twenty years of operations, Finley Kumble had finally done something so dramatically positive that it made the front page of nearly every major paper in the country. The two most hotly pursued politicians in the country were both joining the same hot new law firm. Bob Washington was more full of himself than ever. In one fell swoop, he had achieved what Kumble had never been able to accomplish. He, Bob Washington, a black kid from Georgia, had made Finley Kumble respectable. For Manley and Myerson, recruiting would now be easy. Lawyers with huge books of business such as David Ellsworth, who for years wouldn't even send a client to Finley Kumble, would change their minds and join the firm, bringing all their clients along.

In New York Kumble watched the performance with amazement. To press inquiries, he acknowledged he had had nothing to do with the coup. "You'll have to talk to Bob Washington," he would say. "This was his deal, and he doesn't return my calls."

The only problem was how to pay for it. But Washington had learned well from Kumble. He lit up a cigar and called his good friends at the National Bank of Washington. As a member of the board of directors and a partner in the nation's hottest law firm, one now plastered all over the front pages of the nation's newspapers and trade publications, a $10 million line of credit to cover the new expenses was no problem. None at all.

CHAPTER

19

IT WAS THE LATE SUMMER OF 1986, and by all rights there should not have been a grander moment in the meteoric history of what was now Finley Kumble Wagner Heine Underberg Manley Myerson and Casey.

Bob Washington's coup had brought the firm all the acclaim and attention that had eluded Kumble in eighteen years of ardent striving. There was no doubt, as the partners jetted to southern California for a meeting of the managing partners, that Finley Kumble had, in many ways, become the nation's most important law firm. True, it was still not the biggest—Chicago's international giant Baker and McKenzie had the edge there. But Baker and McKenzie had grown over a century, and its numbers were puffed by substantial overseas offices. And, not being headquartered in New York, Baker and McKenzie really didn't count anyway.

But not only was Finley Kumble second largest in size, it was second largest in fees collected. The success of Joe Flom at Skadden Arps could not be denied. Nearly as large as Finley Kumble, Skadden was collecting nearly double their fees. But lawyers at Finley Kumble felt sure that Flom would one day get his comeuppance. Nonetheless, if there was one thing Kumble was sure of in late 1986, it was that building a strong corporate department that could compete for M&A work was his top priority.

If he needed another reason to feel self-satisfied, it was in the long overdue publicity lauding the firm. The USFL suit, even if a defeat, had increased its profile. The Long and Laxalt acquisitions had increased its public stature in the news center of the world, Washington, D.C.

Opening up a copy of *Fortune* magazine, the most establishment journal of the buisness world, Kumble could only smile. He savored the story that for twenty years he had longed to read. Wrote *Fortune:*

> Traditionalists deplore Finley Kumble's nontraditional ways. It raids the competition, rewards on merit rather than seniority and operates like a big business. But now that it has taken a place among the venerable giants, it is forcing them to change.

Describing Kumble as ''a dapper soft-spoken man who would rather be a practicing real estate attorney,'' Fortune continued:

> In a profession notorious for a cavalier attitude toward cash flow, Finley Kumble is a taut financial ship. . . . The enfant terrible is showing definite signs of maturity, slowing growth, consolidation and a broadening of top management. Finley Kumble has no more skeletons in its closet than any other major firm. Is white shoe status just around the corner?

From his earliest days at the Shackamaxon, all Steve Kumble had ever wanted was to be, as he put it, ''a shoe.'' Now Time Inc.'s Waspy successors to Waspy Henry Luce, a ''shoe'' if there ever was one, were ready to confer on him the ultimate compliment.

There shouldn't have been a grander moment for him, but he knew enough to keep one eye cocked.

At long last, Marshall Manley had decided to devote more time to Home Group and relinquish his post as co–managing partner of the firm. In a way, it was just in time. With the firm coming into full flower, Manley wouldn't be able to claim all the credit, as he had in Brill's famous Finleyman article. *Fortune,* not Steve Brill, had the right spin. Kumble was the Finleyman and with Manley busy managing Scharffenberger's insurance company, any doubts would be erased. But no one knew better than Kumble how closely Manley had to be watched. No one could understand better than Kumble how dangerous a brilliant rival like Manley could be outside of the tent. No one knew better because no two lawyers in the country were more alike in their ambition and professional ruthlessness than Steve Kumble and Marshall Manley. Perched in his new office building high above Wall Street, Manley would have to be closely watched. Because if the situations were reversed, Kumble, who prided himself on being known as "a world-class hater" would himself be plotting takeover and revenge.

Naturally, Marshall Manley had little intention of fading into the world of insurance. And while he was leaving his position on the firm's management committee, he wasn't actually leaving the firm. Although the firm's partnership agreement required that any income earned from outside directorship or corporate positions be thrown into the firm partnership pot for distribution, Manley had used his power on the management committee (a power derived from his control of the Scharffenberger business) to make himself an exception to that rule. His $1.5 million compensation package as president of the Home Group would not be shared. In addition, Manley continued to receive more than $1 million from the firm, despite his absence.

It wasn't a bad arrangement, Manley felt. Best of all, he was getting out of California, away from the terrible pain and hurt that his highly publicized and traumatic divorce and custody fight had caused. He was getting away from the place where his friend Alan Rothenberg had turned against him, without even giving him a chance to defend himself. Away from the place where friend and alter ego Kumble had tried to screw him out of $400,000. Having finally won custody of his young son, the frenetic Manley was getting out of the place that New York lawyers disparagingly called La La Land. Marshall Manley, multimillionaire son of a union organizer, was at last coming home.

Although Kumble was having pleasant dreams of a triumphant Manleyless return to power, Marshall had no intention of giving him that pleasure.

His alliance with Bob Washington was solid. The men were united, not only through the common interests of their legal outposts, but through the entangled financial web that Washington had spun between the National Bank of Washington and Manley's Merchant Bank. Washington had also built a good relationship with Myerson, again through Washington's willingness to intervene with National Bank of Washington loan officials to get Myerson the $200,000 he had begun borrowing back in June. To round out a team on whose loyalty he could count, Manley had remained friendly with Heine. While Heine and Myerson eyed each other warily, Washington's rise in the firm had in some ways been promoted by Heine. So those two were close.

With the total support of the partners in L.A. and D.C. and the New York partnership split, Manley knew that at the Los Angeles partnership meeting, he could have himself replaced as co–managing partner with both Washington and Myerson. It was, of course, far too early to make any kind of a serious grab for Kumble's power base. The lines of credit at the National Bank of Washington weren't yet large enough to bankroll the entire firm, and Kumble was, after all, still the firm's business leader and the contact point with all major lenders. He had to be handled carefully, lest the whole firm be blown up when Manley's bomb went off in his suite. A move to oust Kumble was premature, but this would certainly get the founder's goat. With a squabbling three-member directorship and with two of the three beholden to him, Manley as senior partner emeritus and supplier of nearly $10 million in annual billings figured to lose not one iota of influence. And as for Heine, he too would be rewarded. When the time was right, probably in the early spring or winter, Manley and Myerson would throw their weight behind deposing Kumble and elect Heine head of the New York office.

Kumble had always prided himself on matching wits with the most clever. Yet, at every turn, Marshall Manley had proven to be his match. The 1986 meeting in Los Angeles would be no exception.

Oddly, Kumble's best instrument for maintaining a grip on his firm was the penguin suits he required at the stiff and formal annual partners' meetings. Lawyers are by nature a cantankerous lot, prone to argument and backroom maneuvering. But they also know how to act. They behave one way when dressed in pinstripes in front of a judge, in another way, with sleeves rolled up, in front of the jury. But the way to sedate a lawyer into the most civilized possible manner, Kumble believed, was to dress him in formal evening clothes.

Of course there was more to controlling the minds and fortunes of powerful men than tuxedos. One would have to be a fool to think otherwise. Nothing was more important than maintaining his grip on the annual partnership distributions. And as long as Kumble continued to know more than anyone else about the firm's financial picture, particularly its relationship with its three primary lenders, Manufacturers Hanover, Citibank, and Bankers Trust, his position would be unassailable.

Just as years ago Kumble had used debt to indenture his unhappy lawyers to the firm with what Grutman had called "silk and chains," he now used the firm's debt to make himself indispensable.

It had begun harmlessly enough in 1985. When the 1984 fiscal year ended in February 1985, Kumble estimated that about $1.8 million in accounts receivable would be late coming into the firm. With the number of lawyers expanding fairly rapidly, he figured it wasn't fair to the 1984 partners to hold the receivables over until 1985, when they would be split among a much larger group. Furthermore, why should partners who weren't even at the firm in 1984 be receiving income for work just because some clients were late payers?

To solve that perceived unfairness, Kumble established a dummy corporation that he called the Accrual Corporation. He then sold the borrowed $1.8 million in accounts receivable to Accrual. Then, as the president of Accrual, he went to Manufacturers Hanover and borrowed the $1.8 million, using the accounts receivable as collateral for the loan. The $1.8 million was then pitched into the 1984 partners' distribution. It wasn't a particularly complicated transaction. Indeed, for all concerned, it seemed extremely fair. When the additional fees were received, they were quickly used to draw down and then eliminate the new loan from Manny-Hanny.

But the following year, Kumble calculated that the firm was $10 million short of its revenue projections. Accordingly the bank loan through the dummy Accrual Corporation jumped dramatically. Even so, as Marshall Manley would shortly explain to new recruit David Ellsworth, a $9 million or $10 million liability in a law firm with $160 million in estimated revenues was hardly out of line.

In terms of pure revenue, and that's what really mattered to Kumble, only Skadden Arps, of all the law firms in America, now surpassed Finley Kumble. Operating with nearly the same number of lawyers, the remarkable Skadden was taking in $225 million a year by the end of 1986. Finley Kumble was collecting $158 million.

But what was disappointing was the bottom line. Skadden's net operating income was more than $100 million per year. Kumble's "taut financial ship" was clearing just half of that, $50 million. Looking over the profits of New York City law firms, one could find groups with half of Kumble's staff taking home more money. Cravath Swaine and Moore, the firm that represented IBM, had only fifty-eight partners but showed profits of $55 million annually. Most astounding of all was the performance of Wachtell Lipton Rosen and Katz. With just forty-one merger-and-acquisition specialists, Herbert Wachtell's firm was splitting a profit of some $60 million per year, enough to make every partner a millionaire.

In reality Finley Kumble's financial performance by the end of 1986 was dismal. But the perception was quite different, especially when Kumble could keep borrowing against the shortfalls. As long as partners kept getting their promised draws, as long as the firm could attract and pay important politicians like Long and Laxalt, the firm would be okay. Kumble felt sure that eventually the big names would start to pay off. Russell Long was particularly upbeat about his new situation. Addressing the throng, he told his new partners that they constituted one of the most politically powerful groups ever assembled. He wasn't wrong.

On the evening of August 14, the partners assembled at the Los Angeles Museum of Art for a reception. The next morning at a business meeting, Manley formally stepped down and awarded the reins of power to his two protégés, Myerson and Washington. Kumble could do little about it. But he was not particularly concerned. New York was still the center of the legal universe, and as long as Steve Kumble controlled the New York office, he would control the firm. Bob Washington was hardly a threat. No member of the national management committee from outside New York had ever amounted to much. Kumble could simply ignore Myerson, he was plotting to destroy Heine.

As most partners at the firm had predicted, the August meeting in California changed very little. Kumble returned to New York, still feeling very much in charge. He had always simply run the firm—he had called the headhunters, interviewed the new lawyers, and dealt with the banks. That was one of the reasons Manley had quit. Comanaging partnerships meant little where Kumble was involved. Despite his new title, Myerson avoided any open confrontations with Kumble. Nor would any hostile acts have been advisable. When Steve tallied the firm's year-end results and compared them to what each partner was expecting from his partnership distribution, he found the firm had ended the year some $27 million under projections. So in late January, Kumble made the necessary arrangements with Manufacturers Hanover, through the Accrual Corporation mechanism, to increase the firm's borrowing from the $9 million of the year before to $27 million.

The shortfalls, a function of the firm's continuing fast-paced expansion, did nothing to slow Kumble's insatiable urge to build the biggest law firm in the country. While Manley was bringing in the Ellsworth group from Memel Jacobs, Kumble planned to add New York partners to maintain the balance of power. Kumble had his eye on two major acquisitions. One was Peter Fass, an expert in real estate syndications. The other was Frank Geller, a corporate attorney. Both were coming to Finley Kumble from the same New York firm, Carro, Spanbock, Fass, Geller, Kaster and Cuiffo. Fass's group consisted of thirty-four people, eighteen lawyers and sixteen nonlawyer staff members. He promised to bring to the firm such new clients as the real estate department of Shearson–Lehman Brothers Inc., Prudential Bache Properties, Kidder Peabody Realty Group, and Smith Barney Harris Upham and Company. As for Geller, Kumble hoped he would unseat Heine as head of the corporate section. The outlay for the new lawyers' offices and staff would presumably be covered by the more than $1 million in capital contributions Fass and his five other partners would make to Finley Kumble.

Although Kumble's hope was that Geller would push out Heine, the new man proved to have no stomach for office warfare. His arrival thus became meaningless.

On January 1, 1987, Heine called associate Kenneth Henderson into his office for an important announcement. Ordinarily it was the kind of thing that associates wait breathlessly to hear. The partner of Finley Kumble had decided to bestow partnership on the Atlantan, who had come into the firm with Myerson but been assigned to work apart from the others, under Heine.

"I've decided not to accept your partnership," Henderson responded.

It was not the typical response. Associates simply didn't turn down the golden offer. Heine pressed Henderson for an explanation, but the courtly Henderson simply explained that he had decided Finley Kumble wasn't the best place for him. He didn't like the long hours, he had just become a father, and he was looking to go to a firm with less pressure to produce.

Heine accepted the response but quickly began passing the word that Henderson's decision to decline partnership was the latest and most serious example of the leadership vacuum in the New York office. Henderson, whom many of the partners had never heard of, suddenly was besieged with calls from partners as far away as Washington. Joe Tydings, whom Henderson had never even met, called wanting to know if the real reason for his departure was Kumble. Kumble's people took it as a sign that Heine's corporate department couldn't hold onto talented young people. Kumble himself danced into Heine's office and announced, "Henderson tells me he's leaving because of you." In fact, Henderson had said no such thing. It was clear to him that partners were collecting ammunition for a coming battle, one that he wanted no part of.

By February 1987, the end of the firm's fiscal year, its poor financial performance was visible for all to see, if they would just look. Spending was out of control. Myerson, Washington, and Heine knew that the time had come to make their run at Kumble. Here, at the beginning of the year, there would be plenty of time for the new managers to establish themselves and work out new arrangements with the lenders before the next borrowing period would come, at the end of the 1987 fiscal year on February 1, 1988.

The most important calculation worked out by the three co-managing partners was the annual estimate of partnership draws. Washington and Myerson made sure that their supporters were well cared for. Steve did what he could for his closest friends in New York. But despite Kumble's best efforts, Miamians Tom Tew and John Schulte were penciled in for a mere $550,000 per year, well below the figures assigned to the heads of the other offices. Washington, for example, was now looking at nearly $900,000 per year. Myerson was upped to $1 million per year. Richard Osborne, a management committee member from Los Angeles, was expected to earn over $800,000, and Ellsworth, the new partner, was looking for $600,000. Tew and Schulte didn't think it was fair.

Coincidentally, it was in Miami, at Coconut Grove's elegant Grand Bay Hotel across from Key Biscayne, that the twenty-five-member management committee was scheduled to meet to approve the projected partnership draws. When Myerson and Washington arrived, the Miami partners were prepared for war.

In a mid-February 1987 meeting in Bob Washington's luxurious suite, Tew and Schulte desperately attempted to turn him against Myerson. Myerson, they pointed out, was a spendthrift. During the USFL trial, they alleged, he had charged numerous personal items to his company expense account. Rather than being rewarded with a million-dollar draw, Tew and Schulte insisted, Myerson should be put in his place.

Washington listened, but without much sympathy. He was bound to Myerson, both through his antipathy toward Kumble and their connections through the National Bank of Washington.

When Washington reported to Myerson what Tew and Schulte had said, the litigator became angry. Tew and Schulte could have gotten the expense account information in only one way: a leak from Kumble.

Washington and Myerson knew that the time had come to act.

In a move that surprised both Kumble and the double-crossed Heine, Washington and Myerson pushed through a motion to replace Kumble with Myerson as head of the New York office. It was scheduled for a vote the following morning.

At a working breakfast the next day, Kumble pleaded for time to fight off the surprise move. But the sentiment was for a vote. Slowly he put on his reading glasses and began to speak:

> For twenty years I have been working to build this law firm. Most of you sitting around this table I helped recruit. I think I have had a hand in improving and expanding the personal fortunes and professional horizons of each and every one of you. In all that time I have had the responsibility of running the firm and the New York office of the firm, either alone or with others. That took twenty years of my life. Now in twenty hours you would like me to make a decision which could affect the rest of my professional life and the future of the firm. Well, I'm not that quick. The vote that you have been discussing—there is no precedent for it. The leaders of each office are selected by the lawyers

in that office. When this firm was created it was never contemplated that people from California or Washington would dictate who the leaders in Florida would be—or how many there would be. There is no provision for this vote in our partnership agreement.

A leader or manager is a person who is regarded as such by his peers. I can tell you that within the New York office and outside that office in New York I am looked to for leadership and am so regarded. You can't legislate that away. This vote will have no binding legal or more important, factual efficacy. Most of you have eaten at my table and many of you have stayed in my home. Our families were close. Last night at the cocktail reception for the Florida partners my wife was in tears. I had trouble explaining to her what had occurred earlier in the day was motivated by goodwill and sensitivity. The way you went about this was very strange. No notice, no serious discussion, no item on the agenda. Just twenty minutes to think about my continuing relationship with the firm that bears my name. Meetings in the dark, behind closed doors. No discussion with the individuals involved. I guess some of the things they write about us are true. Shame on us. The consequences for me are difficult to assess. Whether or not we should all stay together or go our separate ways, vote or no vote, is very questionable and so you may have accomplished what you set out to do. But the consequences for the firm are not difficult to assess. They will not be good. The firm could break apart. Banks hate turmoil, instability, and uncertainty. Orderliness—choosing the right representative to deal with the banks—a person whose sense of personal financial responsibility and integrity the banks respect—making a smooth transition—that's important. Recruiters and headhunters love instability. They thrive on it. Depending on how this type of situation is handled, I would expect our people to be bombarded with phone calls. We have a tough enough time recruiting good people without this added problem. And the media—they will have a field day. What the fallout will be is hard to assess—but the effect will not be favorable. I urge you gentlemen not to proceed in this way. It will not be a proud day for the firm. I will take this vote as a statement that a majority of people here wish me to remove myself from the management of the New York office. I would like the time to consider the implications of that for me and the firm. And I will be back to you with my response.

But the partners had learned from Kumble himself how important it was to close a deal, to act quickly to prevent the opponent from squirming out. The vote was taken. By an 18–7 margin, Harvey Myerson fulfilled his pledge to his fellow Webster and Sheffield defectors. In just two short years, as he had promised, the spendthrift Myerson had become the "Finleyman." But for a firm that needed financial belt tightening, it was not a wise choice.

CHAPTER
20

T O M T E W had no doubt on that balmy February afternoon that Finley Kumble in its present configuration was history. His Miami colleague, John Schulte, shared Tew's disgust at the manner in which Kumble had been deposed and couldn't have agreed more. Both men had pleaded with the other members of the national management committee to stop the infighting, to get on with the development of a national business plan.

But it was to no avail. To them it seemed that no one at the Coconut Grove meeting was interested in the firm's perplexing financial performance. Tew and Schulte decided to suggest to their Miami partners that they leave Finley Kumble and strike out on their own. But when they approached their 130 lawyers about the idea, everyone, especially Herb Suskin, thought Tew and Schulte had gone crazy. The Miami office was doing exceptionally well. Rather than being on the brink of ruin, the rank-and-file partners were absolutely convinced that the firm was on the verge of taking off. So try as they might, Tew and Schulte couldn't convince anyone who hadn't been at the Grand Bay meeting that the firm had potentially fatal weaknesses. Unable to make any headway with their partners, the two Miami leaders decided to stick it out, at least for the time being.

In New York the news of Kumble's overthrow was met with worry. He was still, after all, the firm's point man with the banks. Carl Schwarz was one of the first partners to visit Kumble after the managing partners returned from Miami.

"Steve, what happened?" asked Schwarz.

"Just round one," Kumble replied shortly.

Hardly a mindless supporter of Kumble's, Schwarz was a practical lawyer who wanted the firm to survive, and he could see that Myerson had little aptitude for staying within a budget. "Steve, I think you should stay," Schwarz said.

"I can stay and work with Harvey," Kumble replied. "I can't stay and work with Andy."

When that message was relayed to Myerson, he agreed that Heine should be jettisoned to forestall the disruption that a Kumble departure would create. After all, Myerson's alliance with Heine had always been one of convenience. He had needed Heine to help depose Kumble as head of the New York office. But now that he was in control, it became necessary to throw Heine overboard to keep Kumble from destroying the ship.

The extent of Finley Kumble's borrowing—a total indebtedness on January 1, 1987, of approximately $52 million—continued to bother the rank-and-file partners. Those who hadn't read the firm's annual financial statement closely became aware of the situation through their K-1s, the annual form that states how much of their income was earned and how much borrowed. When partners opened the IRS statement and learned that 44 percent of their partnership draw was borrowed, an angry revolt nearly broke out.

It was worst in California, which had become leaderless since Manley's departure to the east. Manley's deputy, Alan Schwartz, brought in several financial experts from Price Waterhouse to go over the reports and assure the partners that the debt was not excessive. Washington did the same in his office.

The chaos strengthened Kumble's hand. If there was one thing Myerson was not, it was an organized financial manager. More than ever, Myerson needed Kumble. But unless he turned on Heine, Kumble wouldn't help. Not only was Kumble sullen and noncooperative, he began floating rumors of his own impending departure, even leaking to a *New York Post* gossip columnist that he was thinking about taking Wagner, Carey, and the entire Miami office and starting a new firm.

The impasse broke in the late spring when someone, widely assumed to be Heine, though he denies it, slipped the American Bakeries documents into an envelope and mailed them to Steve Brill.

After Brill published excerpts from the memos in his gossipy "Bar Talk" section, Washington and Myerson, still struggling to get a handle on the firm they finally controlled, were furious. Their anger had nothing to do with the issues raised by the memos. The new firm managers were fighting the image that the firm was unstable and going through a management crisis. Now here was Heine revealing to the world that two of the name partners didn't even speak.

There was no doubt in Myerson and Washington's minds that Heine's defiant act could not go unpunished. Conveniently, their anger gave them an opportunity to cut a deal with Kumble. Heine had to be punished. So if Kumble would stop the threats and rejoin the team, they would agree to remove Heine as head of the corporate section, a move that would effectively expel him from the firm.

On June 23, at a management committee meeting in New York, the deal was sealed. Heine was at last pitched out. Kumble's comeback had begun.

Gleefully, Hugh Carey announced to the press and public that with Heine's departure, Finley Kumble's long management fight was now over. The firm, he told the *Times,* was now solid and intact and ready to face the future.

Wrote the *Times,* "Mr. Carey said that the 58-year-old Heine had 'voluntarily relinquished his managerial duties so he would have more time for personal and professional pursuits.' Mr. Carey was optimistic about the future. By next year, when the firm observed its 20th anniversary, Finley Kumble hopes to be 'the largest and one of the most competent firms in the country.' "

Everyone in management was certain the crisis was over. While they awaited the income that would soon be generated by new partners such as David Ellsworth, Bob Washington renewed the firm's unsecured $10 million credit line with his National Bank of Washington, assuring his bank in the process that the "material condition of the law firm has not changed" since the previous loan. With that infusion of capital, the firm then declared a distribution of profits to its partners, the surest sign any partner could have that there was money in the till. Washington and Myerson shook hands. "I've think we've crossed the Rubicon," Washington said.

The new developments still didn't completely satisfy Tom Tew and the Miami group. "The total focus here is on politics," Tew complained. "There's no growth. There's no new client development, no crispness. We haven't spent more than five minutes discussing a business plan." Tew pointed out that while Heine was leaving, a move he felt would benefit the firm, there was still no heavyweight corporate partner who could compete with Skadden Arps for complicated merger-and-acquisition work.

Tew's comments received little sympathy from the warring factions in Washington, New York, and Los Angeles. The Miami partners had just moved into enviable new offices overlooking Biscayne Bay. The branch was exceedingly profitable, mostly because of clients sent to it from the New York office. Partners in Miami, where there was no state income tax to dilute earnings, were making far more than other Miami lawyers. In real spendable income, the Deep South contingent, where housing was cheap, was the most highly paid of all the Finley Kumble groups. In the eyes of the New York partners, the Miami group was living well off the capital that the New York had provided to start the branch. More than Washington or Los Angeles, it was their creation. As such, the loud bellyaching of Tew and Schulte was viewed as particularly declassé by Washington and Myerson. Who cared what Tew thought?

Tew's frustration deepened, and once again he returned to his Brickell Boulevard office certain that he and his partners had to leave Finley Kumble. But once again he found no support from his partners. They were as aware as anyone that they had stumbled into a fantasy world of riches. Let the guys in New York squabble, one partner told Tew. Just so we keep getting our checks.

Kumble assured Tew that things would be fine. It was only a matter of time, he said, before Myerson's managerial ineptitude did him in. When it happened, Kumble would come riding in and retake control of his creation.

But while politician Carey had brought the *New York Times* under control, there was still one cannon aimed at the ship: Steven Brill.

Since the publication of the Finleyman article, the invitations to Kumble's estate had ceased. But that was fine with Brill. By the summer of 1986, he had become not only a dangerous investigative journalist, but an extremely busy businessman as well.

Starting in early 1986, Brill had begun a series of acquisitions that would enhance his already considerable influence in the legal world. He first purchased the *Connecticut Law Tribune,* a reporterless little legal weekly in Hartford. For years the owners of the paper had gotten rich simply by reprinting otherwise hard-to-find opinions written by state court judges.

But Brill saw in the paper a vehicle by which he could give the lawyers of Connecticut the same scrutiny that his *American Lawyer* magazine was giving the big national heavy hitters.

After buying the paper, Brill immediately began hiring reporters and editors. He relegated the court opinions to a back section, then began putting exposés and not always flattering profiles on the front pages. Connecticut lawyers were initially appalled and disturbed. But neither could they avoid reading the publication.

The former owners, still wandering around during the transition, just shook their heads at the changes Brill had made and the commotion he had caused.

"We made a lot of money here for a long time doing practically no work," one observed. "Brill comes in here, starts spending all this money, and all he's doing is making people angry."

But Brill was so successful in making people angry—and eager to read his publications—that by August 1986, he was able to purchase legal or business papers in Miami, Atlanta, Dallas, Newark, and San Francisco. He capped off those purchases by buying the Washington-based *Legal Times,* which had been, along with *American Lawyer* and the *National Law Journal,* one of the big three legal publications. Brill the muckraker had become Brill the entrepreneur. The one-time student at Yale Law School was profiled in the *Wall Street Journal,* the *Los Angeles Times* and even the trendy Style section of the *Washington Post.* Not even Kumble had received that kind of national publicity.

Despite the frenzied buying for which Brill was traveling extensively, he continued to produce front-page stories for his magazine. His reputation was still primarily as a muckraking journalist, although his ubiquitous suspenders and fat Jamaican Macanudo cigars sent out a different message. It was said in 1987 that Brill had suddenly grown up. After all, he had been only twenty-eight when *American Lawyer* was founded. The biggest change that had taken place was the birth of his children. Although as irascible as ever at work, he became a doting father, almost always leaving the office by 6 P.M. to spend time with his two small daughters.

It was shortly before Heine was deposed as head of the corporate section, in May 1987, that Brill began receiving anonymous memos raising questions about the state of Finley Kumble finances. Such "over the transom" sources of information were not unusual at *American Lawyer.* But the magazine rushed nothing into print without extensive checking. Although often accused of irresponsibility by those who were the subject of his harpooning, Brill demanded that every piece of information be checked and rechecked before it could be included in a story. He then had a staff of fact checkers examine every factual statement that appeared in his magazine one last time. With a thoroughness rarely demonstrated by editors, Brill also insisted that each person mentioned in an article be given an opportunity to respond.

Not overly moved by the initial allegations about the firm's finances, Brill turned the memos over to one of his young report-

208 | KIM ISAAC EISLER

ers. But after she was unable to come up with much information that would shed light on the firm's true financial condition, Brill decided to take on the project himself.

Looking at the balance sheets that he had been mailed, Brill focused on one item that continued to strike him as curious. The firm had claimed to have collected $150 million in professional fee income. But there was a footnote attached to the figure. The footnote revealed that the Finley Kumble partnership had sold $20 million in accounts receivable to the Accrual Corporation "and recorded this amount as professional fee income."

Of the $47 million in reported excess revenue that had been disbursed to the partners as profit, some $20 million of that income was borrowed, not received at all.

On a summer flight to check on his San Francisco paper, Brill found himself sitting next to a managing partner of a major New York City firm. Brill produced Finley Kumble's financial information from his briefcase, careful not to reveal from which firm the numbers came.

"Tell me if there isn't something strange here," Brill requested.

"This isn't a law firm, it's a scam," replied the partner, noting the borrowings.

Another passenger, a partner from a Big Eight accounting firm, asked if he could have a look. Brill turned over the documents. The accountant's face contorted in puzzlement.

"These numbers aren't possible," he said. "What firm is this?"

Brill wouldn't say but asked both men to write down on a sheet of paper which firm they thought it might be. Both wrote down the same name: Finley Kumble.

Now confident that he was onto something, Brill did a quick study of different accounting methods. He discovered that Finley Kumble was listing their expenditures on a cash basis but itemizing revenues using an accrual method of accounting. That was the inconsistency that had caught the eye of the accountant on the airplane.

Brill then packed up his documents and went to confront Harvey Myerson.

According to Brill, Myerson pulled a copy of what was supposed to be the same thing that Brill had, some of the numbers had been covered with correction fluid, and new ones had been entered. Brill didn't challenge Myerson, but what he had seen furthered his belief that something was being hidden.

Brill now began attempting to talk to just about everybody in the firm, and Myerson knew it meant trouble. Heine agreed to interpret the numbers for Brill, telling him many of the things he had tried to impress on Myerson and Washington in the late winter and spring, especially that Kumble had overestimated the collectibility of the receivables that he was using as collateral for the Accrual loans. Heine had been head of the firm's financial committee and was extremely familiar with what the figures conveyed. All through late July and August, Brill continued to interview Finley Kumble partners, and the management of the firm began getting extremely nervous.

Brill's article was expected to come out on the first of September. Already the rumor mill was circulating the title: "Bye-Bye Finley Kumble."

With no doubt that the article would be extremely damaging to the firm, Manley, no stranger to the power of a Brill article, resigned his partnership effective August 17. In his own modest words, Manley had been acting as a "partner emeritus." But implicit in his final resignation was the threat that the Home Group's legal work would begin drifting off to other firms, further sealing the inevitable. Other partners, including Kumble, formed professional corporations to protect their personal assets in the event the story brought down the firm. Meanwhile, in the Finley Kumble boardroom, steps were taken to minimize the impact. Myerson and Kumble agreed that a preemptive strike might knock Brill out of the water.

Myerson got his opportunity when James A. Finkelstein, the publisher of the *New York Law Journal*, called Myerson to complain that Brill had information that his reporters couldn't get. That didn't seem fair to Finkelstein. It provided Myerson with an opportunity. If Finkelstein would agree to write his article before Brill's, the firm would give him full cooperation—interviews, pictures, financials, even a comprehensive list of how much each partner in the firm was earning. Finkelstein said he would assign Donna duBeth, who had been part of a Pulitzer Prize–winning news team while working out west.

Myerson agreed that assigning duBeth to the story was a good move. It would enhance the credibility of the piece. To make sure that all clients and bank executives got the true picture, the law firm would buy up the unsold copies of the paper so the article could be mailed to clients and lenders.

When Brill heard what the *New York Law Journal* was planning, he moved up his own publication date.

On August 18 Brill received a telegram from Finley Kumble stating that not only were they aware of the planned article by Brill, but had retained legal counsel specifically to deal with Brill and his proposed piece. The firm, Williams and Connolly, was hired, said the telegram, to "protect" the "interests" of Finley Kumble, who were concerned with reported falsehoods and inaccuracies within the article. The telegram ended with a promise—a cryptic threat—that future contact by Williams and Connolly could be expected.

Brill found the threat extremely curious, in view of the fact that *he* had just hired Washington, D.C.'s Williams and Connolly to represent his own *Legal Times* in a threatened minor libel action that had nothing to do with Finley Kumble.

"Get me Edward Bennett Williams on the phone," he barked to his loyal assistant, Patricia Collins.

"This is a hell of a way to treat a new client," Brill told the nation's most famous criminal lawyer.

Williams, embarrassed, said he hadn't known that Brill had retained his firm. He promised to check into it. The lawyer working on the *Legal Times* matter came running into Williams's office. "Mr. Williams, I'm terribly embarrassed. I have this small matter."

"No, you had it first, it doesn't matter how small it is," Williams replied. "I'll tell Finley Kumble we can't take their case." Edward Bennett Williams, who died several months later, was from the old school.

Two days later, Brill's article was published. It was headlined, "Bye-Bye Finley Kumble: The Firm Everyone Loves To Hate is Falling Apart."

It was a grand experiment. Take 198 restless, disgruntled, money conscious hard driving partners from around the country. Free them from the stuffy old firms that insist on paying on seniority or pedigree rather than productivity. Give them 450 associates, 17 offices, huge bounties for attracting business. And see what happens.

What's happening now is $76 million worth of debt that's growing, name partners not talking to each other, at least one key client afraid to send new business, and partner and associate resumes flooding the mails from Beverly Hills to Park Avenue.

The total meritocracy, it turned out, was nothing more than a commission for fees operation soon to fall under the weight of that commission structure. Lawyers got paid most for bringing in business, not legal work and certainly not for any kind of contribution to building any kind of long term institution.

If Finley Kumble were a determined, going concern, the banks would have little to worry about. It has a broad base of business, and its steady cash flow could easily pay down the debt if the firm's management simply forced partners to take cuts for a year or two. But not only has the firm fallen short of projections while continuing to pay out as if it's on target, it's also been rocked by the kind of management turmoil and buffeted by new marketplace forces that could indeed give the banks pause.

It has become a place where lavish new quarters in New York and Florida seem to have been the way the firm sought respectability instead of doing it the hard way by recruiting and paying stellar "grinders" of legal work rather them simply rewarding the "minders" and "finders" of clients. It has become a place where the only corporate culture is greed and where things like pro bono work are sissy stuff.

Its failure will redeem the idea that there's more to law practice than an aggressive business plan—that quality work, real professionalism and liking one's partners aren't sissy stuff—but are essential to building a truly prosperous law business.

On September 1, 1987, the day that Finkelstein and Myerson thought Brill's article would be coming out, the *New York Law Journal* published its story, headlined "Finley Kumble: Success, Change, Some Pain." There, on the front page of the newspaper, was a smiling picture of those two close friends and happy colleagues, Harvey Myerson and Steven Kumble. Wrote duBeth:

> After 18 months of internal strife, a stable management team appears to be in place and the firm is making adjustments to accommodate its fast growth and its success.
>
> Although Finley Kumble's rivals might relish a juicy divorce, it doesn't appear to be forthcoming.
>
> Although there is room for improvement, even the most unhappy partner did not suggest that Finley Kumble was anywhere near the brink of disaster.

The article ended with typical Kumble cheerleading. "By the early 1990s," he told duBeth, "there will a Big Eight in the legal field, just like today with accountants. The Big Eight will be on the basis of size, gross revenues and profitability. And Finley Kumble will be there. Hell, we could open an office in Ames, Iowa, and make it work."

The story was followed by an article in the *New York Law Journal*'s sister publication, the *National Law Journal*. This one was headlined "Finley Kumble: Alive and Well."

But Finley Kumble was hardly alive and well. Nor did the attempt to salvage the situation with the second article help matters. As usual, Kumble and Myerson had merely shot themselves in the foot.

Ironically, the *New York Law Journal* article did as much damage as the Brill piece. Among the information provided to the publication was a complete list of exactly how much every partner in the firm was making and how much they were expected to make in the coming year.

Securities lawyer Martin Gibbs, who controlled $3 million worth of business and made $800,000 per year, was so upset after the publication of the salary list that he stopped coming to work, showing up a few days later as a new partner at competitor Rogers and Wells. Carl Schwarz was at a negotiation when one of his legal adversaries turned to him and asked, "Do you really make that much money?"

"What do you mean?" Schwarz responded. That hadn't been in the Brill article.

Then he saw the *New York Law Journal* article for the first time, revealing that he was making $430,000 per year and expected to make $530,000 in the coming year. No one at the firm had told Schwarz or the other partners that their salaries were about to be made public. Schwarz's face turned red with anger, and he knew that he was leaving the law firm. When he returned to the office, the first person he called was a headhunter.

Around the country nearly two dozen partners followed Gibbs out of the firm. Newly hired partners, including Ellsworth, Peter Fass, and Frank Geller, "went crazy," reported lawyers who observed the confused scene.

Kumble's old mentor, Burton Abrams, working out of the law firm as a senior adviser, not a partner, went to management committee member Donald Bezahler. The two were old friends. Bezahler had been with Kumble and Abrams back at Goldstein Judd and Gurfein.

"When the banks read this, we're finished," he said. "You've got to take drastic steps. You've got to say no partner can leave the firm and that the highest draw any partner will earn is $250,000."

"When word gets out that we are wounded," Abrams continued, "we're going to have a hell of time collecting our bills. People hate to pay their lawyers. What they hate worse is to pay their ex-lawyers." Bezahler just shrugged. He knew it was too late to do anything.

But Myerson and Kumble were soon inundated with more pressing demands than those of an elderly nonpartner. The Los Angeles office was literally in turmoil after the publication of the *American Lawyer* article. In Miami it just served to prove what Tew and Schulte had been trying to tell their partners for months—that the Miami practice could do better on its own. Only in Washington, where Bob Washington began holding small meetings at his northwest Washington home, was there relative calm, although the most difficult partner to soothe was Russell Long. After a long and virtually unsullied forty-year career as a U.S. senator, newcomer Long was finding his picture being flashed all over the country as a main partner of a failing law firm. The one thing everybody remembered about the firm was that Long and Laxalt had joined. To many of them, it was Russell Long's law firm that had failed. Each article that appeared with his picture increased the former senator's anger.

Steadfastly, Washington believed the firm could be saved. For him it had to be saved—his neck was on the line with his fellow directors at the National Bank of Washington. Washington's plan to rescue Finley Kumble involved putting a salary cap on the partners' earnings and drawing down the debt. Doggedly, he called partners around the country, asking them to give the firm until the end of the year to build up the receipts and reduce the debt. Not many listened.

The turmoil of the past year had taken its toll on collections. Kumble had been too busy to do his usual beating on fellow lawyers to collect their fees. Myerson continued to be profligate, still flying back and forth to London on the Concorde, still turning in large and annoying expense requests. On trips to Los Angeles, Myerson insisted on staying at the Century Plaza Hotel, where the room rate was approximately $750 per night. He traveled only in expensive limousines, usually a Rolls Royce.

Rather than suffer any reduction in his life-style, Myerson suggested that the firm simply cut back and retrench. He or-

dered Washington to fire twenty-five people from the D.C. outpost.

In Los Angeles, Alan Schwartz was left trying to keep the
partners from leaving. But they could no longer be controlled.
Few in L.A. had bothered to read the financial reports or even
to consider the implications of the tax forms. The L.A. partners
had become accustomed to Marshall Manley taking care of
them, looking out for their interests. Every partner in the Los
Angeles office had been personally hired by Manley, and most
had placed an almost religious belief in his ability.

But when Manley resigned from the partnership, chaos
reigned. One by one, the Los Angeles partners started leaving.
There was no way to stop them. The firm's once glittering West
Coast jewel was shattered.

But not even quitting was easy. The partnership agreement
allowed for a ninety-day notice of resignation. The time was
needed to find a new situation. A lawyer with important clients
couldn't simply walk out and start looking for a job. It's a
complicated procedure. Clients have to give permission to trans-
fer their files to a new firm, and so lawyers must first have a new
firm.

To halt the exodus, Alan Schwartz announced that any partner attempting to give notice would be put out. A loud howl
went up.

"We're throwing you out the next day," Schwartz repeated.
"It may be a breach of the partnership agreement. You can try
to sue us, but before this case is resolved, the cows will have
come home."

In addition, Schwartz announced, "Anybody caught gossip-
ing about the firm will be fired."

Following the meeting, several of the partners asked to see
copies of the partnership agreement. Because it was frequently
amended, many didn't have updated drafts. The firm's adminis-
trative head replied that she was under orders not to let anyone
see it.

Myerson flew out for a meeting with the Los Angeles partners to try to calm them. "I want you to know that nothing is more important than the good faith and support of our partners," he said.

But the L.A. group was skeptical, especially after learning that Myerson had come out to California on a specially chartered plane.

In Florida the article was all the proof Tom Tew needed to convince his partners that Miami should go it alone. He began putting together a loan package of his own that would support a new law firm, to be called Tew Schulte and Jorden. When Bob Washington got word of the Miami defection, he was incredulous. He had called Tew and believed that he had gotten a pledge that the Miami group would stand with the firm. Washington still believed the firm could hang together and ride out the crisis. But, the second week of November, the banks began mailing out notices to all the partners, discreetly informing them that each one was equally liable for whatever debt the firm had piled up.

On November 12 the *Wall Street Journal* reported that Finley Kumble would be reorganizing. Under one plan it would split into two independent units, one with Myerson, Manley, and Washington, the other with Kumble, Wagner, and Carey. Carey told the *Journal* that no main offices would close, but smaller ones might.

But the bank memo had stirred panic. Myerson tried to still it. He circulated a memo in the office which emphatically denied that Finley Kumble was in deep financial trouble and, as suggested by the slew of recent rumors, that its demise was imminent. In the memo Myerson also reiterated that the firm would continue to operate as usual. At the time Myerson posted the memo, he had already been in contact with headhunters to find himself a new position.

Needless to say, his memo failed to stop the torrent. On November 15 the *New York Times* ran two articles about the struggling firm. "Torn by dissension and debt, its pieces are coming apart."

"Unlike those firms it liked to tweak," wrote the *Times*, "Finley Kumble will never make it to its 20th birthday."

"Since June, 22 of its 250 partners have left. The Florida operation is going its own way. The London office is being closed and the smaller U.S. offices will be shut down," Kumble told the *Times*, "With the exception of the departure of some partners, much of what is happening is an outgrowth of a decision to 'streamline the firm.' " But, insisted Carey, "Regardless of how many torpedoes hit the ship, the firm is going forward."

On November 22 Tew found Kumble and Carey having lunch at the Yale Club. He told them that the Miami office would be going it alone, not aligned with any other faction of the firm. Neither man indicated any surprise. Tew said good-bye and flew back to Miami. While Washington was assuring reporters that the firm would stick together, Carey told the *New York Times* that it was breaking apart. Washington's last desperate attempts to save the day were smashed. He began negotiations with the National Bank of Washington for a new line of credit to start his own firm.

In the confusion Kumble seemed to believe that something would happen to save a firm that would carry his name. He even called a meeting of Wagner and half a dozen other lawyers at Underberg's apartment at Park and Fifty-eighth to talk about starting over. But for the participants, it was a surreal meeting. Kumble talked for two hours about starting over and once again building a national law firm. "We'll learn from our mistakes," he pleaded. But even the once loyal Underberg couldn't buy it. Kumble's plea brought empty stares. "We'll talk about it some other time, Steve," said one of the partners, as they exited.

The banks were estimating a total debt of over $83 million. Among the lawyers hired by the firm's four main lenders to recover its now shaky loans was Joe Flom and Skadden Arps. In letters mailed by the banks to the partners, all were reminded that in a New York State partnership, all were jointly liable for the debt. Should it be apportioned equally, that meant each of the two hundred partners would owe at least $415,000. Nor would any partners be getting back their capital contribution. David Ellsworth's $322,000 was gone.

Feeling lied to and betrayed, Ellsworth filed suit against his partners and in humiliation moved to Philadelphia's Morgan Lewis and Bockius. Finley Kumble has not responded to the suit due to the pendency of the bankruptcy proceeding.

By the first of the year, Finley Kumble's 1,300 employees were out of work, its partners were being dunned by the banks, and clients were scurrying for new attorneys.

Out of the mayhem, Roy Grutman reappeared. He had been hired by a group of partners who called themselves "the mushrooms" because they claimed to have been kept in the dark about the sorry state of the firm's finances. For Grutman it was the opportunity for delicious revenge. But in the world of Finley Kumble, not even successful revenge was permitted. Grutman and the "mushrooms" themselves split up, Grutman claiming the Finley Kumble partners owed him more than $100,000.

Partner sued partner. The banks sued the firm. Kumble's artwork and classic furnishings were sold at auction. And out of the decaying corpse came work worth millions to literally hundreds of lawyers. None would do better than Manhattan's Milbank Tweed Hadley and McCloy, appointed as the receiver by the bankruptcy court. Milbank reaped millions in legal fees from the estate.

While Judge Prudence Abram began parceling out the assets and assigning the debt, the partners continued to go their separate ways. Miami's Herb Suskin took the loss hardest. While being treated at a Miami hospital for depression, he pulled a blood monitor out of his arm and leaped to his death from a twelfth-story window.

Of the major partners, Myerson regrouped the quickest. Taking Alan Gelb with him, he joined forces with former baseball commissioner Bowie Kuhn, who had been practicing at Willkie Farr and Gallagher, and formed Myerson and Kuhn. In just a matter of months, the new firm had nearly two hundred lawyers, with offices in several cities.

But by the end of 1989 the legal press was reporting that Myerson and Kuhn might itself go the way of Finley Kumble. Wracked by fights among its partners, and feuds and suits with clients, the number of lawyers had sunk to less than one hundred. Among those who had been lured to the new firm was Michael Horowitz, a former star general counsel at the federal Office of Management and Budget. Horowitz had been promised by Myerson that there was no resemblance between Myerson's new firm and his old one. But after just a year it had become clear to Horowitz and others that the similarities were stark. Horowitz quit, publicly denouncing Myerson and Kuhn in the *Wall Street Journal* as "a nightmare."

Unlike the California office, which split in a hundred different directions, the two other major branches remained recognizable. In Miami Tew, Schulte, and James Jorden began operating as Tew Jorden and Schulte. But after operating independently for little more than a year, Tew put out the word that his new firm was on the auction block, available as a merger target.

Bob Washington and Paul Laxalt dumped Joe Tydings and formed Laxalt Washington Perito and Dubuc. Russell Long refused to participate and formed his own firm, aptly named the Long Law Firm. Winning the chutzpah award for 1988, Washington then attempted to oust Luther Hodges from the National Bank of Washington, claiming he had hurt the bank by making too many bad loans. As Washington well knew, the worst loan Hodges had approved was the $10 million credit line to Finley Kumble. It had not been repaid after the firm's demise.

Kumble moved a block away to a law firm called Summit Rovins and Feldesman, where Len Toboroff had also gone. But he began spending most of his time on business deals, as well as dealing with court-appointed bankruptcy trustee Francis X. Musselman.

For several months the maze of what had been the Finley Kumble offices became a ghost town. The gold letters that had once spelled out the long name had been taken. Finally only Burton Abrams remained in the $11 million offices, now controlled by Musselman. Kumble's first legal mentor had just come to Finley Kumble as a senior adviser. But no one had listened to the old man. Everything had happened too fast. Now only

Abrams's light dotted the darkened corridor. "I had the wheels taken off my file cabinets," he said. "I'm not going anywhere until somebody throws me out."

Eventually the New York real estate department of Mudge Rose Ferdon Alexander and Guthrie did come, and Abrams was finally forced to find a new haven. Assigned to Leon Finley's old office was an early partner, Bob Peduzzi.

"It's a little weird coming in here," he said. "I think I need an exorcist."

The hell that was Finley Kumble, for the 1,300-member staff, for the young associates in the tiger cages, and for the image of law itself, had finally burned itself out. From those who admired the law, there were no tears.

SOURCES

W HEN I BEGAN the research for this book, I assumed that the number of lawsuits that had been filed in connection with the breakup would provide thousands of pages of sworn depositions and affidavits that would provide the bulk of my source material. But Prudence Abram, the federal judge overseeing the dissolution, stayed all litigation during the pendency of the bankruptcy. The result was that very little in the way of sworn depositions was available. I then attempted to contact as many of the firm's partners and former partners as possible. A majority were reluctant to speak about the case while a settlement was in limbo. Those who did agree to speak with me, did so, almost to a person, with the understanding that their names would not appear in this section of the book as sources. Several expressed a fear of retribution if the senior partners in the firm managed to become powerful again after the bankrutcy. Some two hundred persons were eventually interviewed for this book. The presence of a name in the text does not presume an interview with that person.

After interviews, the majority of the research for the book came from court files. This is especially true of the early chapters involving the Persky problems, Microthermal and Newberger Loeb. I was also able to find the New York State court file dealing with Kumble's breakup from Amen Weisman and Butler (*Weisman v. Finley;* Index #13005/1968).

Among the court files on which I relied:

Dobbs v. Vornado, 576 F. Supp. 1072 (1983)

U.S. v. Persky, 520 F.2d 283 (1975)

Newberger Loeb v. Gross, 611 F.2d 423 (1979)

Matter of Arlan's Department Stores, 615 F.2d 925 (1979)

In Re Sambo's, 20 Bankr. 295 (1982)

BusTop Shelters v. Convenience & Safety Corporation, 521 F. Supp. 969 (1981)

U.S. v. Bronston, 658 F.2d 920 (1983)

In Re Eastern Sugar Litigation, 697 F.2d 524 (1982)

GAF v. Union Carbide, 624 F. Supp. 1016 (1985)

GAF v. Heyman, 724 F. Supp. 727 (1983)

Leist v. Simplot, 638 F.2d 283 (1980)

Allegheny Pepsi-Cola v. Mid-Atlantic Coca-Cola, 690 F.2d 411 (1982)

United States Football League v. National Football League, 644 F. Supp. 1040 (1986)

I am also indebted to the fine reporting in a variety of publications, especially Steve Brill's work in *American Lawyer* and the fine continuing coverage of the breakup by the *National Law Journal*'s Rita Henley Jensen. Specific articles from which I was able to gather leads include:

Charlotte Low's profile of Marshall Manley in the *Los Angeles Daily Journal;* March 14, 1983

Ellen Joan Pollack's profile of Alan Rothenberg in the December 1983 issue of *American Lawyer*

Steven Brill's account of the FBI's attempt to muscle him, "Muscled by the FBI," appeared in *Esquire,* October 10, 1978

Brill's article on "Jimmy Carter's Pathetic Lies" appeared in *Harper's,* March 1976

Connie Bruck's profile of Steven Kumble, "Steve Kumble and the Art of Empire Building," appeared in the August 1983 issue of *American Lawyer*

James Stewart's article on "The GAF Proxy Fight," which I used in connection with the chapters on Samuel Heyman, appeared in the *American Lawyer* issue of July/August 1983

Mary Billard's article "Kumble's Tumble," which appeared in the January 1988 issue of *Manhattan Inc.*

Deirdre Fanning's "Fall of a Rainmaker," from the June 1, 1987 issue of *Forbes*

INDEX